"This book is dedicated to all those who shaped me."

FROM BEHIND THE CHAIR

A memoir by Tom Sharpe, as told to Mariette Papic

FROM BEHIND THE CHAIR

A memoir by Tom Sharpe, as told to Mariette Papic

Hardcover: 979-8-9852589-3-6

Paperback: 979-8-9852589-4-3

Digital: 979-8-9852589-5-0

Cover design/layout: Jessica Stooksbury

Illustrations: A.A. Kopsell

Editor: Kristi Bumpass

Proofreading: Audra L. Humbard

Published by Auguries & Alchemy
auguriesandalchemy.com

CONTENTS

I'm Always Driving

I'll tell you right now that you're reading the story of a gay haircutter from a small town. I have a house, a Porsche I bought outright that mostly sits in the garage, and an SUV with payments left on it that I drive all over. In the back of the SUV right now are a whole lot of paper products I picked up at the bulk store, and rattling around next to that is a statue of Holy Death, decked out in rhinestones, which I can explain. My story is simple, actually: I was born in New Jersey, and I still live there.

I'm probably a lot like most people, growing up and living in more or less the same place for most of my life. I work, I watch some TV at night, usually history stuff or something else that's not too mind numbing. Regular life has plenty of drama, so the reality shows don't do much for me. I like to stay busy and do things around the house. I make to-do lists and bitch about them. Most of the things I put on the list get done, but every so often some task gets left dangling. That's kind of where the statue fits into the story. She is on the to-do list.

I spend time with my friends and family even if they drive me crazy. I know, it all sounds familiar, nothing too wild. I grew up on simple food, and I still like simple pleasures. I take half-and-half in my coffee. I like name brands; ones I remember from childhood. I am like most people you know; except for the guy in front of me at the light right now, the one who sped up to cut me off and then had to slam on his brakes. I'm nothing like him.

I'm just your everyday Tom, a guy with ADD and a mortgage. I'm the neighbor with the nice lawn ornaments and wisteria winding along my front porch. The younger version of me wrestled those plants into something functional, and now in the summers I get to admire them. I'm the single guy of a certain age, maybe lying there on his hammock, drinking an iced tea on a Sunday, admiring the purple and pink flowers that climb up either side of the porch and meet in the middle. I'm a regular guy obsessing over the garden, the lawn, and the leaves that might be stuck in the gutters. I spend way less time in that hammock than I want to admit, but every once in a while, you might catch me there, actually relaxing. You might even catch me by my little pond right there by the front porch, and see me feeding the fish. You could even come by and hear the sound of the running water, notice how it makes tending the lawn kind of peaceful. I'm your normal neighbor on the corner lot, first to get the lawn into shape every spring, up at dawn most days all throughout the year.

The fact that I've got that angel of death – excuse me, *Holy Death* – rattling around in the back of the SUV is probably the only thing that might make you or someone else wonder what I'm all about. Of course, if someone really got curious about my life, they'd notice all sorts of things about me that aren't your everyday normal. Truth is, most people are unconscious or busy as hell just trying to survive, so nobody's got time to pry into my life. Unless I open my mouth and start talking opinions, I don't draw a lot of attention, and I like it like that. I keep my hair short and my conversations with people I don't know even shorter. With the ADD it's not that hard to move on from one to the next. Sometimes with the ADD I might slip in an opinion without noticing I did.

You're maybe wondering right now why this asshole with a fish pond and a hammock thinks he has anything to say. Maybe you're wondering why I don't pull the car over and adjust the statue so it stops rattling around. Well, everyone's got a story to tell, and I'm telling mine because I promised my friend Cheryl I would. Cheryl's passed now, no surprise around that one. Cancer got her, and it got her fast. I am here spilling my life's story to you because of Cheryl, because I promised we were going to do this thing. Only problem is, Cheryl was supposed to live. With Cheryl dying, the whole vision we had, of her beating cancer and living to write about it, changed.

To be honest, it's not like we did a bunch of planning on this. We would talk about it, and Cheryl would get some real excitement in her big, brown eyes, and then we'd move on to something else, like dinner or planning doctor's appointments. Being sick takes a lot of stamina, just keeping up with the doctors, much less the bills. So, you're going to get more of me in this story than I thought you would. You're still getting a lot of Cheryl, just in a different form. You see, Cheryl is in between the lines of everything right now. She's passed on to the other side, but she wants me to tell our story the best I can manage.

Cheryl's the reason I've got Holy Death rattling around in the back of the car, of course. She's back there with her rhinestones, all dressed in white, catching the light as I drive, shining little prisms onto the back of the upholstery. Cheryl's waiting while I figure out what to do with her, while I drag my way to telling you all these stories from my perspective. By the way, Cheryl told me exactly what to do with the statue, I just haven't been able to do it. One day I'll do as she asked, but for right now, I like having the statue of *Santísima* around. Her full name in Spanish, if you don't know, is *Santísima Muerte*, which translates to "Most Holy Death," but we call her *Santísima* for short. I know. It sounds kind of wild, but it is what it is.

Cheryl is the reason for a lot of things, including this ridiculously cute dog in my lap. His name is Napoleon, and he lives up to his name: He weighs almost nothing, and he's incredibly possessive and controlling. He's got pretty much every neurotic malfunction you can get from having a traumatic puppyhood, and I guess me and Napoleon relate. I don't want to even think what will happen if he leaves me one day. I can't imagine his passing any more than I wanted to imagine Cheryl's.

Cheryl was going to juice her way to health, and everyone who heard her story was going to weep with joy. Eventually we would go on tour and put a juice bar in the salon when we came back home. We had so much fun coming up with ideas, how we would come out with our own book of recipes and spells for longevity. How we would make a children's book on magical thinking, and another one on dogs. Cheryl was going to be a miracle, beating sickness through prayer and nutrition. It was a long shot, I'll be honest, but I believed it could all come true. I gave her every ounce of support I had in me. Cheryl, for her part, gave it all that she could. Sometimes the story of life doesn't go the way we want.

You see, Cheryl was a haircutter just like me, although I think she preferred to be known as a hair *stylist*. We met when she came to work at one of my salons. Now, these are not your fancy salons where you book weeks in advance and pay half a paycheck. They're the kind of salons the whole family walks into to get themselves cleaned up for the holidays, visiting Grandma or the beginning of school. These are the kinds of salons that run on price point, not so much on style points, and I imagine coming to work for me was not exactly the ultimate expression of Cheryl's career goals. It happens.

Cheryl and I had this idea that she'd get better despite the illness she had, the one that came *before* the cancer. We had this idea that if we kept really positive, all of this would get better. We had these ideas built all around that day in the future when the tumors would have shrunk to nothing, when her Lupus would have disappeared. So here I am telling this story without her, without our triumphant ending. To be honest, I'm not in the mood to do this, but I promised I would try.

You know how I said most people are unconscious? Well, Cheryl was pretty fucking awake. She was born that way, with gifts that most of us don't have. Cheryl could see people's energies, you know, their auras. She could tell what was haunting them, too. She'd see old relatives and see childhood pets hanging around the living. Whatever your otherworldly entourage might be, Cheryl saw them. I witnessed it many times at the salon. Her head would tilt a little or her eyes would widen a tiny bit as the person got into her chair.

Sometimes she'd start asking the person questions, offering them the tiniest suggestions or offering up ideas on what really mattered to Grandma or Great-Aunt Sally. It was subtle, and it had to be quick, because Cheryl was making money for cutting, not for her psychic consultations. She could have made money doing that, too, but Cheryl loved cutting hair. She liked things that made her normal, and she loved looking good. She couldn't turn off the rest of herself, the psychic self, so she just wove those parts of her together. From where she stood, Cheryl could keep her hands busy tidying up the look of a person, while the rest of her helped clean up the things they couldn't see. Showing clients that their split ends were gone was easy with a turn of the chair and a couple of mirrors. The look of sudden relief or total frustration on the face of the visiting deceased, Cheryl kept to herself. You have to understand, some people don't take the hints.

Cheryl was a witch by birth. She was born into a family of women with some kind of "gift" and hers was the strongest. It happens like that lots of times. Her mom was definitely psychic, but maybe not as much as Cheryl. She had powers to see, hear and feel all these things that most people spend their time learning to do. Sure, she had to learn about ways of putting her gifts into action. Spells and potions, methods for clearing her energetic space; she had to learn those things. She learned a few things at home, but it wasn't enough, so she studied books and talked to old ladies at shops to keep figuring out what to do with the gift, to figure out how far to take it. That way of seeing and feeling the other realms – that was not something she could ever turn off so she grew with it. Cheryl was born into the thinnest part of the veil, the one that separates the world we see and the worlds we don't. This world calls that "being a witch," but to Cheryl it was plain old being human.

To be totally honest, if Cheryl were still on this side of life, there's no way she would be comfortable with me telling you this. Just me mentioning this would get that look from her, the one that said, *"Fuck off"* without saying a word. I miss that look. I miss the shit that came with it. Cheryl had a haircutter's mouth, a Jersey girl's mouth. She didn't mince words, and I can only think she's throwing daggers at me telling you this part, or maybe she's not. Maybe she's at peace with who she was because none of that normal human ignorance can hurt her now. No one can thump a book at her, acting like her very life was a crime instead of an act of God.

Cheryl was an everyday person, just like me and you. She had a constant show going on, with spirits and situations popping from every corner, but other than that, Cheryl was normal. She made cash money and stashed a few bills in her bra. She paid taxes on most of it. There just wasn't anything Cheryl could do about the things she could see, nothing she could do about the spirits parading around in places where you and I might never expect them. When she wasn't scared of people finding out about her natural gift, I think Cheryl got a great big kick out of life, listening to music and telling jokes. You wouldn't know how she worried. Dressed in black, sexy outfits like some kind of cool girl, Cheryl made noise with her fringed boot and jewelry. She could intimidate people dressed like that, and that was the point. Every bangle and hoop earring, every swaying fringe was like some kind of armor, since Cheryl was scared of most normal people.

Cheryl was sure a cross would be burning in her front yard at 3 a.m. one day. Speak too loudly about the cards or auras, and Cheryl would shush you. Say too much when a Book-thumping type was in her chair, and she would shoot you a dirty look. Sad to say, Cheryl's mind would go to the worst scenario for every situation. She kept a lot of what she was thinking or seeing to herself because of her feelings, because of what she had seen in movies and heard about women like her. She thought with one wrong move, and her life would be over. Considering the way the world works these days; Cheryl was not totally paranoid.

The more we got to know each other, the more normal it all seemed to me; the spirits and auras and all the past-life talk, but for Cheryl it was clear that this was not normal. The more I came by to hang out or check in on her at home when she was sick, the more I noticed things, like how for a while she kept the blinds down.

She needed fresh air and some sunshine but when I went near the blinds, she looked like she was ready to deck me.

"Why are your blinds closed?"

"The old lady across the street."

"She's not home."

"Not her. It's her dead mother."

"What's she doing?"

"She's standing there, flashing a light. Waving her fist. She's mad at me."

"What does she want?"

"She wants me to tell her daughter it's time to move on."

"So go do it."

"Let me get this straight. You want me to go over there and say, 'Hi, how are you? I'm from across the street. Your mother is telling me to tell you to move on.'"

(Blank stare.)

"You just don't do that, Tom."

"Why not?"

"You don't know how people are, Tom. I could wake up at 3 a.m. with a cross burning on my front yard. I've died like that in other lifetimes, Tom. Do you think I want to be burned like that again?"

Cheryl was genuinely worried about a cross burning on the lawn, and who's to say she didn't have a point? Who was I to tell her it wasn't possible? People burn crosses on their neighbors' lawns for all sorts of reasons, none of them good, but that's what they do. All the ghost lady wanted was for Cheryl to tell her daughter across the street to move on, to stop grieving, but as far as Cheryl was concerned, that was too much to ask. I get it.

Sometimes you have to pull down the blinds and pretend you don't see something like the ghost of an old neighbor lady raising her fist in your direction, waving her flashlight but that doesn't mean it's not behind the window, waiting for you to deal with the message. And I guess that's why me and Holy Death haven't parted ways even though – yeah, you guessed it – she's supposed to be at Cheryl's grave.

Your Potion No. 9 is Ready

Cheryl gave me everything she had as a friend. She rooted for me, and when she could, she did magic for me. Cheryl put parts of her soul on the line for me. One day she even made me a potion and, of course, didn't want anything for it. It wasn't the last time she would go out of her way to make my dreams come true. That is why I'm over here trying to talk to you.

Some people lust over shoes, or over their neighbor's car. I lust over finding the perfect soulmate with the perfect abs and a full head of hair he shaves down to nothing. Cheryl understood that in a suburban world full of families and straight guys, my search was not going well. I could have moved to the city, I guess, but I like a quiet life. It's what I know.

For years I would dream of just one perfect smile and a set of eyes that would immediately pierce my soul. By the time I met Cheryl, I had modified the dream. In fact, the dream was kind of up on a shelf, next to the self-help books. You could say I was set in my ways, and settling for way less than I thought I would. My dreams had taken a detour while I made my way, and paid my mortgage. I was never too boring, just stuck in some drama a lot like the last one. I was stuck in a world of repeating relationships that were never going to work. Straight guys would bend my way here and there, and that led to sex, if not fulfillment.

Maybe my standards were too high from the beginning. I dreamt of the ultimate never-ending date. I believed in a 100 percent perfect relationship. It's not easy, because I hang out with so many straight guys, lots of them partnered, so I could watch them live out their marriages while fitting me in on the side. I kept a better house than half their wives, but I wasn't socially acceptable as a partner. So, back and forth I went, living between my dream-guy fantasy and my everyday world full of men who have no abs, no interest, or no guts to live like they want. At best, I get the guys who want to experiment but who don't want to commit and this, my friends, is one of the oldest heartbreaks in the books.

Cheryl had some serious empathy for my situation. She knew what it was like to want someone in your life full time. Cheryl knew from her own series of relationships that you could conjure just about anything, but you could never make someone do something against their will. She knew, like lots of women do, that you sometimes wait for a man to come to his senses – until you realize his sense is limited. When Cheryl got sick, she put a lot of her romantic efforts into making my love life what hers was not. She was heavy on giving me everything from potions to on-the-spot card readings for every new twist and turn in my love life. Cheryl wasn't just my wingman, she was my witch, my *bruja*.

She gave me the potion, which was a kind of spritz. It was light brown, and I have no idea now what was in it, except for the glitter she added. The glitter was a sweet touch, and maybe it was important; I don't know about that. I do know it kept clogging up the spray action on the bottle, so the spritz sputtered. Cheryl gave me a Come to Me oil that you put on from the wrist up the rest of the arm. It was like a literal roadmap for the object of my affection and it worked. Too bad that one – who shall remain nameless – well he was impossible. Perfect abs, perfect face, sweetest heart – but, boy, did he have issues. So, into my arms he went, and he ran back out of them just as fast as he could.

I keep myself busy, probably too busy, trying not to think about it. He's there. He's always there, but to keep myself distracted I play games of my own. In the back of my head, I'm usually thinking about fairytale stories like the one about Christian Gray, the "50 Shades" one. I liked the book, but the actor who played him in the "50 Shades" movie looked even better than I could have imagined. I have watched that movie at least 75 times, and I am not ashamed.

After a long day of work, I could just turn it on, witnessing the couple's matching hang-ups, their complementary hotness. I like the lamb-that-heals-the-devil type of scenario – you know, the innocent one and the worldly one type of thing. I like seeing the lamb and the devil reflecting parts of each other, realizing they need each other. Sure, maybe that's corny but fast-forward, and in a few years, I'll come home and stream Korean pop dramas with completely different storylines, and I will be just as obsessed. Street singer meets studio musician? I am so here for it. I am here for the future, and always the romance, for all these spins on the *impossible but fated* love story. I'll even spend my time learning Korean on social media, just in case some hot guy jumps off the screen and into my arms.

Cheryl knew my obsessions. Whenever I was down, she reminded me that some people really do get lucky. Some people get hot sex and a relationship, too. She was determined to help me get lucky like that. "Tom, *this will work,*" she would say with her hand outstretched, her perfect eyebrows arched around her deep brown eyes. Her skin would be glowing. She was like a serious porcelain doll, handing out magic. There was nothing spooky about it. There would be sunshine and birds outside, and Cheryl would just stand there, offering me her heart's and soul's efforts.

Problem is, sometimes the magic works in ways we can't predict, and other times it works perfectly, but then it takes a turn. That's when you have to wonder if somebody somewhere might be working magic of their own. I know it sounds dramatic to think of magic spells floating around all the time, especially in the suburbs, but lots of time magic isn't what we think. Magic is all about intention and focus. Well, that bitch who stares you down at the bar when you're competing for the same guy, that bitch can have all the intention she needs to mess things up for you. Those unconscious witches can mess up a lot with their concentration and the things they say under their breath. They don't need a book or some charged-up oils, they just need to be focused, and then, let me tell you, the game is on.

I still imagine it's possible to find myself lost in the arms of some perfectly fucked-up soulmate like I see in the movies. I mean, I'm not looking for a perfect guy, just one perfect for me. I believe in that kind of never-ending romance, or drama, or whatever it is that makes two people into a couple. I know that the "50 Shades" thing doesn't sound healthy, but it's one example of what works for me as far as the sex. I know it was written by a shy British housewife and people get down on it for being too traditional somehow, but I can put my gay spin on it, and I have done exactly that at least 75 imaginative times. I will do it forever most likely, spinning the straight stories and even the gay ones into things I can relate to here in the 'burbs by the highway where I don't know the last time I met a musician or a CEO with a jet.

Anyway, can you imagine being me right now? Can you imagine having a high, gay sex drive, while being raised conservative in every way possible? It was like growing up in the eye of a hurricane that no one is willing to see or mention. You don't want to think about it, I know. Sounds crazy-making and complicated, and it was, but I survived. There was some internal devastation along the way, but I learned to get creative.

Eventually, though, I got settled, put my dreams up on the shelf, like pretty much every practical, working-class person I know. I managed to settle down in every way but one. I guess I never lost the idea that somehow everything I truly wanted came with a battle. I never managed to pick a guy who was calm or able to commit. I was ready to fight, and Cheryl was ready to fight for me, but the playing field was not level. I was programmed to dream on one hand but to value paying off my mortgage on the other. I was programmed to stay close to home, even if that home was going to turn into a kind of a dating minefield. I was taught that love and power were tied together and when they got knotty, the only way out was to cut.

Anyway, when your version of fun and fulfillment is demonized by the TV and the radio and the preacher at church, you learn to deal with it. Sometimes you learn to deal with it by being single, by watching some porn before bed or indulging in some light fantasy S&M where everyone has a killer body. Maybe you hang out with a friend and watch hours of DIY home-decorating shows and eat snacks. Before you know it, you might even stencil the front porch floor and repaint all the ceilings while wishing on your dreams. Your house gets gorgeous while you end up mostly sleeping alone.

Some people might read about my life and think, "Of course, sex is all he thinks about. He's gay, he's got no boundaries." But sex is all about boundaries and who gets to call them, and that part of sex is universal. I know plenty of gays with boring lives and low sex drives. I'm just not one of them.

Anyway, being gay is kind of like being born a witch. It's not something you ask for, but it's something that shapes how you see the world. That's kind of the point of me telling you this because nobody asks for certain gifts; you're just born with them. You might think being gay is a curse or being born a witch is a curse, not a blessing, but that's really you judging. I don't blame you, though, because that's the thing society teaches us: to judge. Only problem is, it's kind of a no-frills judgment we pass on each other. We don't get training on doing it right, just doing it fast. Rushing to judge is the worst kind and the most popular.

A lot of people are scared of gays, and let's be honest, who isn't at least a little scared of a natural-born witch? Gay people can't do anything to you, so I don't understand that fear as much, but witches or clairvoyants, real psychics – they can tear you apart. They can see your soul. They have power and potions and those oils and cards, and more than that, they have intuition. They have extra eyes no one can see, but you can feel them on you. I know the other cutters in my salon felt it with Cheryl. One look at her, and she was bright somehow. Dark hair, dark eyes, and somehow, she beamed this electric kind of light. That girl had presence.

I never worried about Cheryl getting mad and hurting the other women even when they were horrible to her, because she really didn't want to hurt a fly. I watched her stuff steel wool into all the holes along the outside walls of the tiny house she rented because she didn't want the mice coming in; she would have felt guilty for catching them in a trap that would hurt them. She religiously stuffed up all the holes, which took a lot more work, but it was worth it to her. Cheryl measured out a loaf of sliced bread every week, rationing out the 24 slices so there was something to put out for the birds each day. The squirrels got nuts and a bowl of water, *every day.*

She had a couple of rabbits out there too, in the yard. They were your standard little brown ones, and she would spare some of her organic juicing carrots for them. Watching them eat gave her so much joy. I helped her buy those carrots because Cheryl couldn't afford organic, but I couldn't be mad she was sharing the wealth. She took solace in nature. Being born out of the norm can mean you're always looking over your shoulder. I wasn't about to begrudge her treating the rabbits like royalty instead of pests.

Whatever you think about me or my friend, being born different from you, that's your business, but trust me: If you were in trouble – I mean r*eal trouble* – and we knew each other, me or Cheryl would be the people you would want to call. Remember, the unconscious witches and the people living in denial are the ones you want to watch out for. The eccentric woman in her sweatpants feeding the outdoor bunnies organic carrots is not your enemy. The guy tending his lawn and obsessively winding his wisteria plants up the porch – me – does not give a damn about your private life. We are the ones who mind our business. It's the people hung up on being normal who should terrify you, because that idea that "normal" even exists is terrifying.

The point is, everyone has psychic power, if not exactly the same gifts Cheryl had. Normal people do hateful shit all the time, and that stretches far and wide just like a regular spell. Sure, a spell or a potion is bona fide to do what it is supposed to do, but a normal cup of tea brewed with spite can make a person choke and cough all the same. You want to be careful the kind of people you let in your life, because all their secret thoughts can get you. Be very careful of the perfect people, because they might need you to stay stuck in a bad situation so as to make them look good. I know that sounds intense, but you know you've seen it. It's like that pretty girl who puts down her best friends all during high school. Well, she can grow up and become your extra sweet neighbor or maybe she takes a job answering phones for you. Next thing you know, things are off and you're not sure why. Well, the answer is, she's cursing you and everyone else out behind that façade of neutral palette cosmetics.

It's the morning, and I've got a million things to do today. My phone has been beeping and buzzing from the crack of dawn. Petty shit keeps the world moving. At work someone wants to leave early for their kid's game; another cutter needs to leave for the doctor, and they can't believe that I'd be so insensitive as to not accommodate it. They look at me, appalled that I can't understand their needs, but I don't think they understand that although I don't have a wife, I sometimes feel like I have 16 wives. From the salons to the restaurant I own, I am surrounded by women who need a lot of support. I holler about it, and I try to help, but I am overwhelmed. I'm just tired, you know? When did it start that every parent needs to make every school play? I'm not saying it's wrong. I just wonder about things.

So, here I go again, leaving a friend's house after some late-night encounter, wondering why I do the things I do. I wish the world were different, but it's not, and the level of stress and shit going down is giving everyone the jitters. I flick on the news, and then I turn it off after I find myself screaming at the air. The radio doesn't know and it doesn't care if it's making me crazy, and I have to remember this. I don't need a heart attack, and definitely not one brought on by a bunch of politicians who use rage to stay in business. They just keep talking and talking, but we have to keep on working to pay for them. I switch to music because it calms the savage beast. God knows I was a savage last night. Then, of course, my sexy thoughts are interrupted. Holy Death has something to say about that guy. I can't tell what it is now, but eventually I will.

I'm at that point that comes around in life, where I wonder about where I've been and what it's going to look like for me in the future. Here I am bending a straight man for a night or two, and it's starting to bore me. Here in suburbia most gay or bi men hide instead of living their lives "out" like they do in the cities. Even bi-curious guys who go this way or that a few times are quiet about it. I have bent friends, some clients and long-time acquaintances, most of the time without really trying. As far as I'm concerned, any guy I trust is fair game. I'll let them hit on me. I hit on them, too. But don't kid yourself, it's not all me, and for these types of casual things it is never influenced by a potion or oil. It usually starts with a joke, and it ends up with us eye to eye. Then there's the unspoken pause, and then you know how it goes.

Imagine the Luggage

I don't hook up with guys I just met. I never do the bar thing. I don't use apps or the Internet either. I let things happen naturally. I happen to be the token openly gay guy in a lot of straight guys' lives, so I have generally gotten a very decent amount of play. I don't worry about the wives or the kids as long as we keep things clear between us: I am their adventure, not their destination.

For me, sex and hookups are mostly like catch-and-release fishing. I don't want to keep them; I just want a few moments to appreciate my catch. Of course, I tried love – tried very hard a couple of times, at least. Those relationships are my luggage, the reasons I try not to get too close most of the time. I remember dating a guy not too long ago, an actual out-of-the-closet gay man like me, and he seemed good on paper. It's amazing what looks good on paper.

He liked older men, and he was kind of cute; maybe not my ideal, but he was out of the closet without being a super fairy. I was in this mood to commit, to do it all differently, so I was really taking this guy seriously, looking at the pros and cons. Two weeks in and no sex, no rush. We were doing regular dating, and I liked it. In the end, I had to walk away, because he was not my kind of driver. I mean that literally.

This well-groomed guy in a button-down shirt got behind the wheel of his RAV4, and I got in the passenger seat. I was excited, thinking this was a big moment. He put the music on. We buckled up. The car wasn't my style, but I wasn't judging. The first couple of turns were nice. The traffic lights leading us to the highway felt like they were timed with the music. Then we got onto a small local highway, and everything switched. This guy went from normal life to a driver in some video game. He barely managed to stay 6-12 inches away from the bumper in front of him. He inched and braked and moved from lane to lane. None of it was smooth. The rhythm was off. I saw my life flash before my eyes in his passenger seat – and not in a good way.

No amount of house music thumping on that radio was able to distract me. In fact, the heavy bass started to add to my anxiety. I feared for my life with this guy, and I just let out a sigh. It was nothing personal, just too much pent-up rage on his part. Sure, he could have just yelled at the unconscious assholes like I do, but riding up on them like that was a move too far. Losing his cool, literally starting to sweat over nothing – it felt like a window into this guy's true mental state. When he finally pulled off the highway and into the parking lot, I was depressed for a few seconds.

We attract what we put out.

I had attracted this seemingly relaxed guy to me. I had put out the energy of love, and here it was screaming at the Subaru looking for the exit. I was a thousand percent calm as we came to a stop and my date turned the key, finally giving the engine a rest. When I asked him what was with the horn every two seconds, it didn't go well.

"What was that?"

"What?"

"What??"

Silence.

It was over right then. You see, I don't just have baggage; I have luggage. I have an old travel chest and a few big suitcases. The rollaboard of issues and quotations was bulging at the seams. It's like I could see all the luggage tumble with me as I opened my door and vacated that death trap. I could hear my dad saying, "A stiff dick has no conscience." Seemed like an odd moment for that tidbit of advice to surface.

My father always said, *"A stiff dick has no conscience."* Maybe it was a warning. My father died young, and I have never wanted to follow his footsteps into an early grave. Maybe my father was with us, I thought. Maybe this guy gets off on this kind of driving. If that's true, then there is no way I'm going to fix this. Still, what the hell kind of advice was that in this moment?

Knowing where my stiff lack of conscience has landed me, I always thought a monogamous partnership was going to be my salvation. As we sat through dinner, I counted the minutes. I really was thinking if I could get this guy to drink a few then I could get him to give me the keys. I was thinking of Mom taking the keys to drive when my father had a few too many. I wondered if my father would have preferred I couple up with someone like this or keep living the "crazy" life I have. Maybe my father could see all my hookups from the other side of the veil, and after seeing this jerk drive, he was huddled with Cheryl and Mom, figuring out some next steps. You see, from what I have heard, now that my father is on the other side, he wants to help me. I can't even think about it too much. The potential lack of privacy freaks me out.

The point here is, I'm working out issues, plus the issues of some people no longer with us. In talking to you I find myself going back to the stories of my days of growing up. As dinner winds down, I find myself wondering if all stiff dicks have no conscience, or just mine. Some stiff dicks know how to drive. Anyway, it was this swirl in my head and my father was not my favorite driver, and car rides with him were not a joy. Anyone who thinks I'm going to put my heart in their hands when they can't even make a trip to the restaurant pleasant is sadly mistaken. As crazy as my life may seem, I am not a risk taker.

I've got luggage like I've got ghosts all around me. I know my luggage just like I keep track of my ghosts. I understand that I am the one who screams at the radio, not the one who listens to someone else screaming. I am the one who doesn't drink, because my father did. I am the one who is probably inclined to be an enabler because it's just easier. I am also the one who knows that you can escape that pattern through hard work and by confronting problems as they arise. You can also escape those patterns of stress by walking away right at the beginning, by getting out of the car with your keys, your phone and all your luggage, and closing the door with a smile. Listen, I am not saying I'm perfect – not now, not ever. I'm saying it's important to *know thyself.*

Knowing the Road

Sometimes in life, you end up taking an off-ramp that leads into a detour, and the thing you realize then is that you have to go with the flow and follow these signs you don't recognize. Life is full of unfamiliar territory, and it usually sits just to the edge of your familiar life, your comfort zone. Thinking back now, I figure I took my parents off the road they were on and pulled them into these unfamiliar places, and I did that a lot.

I remember feeling, for both of my parents, a sense that I hadn't been exactly what they wanted as a son. I knew they loved me, but it was likely they suffered from things I couldn't change. They wanted the regular things for me, and in some sense, I wanted those regular things, too. In fact, a good job, a nice house with regular trash pickup – those are still what I like. Nevertheless, something about me was challenging, and I don't know if it was all about me being gay. Whereas my twin brother, Charlie, kind of let things go, I was this firecracker popping off whatever came to my mind.

I think about the ties that bind, about living with a child who keeps setting off fires with his comments. I think about my mom sometimes, see her in the casket, and I think about my father in his. With my father, I remember feeling free for the first time in my life. As I stared down at him in his suit and starched white shirt, with his wedding ring and his Masonic ring both on his hand, I felt something come over me. At first, I had no idea what that feeling was.

My life story started a whole new chapter at the age of 21. I remember thinking that me and my twin brother were the men of the house now. Along with that weight of responsibility, I felt freedom. It was this feeling, like being high for the very first time. I had no idea what it meant to be my own person. I remember telling Cheryl about my father, how I wondered what he thought in those last moments of his. I would tell her how I didn't want to go out young and angry. At first all Cheryl did was listen.

I wonder about people and why they do what they do. I drive past an older development full of retirement homes and wonder if any of them remember a day when they thought, "I am free." It's kind of a ridiculous thought but being free sounds good. Out of the retirement village, I'm driving out to the main road. It's early; I guess I could take a drive to the beach, but I probably won't. I sit at the light with the *No Turn on Red* sign and wonder some more. I wonder about how many guys think about me when their wives go down on them. I hear Cheryl's Holy Death in the back, and I wonder if Cheryl's huge tits influenced her entire life. Then I make the turn, and I wonder when I'll see my friend again, the one I'm just leaving. I weigh the possibilities he'll want to risk another night with me. I figure I can get errands done and not feel pressure.

I'm not wondering if something broke in the middle of the night, not thinking anyone is going to call me in a panic saying they can't make their shift. I'm just wondering about random stuff, like labels and sayings. I wonder about Cheryl and whether she's sending me any messages right exactly now, or if she's dealing with my father, arguing over what's right for me. Maybe she's doing her own thing. I imagine she can see what's doing with me whenever she feels me calling.

I put my foot on the gas and finally make the last turn toward home. I hear the statue of Holy Death hit up against the side of the interior. I wonder if I'm spending too much time thinking about death and sex. I don't want to bore you. I don't want to dwell. In fact, I promised myself not to dwell. Every death is special, and each person is, too, even the ones who annoy you. I know that certain deaths come back to me, and then so do all the memories. First comes the last time I saw them, then maybe the first time, or the time they were sick, maybe the time you sang the best karaoke of your lives together. People flash before our eyes. Our lives flash before us, too.

Napoleon is on the seat next to me, snug in a car bed. He's like an only child with me. He barely weighs 11 pounds, but he's my boy, my number one, and he knows it. It's not easy being Napoleon, because he's super tiny, but I try to insulate him against that feeling. I keep him close. I bought beds and blankets, and I have them ready for whatever we're doing. And we go everywhere. I have to say on the legal papers that I would go nuts without Napoleon, but the truth is he has his own frightening level of anxiety. Making sure he can always be around me is something I could arrange, so I did. When you take your dog everywhere like I do, managing his needs while not killing us through distracted driving can be a challenge. That's just a little note, in case you were wondering.

When Napoleon leaps over the seat without warning, crushing my body with his sharp little paws, it tends to break my train of thought. That might be a good thing, or it could result in an accident one day. We don't know how many times we've got before he jumps hard onto my thigh, or maybe on my genitals. If he isn't crushing my balls, he's potentially hurting himself, so either way I lose if Napoleon is unsure of his surroundings. Someone cut me off once, and the dog slid off the seat like he was on a slippery slide. He rocketed onto the floor, and I couldn't stop him. It was terrifying, and it was kind of funny. But we took no chances after that and found the perfect bathmat in the house. We turned it into a bumper so the slip-and-slide wouldn't happen again. The mat is kind of ugly, but it saves us both trauma – and me the guilt of Napoleon's really offended looks. As a companion animal, Napoleon has standards, and he is not scared to express them.

My ultimate job as far as the dog is concerned is to not lose my cool. People slam on their brakes, miss their exits, and swerve in and out of lanes. It's their job to get where they're going. My job is to navigate all their crazy without bouncing Napoleon around the interior of the car. Cheryl told me this once or twice, making sure I got the message, but trust me his wide eyes and drooped head transmitted all his disgust at my regular performance. I realized I had to do better.

To do this job, I have to deal with others, including all the retirees with the handicap plates. I have to adapt to their undying love of the brake pedal. I deal with them and their clueless driving, with the unpredictable rhythms of their mind-to-foot conversations. In addition, I have to tolerate all the younger drivers, the ones who are usually texting their coffee orders or managing their exes while changing the music and their mind about which lane they want. The moms working out childcare on their way to work – I don't bother them. Those working moms honestly look right through you.

The biggest threat on the road around here isn't someone stopping short or rear-ending you directly. It's the lane floaters, the ones who forget to look, and then before you know it, they sideswipe you. In the summer you've got beach traffic and those lost souls floating from lane to lane with bored kids and sunburns. In the fall and winter, you lose the beach people and get the cars heading to the flea market for deals on junk and antiques. Before a big storm you get the ridiculous behavior of everyone stocking up on bread and milk. No matter what, you get someone not paying attention, all stuck in their head. Before you know it, there comes a float, past the lane into another one. Then like a useless "excuse me" they squeeze out a quick brake light, resulting in a horrible parade of those lights going down the line. In no time at all, that one disturbance ripples, and your day gets complicated.

Nothing is an accident, and nobody comes into your life without a purpose, even if they come in with a bang, even if it happens because nobody was looking. They say everyone sits just a few degrees apart from each other in this web of comings and goings, and at the center sits God. It's like a cosmic highway as much as a web. When you realize how things are connected, you realize you're never alone in life, and all roads have the potential to lead you home.

Cheryl came to work for me after she got sick and moved south, after she had no choice. Her parents were getting older, and Cheryl came down this way to be with them. She said that decision to move was her path to doom, because that's when she got sick, first with lupus and then with the cancer. She left her best friends behind, and even though they weren't that far away by car, it was still far enough for Cheryl to end up mostly alone.

Cheryl said she knew we could be friends right away, and after a while she knew she could trust me not to judge her, but she stayed mysterious. Old friends and new friends — not everyone was allowed to meet and hang out together. No, Cheryl would mention the person, maybe let you say "Hi" on the phone, but that was about it. Going to Cheryl's house for the first time was a big deal, too. Cheryl had certain friends for years, but in some ways on the highway of life, Cheryl was a lane-floater. She didn't do it on purpose. She just happened to do it.

Cheryl sideswiped me, but I didn't mind. She floated into my life, and the next thing I knew, we collided, and our lives were linked. At first, she was a cutter who needed a job, but by the end she was my eyes and ears at a whole other level. She started off slowly, by predicting the dog and by giving me details of what she saw. The new dog coming my way *was in love with me*, she said, and sure enough, he was. It was a clingy love, a battered-by-life-and-in-need-of-a-rescue kind of love, but there it was. As if I needed more proof, one day I came home and this other girl, Aubrey, was sitting inside the house with some friends of mine. Aubrey was kind of sultry with this velvety voice, and she said that little dog was definitely in love with me, and that this was part of his problem. He loved too much, she said, and I have to say it sounded right.

So, Cheryl came into my life out of nowhere, and so did Aubrey, telling me things that helped me see the web between people and everything else. These are the kind of people who run into you on a normal day when you're doing normal things, and they tell you things that aren't really normal. People like that find their way to you, and what you do with them is up to you. Like Cheryl said, some people like

33

to burn the special people; historically, that's true. But I'm proof that not everyone wants to burn the messenger.

Now, I like to bitch about life. And I work with a lot of women. So, I bitch about women a lot, except for those women who hold onto their intuition. I can't help but listen to them because just saying what they say is risky. Women who use their intuition are some of my favorite people on earth. When a woman holds onto that intuitive side, her witchy side, you can't touch her. So, I believed that Napoleon loved me, and I kept him, no matter how much he marked his territory or guarded the perimeter. I outfitted my nice car with an old bathmat for him. I even had him certified as a service dog, not because I really needed him, but because the dog, all 11 shaking pounds of him, needed me. I did all that because of these ladies who showed up in my part of God's highway system.

Aubrey, I should mention, started stopping by my house on her own. It was like she would sit there and read the dog moment to moment. She could interpret his behavior dead on. She said he didn't know I was leading the pack. She said Napoleon was out of his mind because he felt he needed to be tough. It was obvious to him that he was really small, and he was worried to death. I told her to tell him that I was the pack leader and that he was totally fine. Aubrey said she mentioned it, but Napoleon gave her a look that said something like, "Have him prove it." At that point, I got annoyed. I thought I was his salvation, and now I was hearing that the dog was still attached to me, in love with me, but he didn't think I was alpha? It wasn't cute. It was hell on both our nerves, and Aubrey knew it. He was like lint, relentlessly clingy, and although I loved every ounce of him, I pitied him, too. I also imagined my sex life coming to a complete stop if I didn't do something about it. How could I lock him out of the bedroom without a tantrum? How could I leave him for even an hour? Thank God for Aubrey.

Like Cheryl, when I met Aubrey we clicked immediately, while talking about some line from Eckhart Tolle. Our friendship was sealed in the way it was with all my friends, a way you couldn't force. Aubrey was into her thing, and she knew things, and I felt lucky to know her. I loved the way she changed her hair color pretty much all the time, almost as much as I loved her for helping me with Napoleon. Aubrey with her heavy, penciled-in brows and the purple hair with the yellow streaks, or bright red, or some other colors – she was a type of angel. She was 26 when she heard the words "Stage Four."

She didn't have children – she wasn't even married – and within a year of getting diagnosed with colon cancer, Aubrey had passed. She had just finished the chemo and gone down to Florida with her aunt. She had just finished the gauntlet of getting needles stuck in her week after week, enduring these infusions of killer drugs, and was resting by the beach. She was having a moment to think about what was next, and then she was dead of a heart attack. Nobody who knew her took it well, because you felt in your bones how much more she could have done.

I wasn't that happy through my early life, but the dogs I had taught me how to get at love. First with Halston, who I thought was trying to spite me all the time, and then with Napoleon, who was so protective he almost killed my social life. The dogs pushed my buttons, and that made me change how I was doing things, made me change how I saw the world. If it weren't for the women who came with the dogs, like Cheryl and Aubrey, I wouldn't have known how to change things up. I had to do the work, but they were like guides, like angels who still said "Fuck."

Aubrey once said to me that spelt backward, "dog" and "god" are the same word. I know you've heard that before, and I had, too, but something about the way and the time when Aubrey said it made the words feel strong and new. Maybe it was her multicolored hair or the dark eye makeup, but when Aubrey said things like that, it felt like an announcement, like you forgot the memo and someone was reading it out loud to remind you. Yes, it sounded ridiculous, and yes, it sounded true. Staring into Aubrey's face, I decided to be serious and not to laugh.

Napoleon, being a dog, has a memory span that is supposed to only be about ten minutes, but somehow, he still remembered that he had been hurt and had to be careful. I thought about how that must make him feel crazy, acting out from things he couldn't actually remember. I don't even know if what I'm saying makes sense, but to me it does, because there's some bit of God in Napoleon, and in me, and in you. Watching him do things that made no sense, like bark incessantly at the back door, started to make me think about life. As soon as I could get him to stop, I would wonder what about me didn't make him see me as a leader? As soon as he was not piercing my every thought with a whine and a yip, I could wonder if the way I talked to people, the way I lived, had its roots in who I was as a child. So here we are, exploring the depths.

Look, I love Napoleon for being crazy. I love him for throwing himself into my arms that first time I took him with me, away from his situation. I'm pretty sure he watched me for a while and felt nervous about it, but when he made that leap, he never looked back. The first year I had him, he lived under a blanket whenever he was in the salon with me, and to this day he has to work at being social. The mail lady brings him a biscuit when she comes, but he won't even get out from under the blanket sometimes to take it. On top of everything, Napoleon is a picky eater. Go figure.

Aubrey is gone, so I can't ask her what Napoleon wants for dinner anymore. It's all trial and error now, because this dog seriously does not eat everything. Cheryl and some of my favorite clients have passed now, too, a lot of them from cancer. The dog is still here, but chances are he will go before me, and then I will have to deal with that huge emotional loss and the change in routine. So be it. All the things this dog does now to make me crazy will be the things I miss the most when he goes. I will remember him barking up a storm outside, just like I remember things about my parents, friends, former lovers. I know how grief works. I still laugh with my brother and sister whenever we think of Mom raising her one eyebrow. We hated that eyebrow because it meant Mom was beyond annoyed. Now, we can't help but laugh about that eyebrow and make that face ourselves.

Change is the number one constant in life, and we secretly fight it. Cheryl told me about Napoleon, and she told me about love. She even said that if this guy, this one I was seeing when she met me, if he didn't work out, she'd send me someone else. She said she would work from the other side to send me someone better. I said, "How do you know you'll be able to do that?"

"My father sent me to you after he died. So, I should be able to help you."

"Just like that."

"Sure."

"Your father sent you to me?"

"Yes."

"When did he die?"

"Six months ago."

"What did he say?"

"He would find me someone who would take care of me like he would."

"Was your father a witch?"

"No, Tom, he was my father."

It's been on my mind for months as I drive past the shops, the hearing aid outlet, radiology centers and scrub pines. I'm driving around with less yelling at the dashboard and more time breathing in and out these days. First, I did it for the sake of the dog's sanity, since he absolutely hates the yelling. Then I did it for myself because it's pretty amazing what happens when you don't yell so hard that the little veins on your neck pop out. Little by little, the changes do come.

Sometimes these days I don't have any yell left in me, so I stop. It's really that simple; I feel pretty good. For a few seconds I don't know what to do with myself, because the car gets quiet and all I can hear is the engine, but then the phone rings again and I go through the whole dance back and forth. Sometimes I wonder if I'm surrounded by women because I have no interest in sleeping with them. Maybe I'm like a father figure or a godfather or something, but not in the mafia way − more like in a Cinderella-getting-ready-for-her-big-night-out kind of way. Cheryl had this vibrant appearance, plus she had these God-given huge tits. Aubrey was sexy as hell if you were into that kind of futuristic punk-goth-angel look. Sometimes I wonder if having just one man they could trust was something they each needed for different reasons. Looking around at what passes for decent male behavior, I have to believe there was something good I gave them. Friendships are what make the road to God seem real. Love at its best doesn't need to have anything to do with sex.

The Devil You Know

What you resist, persists. That's not a demon; that's right inside you. The more my father resisted me having an opinion, the more I had to share it. The more he said for me to shut up, the more I had to open my mouth. It wasn't even conscious. It was a reflex, like breathing. Of course, there are different types of breathing, but I didn't grow up with explanations on that. Nobody took me aside and shared some deep knowledge on how I could change our patterns of arguing. My father would deal with me, then he'd fire up a cigarette and look away into space. I don't know where his mind went when he did that. I just know it was usually a good time to shift gears or get the hell out of the room.

Now I know how to breathe better, but I sure deal with those persistent demons. I have them hiding in all the corners of my life, like some damned dust bunnies I can't quite reach. The more I want peace and quiet, the more the phone rings. The more I can't have a guy, the more I want him. That's one of those demons I can't fix. No matter how many self-help books or videos, no matter how many candles I burn or whatever else I try, I pick the one guy in the room who is absolutely the most unavailable. In this regard, Cheryl and I were twins. Her parents were way calmer. Her dad didn't yell, and still we both had this thing, this horrible talent of picking out a match that brought out the worst in our lives.

One of the things we would do as friends was compare our horror stories to our hopes and dreams. Cheryl would talk about soulmates and twin flames and people confusing the two. Cheryl would show me the things she bought to keep her man happy, even if I never got to meet this man. He'd be gone soon, she said. He would go back to his ex. She knew what he was going to do to her, and still Cheryl kept the fantasy alive. She played the game, trying to make it better each time, but it took a lot of effort. The sicker she got, the less energy she had for heels, outfits, even for makeup, and true to form, her man called less. The more ill Cheryl got, the more the phone stayed silent, the more she wanted me to have the fantasy life, the one she knew she wouldn't have.

Despite liking the movies, I don't need private jets and superyachts in my perfect world; they'd just complicate things. Adding even one private plane to my fantasy life would require me to start thinking about the power washing. I would begin to obsess about the maintenance and whether the staff would be doing that right or if I'd have to go out on the damned wing and do it all myself. Yeah, none of that sounds like more fun, just more headache. My perfect guy, that one in my dreams; I don't even know what he looks like, or what he owns but I know how he makes me feel.

Reality is, that type of partnership, the one that feels right, would probably be too much on my nerves. I don't know how to relax. I am juggling my life. I am juggling the past. I'm a juggler of all this emotional luggage that I can't stand. I can't get rid of the damned things either, so instead of baggage, you might notice I call them *my luggage*. Sounds nicer to think of my bullshit wrapped up in some matched set of designer leather while breaking my back as I keep it suspended in air. Let it land and it might open, overwhelming me and everyone else.

I am juggling this luggage in all these crazy shapes that make it a shit-show of a balancing act. I've got luggage shaped like anxiety, ADD, definitely some control issues and probably some extra testosterone – all pushing to take over my balance. I am juggling every single day, and it feels like I am trying to do it in the eye of a storm, the one I have been in since forever. Now that I'm an adult, the storm is calmer at the center, but it also has more powerful rain, sporadic hail and wind gusts that have names like taxes, water bills, the cleaning lady, that asshole who cut me off while I was trying to merge like a normal person. The list goes on. That's my life – nothing special, just a day-to-day struggle.

Now I realize the key to making life better is to not explode at myself. When I drop a piece of luggage and watch the contents spill out, I calm down and take a breather. It's amazing what that can do: the breathing, the kind you think about. That kind of breathing lets you appreciate the pieces. When you breathe, you can be the observer. Then all of a sudden, you're not panicking when your anxiety comes tumbling out at your feet. The anxiety really has been with me forever, and you can tell it's packed pretty solidly in there. When I look, I can see the *"Daddy's on his way home"* pieces and *"The school called"* pieces, for starters. My ADD luggage is more like its own set of mini bags, all attached. The ADD can make a jangling sound like all the bags are pulling at each other. It's amazing, the shape of things when you slow down. Time allows you to sort the luggage, and every once in a while, you can let things go and lighten the load.

So, yeah, I believe in letting go of the perfect and letting go of the luggage. I believe in a day when that shit is smaller and lighter, like something packaged for actual travel, not just a daily commute. Yeah, that's it. I believe that the longer I breathe and take a good inventory here and there, that someday the luggage is going to be smaller and lighter, and my reflexes better than ever at juggling those few tiny cases. You see, to me that's reasonable progress.

I believe in myself and in a place and time when the luggage is not so important. Sex and work, – all good on the luggage juggle. Sex and money – not bad, a little strain on the juggling shoulder. Sex and love – watch the whole goddamn thing fall and all the seams open up and the damned *"I told you so!"* demons run all over the room. Pandora's got nothing on me when that luggage of sex and love opens. Those demons sure are something to get back into their neat and tidy package. The worst thing is, you have to be nice to them or they embarrass you more.

You see, I'm a product of my history, and I'm a product of history. For a long time, sex had nothing to do with love for me because there was no gay love and no gay marriage, and all I saw was sex and more free sex. You might think that sounds decadent, but welcome to the '70s and '80s. Welcome back to a time before social media, to a time when you could be in the closet all week, and then come the weekend you could go sweat with a few hundred of your closest friends and nobody, but nobody, would have thought to stick a camera into the middle of things. And then, once you broke out of the closet, dear sweet Jesus, there was nothing better than going out before AIDS. You couldn't have felt more goddamn gorgeous and free than being in room after room full of hard-working, hard-playing boys.

The only mistake I made at that time was falling in love, because our models of love weren't shaped by us. Our models of love were shaped by television shows. I made the mistake of falling in love without even asking questions. Not everybody came out of the closet back then, just like now. Not everyone felt OK to be themselves because it could be such a fight with the family, with all the loved ones. There was no "bisexual" back then. We were told that was a myth. There was no polyamory; we were told you were a whore, or you had yourself a significant other. We were all just doing our best, and I was at my best when none of the love stuff came into my head. I was at my strongest when I was just living in the moment. Because the second you fell for someone back then; all that undigested shit from the movies, from the storybooks, from the pulpits, all of that came rushing back. We barely had self-help back then, and we sure as shit didn't have self-care.

My heart got broken with my very first boyfriend, and my love life kept going downhill from there. But don't cry for me. I was who I was. I was cute as hell. I had these steel-blue eyes that made men and women stop. I got offers all the time, at least for a night. I didn't know what I was doing at all, but I didn't care because it was a different time. Remember, only the rich kids had therapy. The rest of us were working. We took our weekends when we had them, and I, for one, packed up all my best looks in the trunk of my ride whenever I had a couple of days off in a row. With bags and outfits packed, I was ready for anything. I had that fury and rage at my dad. I had the grief of missing him. I had all that seething emotion and my own far-off stare. Back then, that made me sexy as hell.

While my love life went steadily down, my sex life went up and up. Even though I was a guy looking for another guy, I still wanted the fairytale relationship and all the amazing sex that I just knew went with it. I mean, how could it not? I wanted me and this magical man of my dreams, living together in some kind of bliss that my parents never had, but that I saw in all the movies. I saw it in the John Wayne movies my dad loved. I saw it in those damned soap operas Mom couldn't stop watching. Maybe I don't have to tell you now that things didn't exactly work like that in real life, but we were naïve. We were hundreds, thousands, even millions of kids who had no idea what manipulation really meant. Trust me, the straight kids were in the same situation. Later, when the divorce rate skyrocketed and no one even tried to stay married, I knew the deck had been stacked against us. We had been driving through a trap, on a road where all the posted signs were pointing in the wrong direction. The billboards with their cowboys and their faithful women wearing aprons were nothing more than a very good-looking lie.

When L, my first serious boyfriend, moved in with me, he had this hot Puerto Rican attitude and a body that matched it. I was ready to give him closet space immediately. In fact, I was in the process of converting the whole house to be more comfortable for him, at least mentally. L could dress, and he could dance, and I was ready to do life together. What I wanted was a fairytale; what I got was him going off to the bar to meet random guys. He did it over and over again until one day he left. There was no big breakup talk. I knew it was coming, I guess. You couldn't tell me that then. Back then I stood around bitching about L sleeping with guys he picked up at the bar while I waited at home. I didn't think he would leave, and pretty much all I wanted was for him to stay. Seeing how everyone I knew as a kid got together and stayed together, I really thought L was it. We didn't have gay marriage, so we weren't married, but I thought two people who got together stayed together. This playing-the-field thing he did changed me.

My heart turned cold as soon as that first big, sticky rejection set in. All of a sudden, I wanted more of everything: more men, more kicks and lots more excitement. I would book flights to Vegas for a weekend of glitz. I headed to Florida and stayed in Boca Raton, hanging out by the pool. I would trek out to see friends on Fire Island, to see hot guys wearing next to nothing, to get lost in the sweat and the sounds of the dance floor. All of it was fun, and none of it felt real.

The years after L left me high and dry, I had other men live with me, and we would go on adventures together, but nothing lasted, and nothing felt like I could trust it. My life became a drama where I knew the script. One by one, lovers left, or I sent them away, and that was more or less fine. It took me years to learn the words "self-fulfilling prophecy." Took me longer to say them into the mirror. This newfound self-knowledge, however, did NOT mean I knew how to stop it. Along the way, I got hobbies to keep the lows from getting too low or the highs from getting too exciting. I mean, you need to see my garden, and those fish in my pond. Routine is my safe zone.

L, that sexy, beautiful son of a bitch, he's passed on, but I still think of him a lot. I don't like saying *he's dead,* because in my mind it's cold and inaccurate. He's somewhere, still dancing, still twirling in circles, shaking that ass for someone. He's not dead, because nothing dies, and people; when they pass on tend to leave a trail, like strings of light. I know that we have a thread between us. I know it stretches between the worlds. I don't know why I know, but I know. I don't know how, but it works. I mean, what's so hard about love never dying? What's so hard about people shining like stars across space and time?

Even if I didn't forgive L in life, I had to forgive him in death. But for the record, I did forgive him in life, for taking numbers behind my back and borrowing money he never returned, for leaving the house *for days* without telling me where or who he'd been with. I forgave him for smelling of other people's colognes or perfumes. I forgave him for never really coming out to his family and for making me date his sister as a cover. *Yes,* he made me date his sister. No, I didn't *want* to fuck her. You know, those were crazy times, and the world made us even crazier with its stupid rules against nature and God.

No way God made people like they are, all different, for each of us to be stuck living out our days the exact same ways. Nothing about being straight or middle of the road is wrong. It just doesn't work for all of us. You see, people are made of light just like stars are, and nobody tells them where or how they can shine it. My L, he knew that, too, that people have to be free to find their own way. I guess that's why I had to love him. He wasn't perfect, and neither was I, and maybe neither was our love, but it was real. Real enough to hurt like a Brazilian wax on my heart when he left, and real enough to forgive once that pain gave way.

I forgave every one of L's "encounters." I forgave every way he would hurt me and satisfy that drive in himself. I've forgiven him because it doesn't matter now, because I understand him better than I did, now that I went out and lived like that myself. In a way, we were both living out what we had seen in the movies, and since they never showed people like us "happily ever after," I guess it makes sense that we didn't end up that way. I mean, my baby, he wasn't even white, so he barely saw himself on TV in anything but a knife fight or a carjacking. So, what was he supposed to think about a nice lawn around a suburban home where we grill on the weekends in matching outfits with absolutely nobody yelling? Things were different back then.

The Devil card in Tarot is about things like sex and addiction, about things like bad relationships and codependence. Sometimes you can see the devil, the addiction or the bad relationship, and lots of times you can't, not until you get a wake-up call. I'm bringing up the Devil card now, because the devil inside us isn't as simple as we like to believe, since the devil's roots stretch right down to the first time someone made us choose a side. *What part of you is bad, and what part of you is good?* What part of you is the victim, and which part is the perpetrator? The devil is easy to spot in the movies, but spotting the devil inside each of us gets a lot harder. We're shadowy fucks.

It all starts in our early life when we learn about love. What I thought I knew, what I thought I saw, was my mother and my father in these simple roles where he was pretty much always wrong and she was always right. Where he was hard and judgmental, she was soft and kind, and to me that was all there was. We try to resist that life we think we witnessed, and so we torture ourselves trying to grasp, to give everyone roles. When I think about the Devil in this way, I find myself thinking about how easy it seemed at the time to side with Mom and hide from my father, but I also see how no matter how inevitable it all was, taking sides came with a cost. Cheryl would be so proud of how far I've come.

"Tom, pay attention."

"I am."

"No, you're not."

"I was spacing out the window."

"I don't care. Tell me what you see in the picture."

"The Lovers are chained."

I tried to act like it was no big deal. I tried hard to make sure my eyes didn't flash all big. I'll admit it now, the first time I saw the Devil card I was scared. Shitless. What with those horns and the sermons from when I was a kid flashing in my head like a goddamn electrical storm. My ADD and my anxiety flickered in all the parts of my brain within seconds, but I just took another drag off my cigarette.

Cheryl must've known I was freaked. Having grown up Catholic, she must have freaked out herself the first time she saw it with the Lovers shackled up like prisoners, their guard behind them. She didn't let on a bit, but she did start explaining some things, the slippery, shadowy stuff. After that I kind of got into the sexy parts, with the couple standing at the devil's big, demon feet with these chains and collars around their necks. With Cheryl egging me on to tell her what I saw, I learned this is a card about our minds and how our minds shape our world by causing ripples. Can you imagine? All this about our minds being our biggest prisons, it's literally true.

I liked the sexy, but Cheryl wouldn't let it sit there. She'd get us into the deeper stuff, the psychology, the moral implications. Good grief, the moral implications took all the fun out of it, but that's life. No free rides.

"The cards don't take away responsibility; in fact, it's the opposite. They make you more aware of it; by making you see your power."

"Well, I like seeing my power."

"Then you have to see how you're making your own hell."

"Oh."

"Well, that's not as much fun."

Cheryl would smile, shake her head. She was such a fucking sport.

Long story short, The Devil card can take away a lot of the guilt you have for being alive, and it can make you let go of your need to control or be controlled. It can make you look at your own power, and it forces you to figure out how you give it away. *Hating yourself is how the devil gets his claws in you.* Turning you into a victim for your whole life is how he can stay. So, what I mean is, we can't give into feeling like victims. Or maybe the amount of time we feel like victims has to be balanced out by how much time we let shit go and move on with our lives. It's not the feeling that's bad, not even the lust. It's getting lost in some feeling or getting lost in the lust that poses some serious problems.

Now, let me explain something – I'm living in a typical suburban community. It could not be more normal. There's the family across the street with the plastic jungle gym – they're fine. There's the neighbors and their teenagers, and nobody there gets on your nerves, either. One asshole doesn't take in his garbage cans all the time, but for the most part this subdivision is nothing different. To take it a step further, we're surrounded by other subdivisions, and on the other side of the one-lane highway running east to west, there's an old folks' development. Up and down for miles, there's your medical testing plaza, your convenience stores and all the typical chain stuff that lines all the small highways from here to California.

It's in this strip of New Jersey, in a place that looks pretty much like every other town all over the country, that these statistics grow in between everything. You know the ones, about depression and illness and small-town clusters in these big epidemics. Somewhere between the flea market on the weekends and the Starbucks open every morning, these statistics grow. Like invisible vines they grow, with nobody noticing, and then one day it pops up on the news: Heroin use is on the rise. Overdose deaths are up.

We got other invasive statistics growing here, too: the lots of innocent kids-getting-cancer list. We make that list every so often but nobody knows why, or if they do, they don't talk. Every day around here, statistically speaking, those kids on the plastic jungle gym with no sharp edges might end up sick or drugged to death. We may be in the lead of some trend, seeing as that's what can happen with this many people living this closely together, but we are not alone in this statistical bullshit. New Jersey is not some foreign planet, no matter what Hollywood tells you. This terrain is familiar despite the accent.

All around here, grandparents who lived regular lives wake up with messages from their adult kids crying and screaming about problems way bigger and stranger than what meets the eye on the way to the Walmart. Parents wake up like that too, staring into their phones with their eyes big. From the headlines to that last message from the specialist, this place has its share of dramas being lived by people who have spent their whole lives being normal, not extra. They dress like normal people, go to the coffee shop and get bagels and pizza, all like their neighbors, like most of America. Still, their lives take all sorts of turns.

Strip mall after strip mall, you have to decide, is it worth the line, the crowd, fighting for a parking spot? Ultimately, every turn you look at the sign and ask, "Is this worth my time?" I mean, that seems to be the fucking question these days – is anything or anyone worth wasting your time? Life is so goddamn short. The statistics keep creeping up on you. So, newsflash: There's more to life than sex, or getting ahead of the next guy in line. There's even more to life than those crappy little fairytales, though don't ask me to give them up. There's way more to life than errands or even your first broken heart. When you're staring down your life trying to figure out how to pay the bills while staying alive, everything registers. Add a pandemic or take it away, add a drug addiction or leave it – it's all just drama, and how you deal with it, or stay stuck in it, is the key.

"You're being your father right now."

"No, I wasn't."

"Tom, yes, you were."

"Well – "

"Tom, NO."

"Ok, fine! Whatever – *you hungry?*"

Cheryl never knew my father, but every time she said I was being like him, I have to say she was accurate. I don't know exactly how she knew, but she knew when she knew. She could see him in me somehow, or feel him in me, or maybe she saw his face mixed over mine. She didn't tell all her secrets. I didn't ask all the time, but I looked to get myself unstuck from whatever I was thinking or feeling, *real fast.* I couldn't help but see those eyes of hers on me. I couldn't help but notice how they changed when she saw me like that. She looked at me big-eyed and strong, like she had a special window, like she could see a whole other type of movie with me inside it. It was like she looked inside me and past me all at once.

Cheryl was good at knowing, and seeing, and I swear when she saw that hard set in my jaw, she was tenacious. This one time, just before Cheryl died, I was talking about my father. I don't even remember the story, but Cheryl barely let me finish, and I was surprised. I wondered if I had come across angry. I was really confused, because I was remembering something small, something stupid about him.

"Tom! Your aura changed, just now."

"Oh, yeah?"

"Yeah. It was like light all around you. My God, Tom, it was beautiful, bright blue and bright green."

"Did you ever see that around me before?"

"No."

"Why was it different?"

"You were speaking the truth from your heart when you spoke about him."

"You saw — "

"I saw the love, Tom."

That was when Cheryl was really close to the end, and her intuition was off the charts. It was staggering to hear her come up with stuff about people she'd never met, people who had been dead a long time. It was like she was swimming in some kind of ocean, like she was floating in and out of that movie screen she went into. She started me talking about things in a whole new way, like memories were plain old objects in films. She could pick something up from the past and show it to you like it was happening right now. She could pick up that moment in time and turn it around in her hand and look at it from all sides.

The truth was, I sided with my mom because she sided with me, but I wasn't much like her. I liked cars, and Dad liked boats. He drank, and I decided, "No, thank you." I did everything and liked everything opposite from him, but it wasn't maybe as opposite as I had thought.

I had a lot of the same tendencies as my father, but it wasn't until Cheryl was close to the end that somehow all that became clear. Hell, that crack addiction I got was pretty crazy, and probably the only way I broke it was because I was hard as nails when I had to be, just like my father. I wasn't missing work and losing my house for no drug.

Inside our minds we have all sorts of closets, and inside those closets are things we hide from ourselves. We unlock those doors one by one, looking into the closets, seeing our memories or hearing names from the past. You might open a door you never noticed before and hear a question echoing all through your brain, one like, *"Don't you think at all?"* and you suddenly remember why you closed that door in the first place. Shining that first light can be hell, but not shining it on those closets in our mind is usually worse.

I'm going to tell you that was part of what made me love Cheryl, the fact that she knew being me was hard. She knew that being out of one closet didn't change the fact that I had those threats, that anger from my father lodged in parts of my brain, hidden away. Like a good friend, she saw where I was barely functioning, and she was patient as fuck. Like a best friend, she tried to make the truth easy on me.

Cheryl had her own inner voices, ones that made threats and kept her in her own type of closet. She tucked herself into her closets as hard as anyone. Sure, she knew better, but she was only human. Like you and me, Cheryl had closets from this life and ones from beyond. She knew she saw things other people didn't. For Cheryl, being at home was safe, but being out in the world – that was always a shit-show.

Can you imagine being born seeing people's auras and then one day learning about the witch trials in school? I mean, the church you go to doesn't like the cards, you learn that pretty early on, with them teachers telling you not to even think without the priest. They talk about souls and heaven and sometimes the Holy Spirit, but that's it, and meanwhile you see these rainbows all over the place. Imagine sitting in church and seeing all the faded-out auras, the ones that look like they've been through some washer too many times, and then maybe they sing a song or something and those rainbows light up again. Imagine how beautiful that could be, and then you realize you can't talk to anybody about it. I mean, you can maybe talk about it with your mom and your grandma, your aunts, but not anybody else.

Imagine realizing how fake the world is, how stupid crazy it is trying to tell you that you don't see what you see and you don't know what you know. Then they get out the history books and teach you all about the evil witches and those horrible trials. Sure, nobody burns witches in America now, but what if they decide to change their minds? After all, they did it before, and sick motherfuckers would do it again. People are jealous like that. If they can't see your aura, nobody should.

Auras are natural, Cheryl told me. She said they're something like our natural electricity showing through our skin. Every aura burns a different color or shades of colors based on our magnetism, our composition as spiritual beings. Some auras are tight to the body, and some walk into a room 10 feet before you. To someone who reads them, they are as regular as daylight. They sprout off people like electric vines, sort of like neon, but softer, and they arc around each one of us like we are walking trellises. Auras are like atmospheres, but personal-size.

Auras are the light of who we are on the inside no matter what we look like on the outside. Our mood can change our faces, and our auras change back and forth, so people who read them can tell who you are most of the time and who you are in the moment. Imagine seeing all that from your first day on Earth and never losing it. Imagine knowing all that and not being able to tell any of your friends. Picture seeing something as bright as the Northern Lights, something like a halo hovering all around your friend's head, and you learning to just sit there without missing a beat, not saying a thing.

I imagine Cheryl growing up and seeing these types of lights, waiting for other kids like her to show up at the playground. I think about her waiting and waiting until she stops trying to mention the lights and sticks to the program. I can see it as she stops saying what's on her mind, listening to, repeating what the other children say. I wonder if that waiting-for-someone-who-never-comes kind of feeling is what stuck with her. I wonder a lot if that waiting became her own addiction. I wonder if that's where it started, with Cheryl waiting on slides and swings for a friend who never showed.

They say a person should list their intentions to get in touch with the kind of life they want. They say it beats the devil on the inside if we stop focusing on the things we don't want and start looking at what we do want. The trick to knowing what you really want seems to be about letting go of all the things you fear. Lately, all I want is a simple life without drama, and maybe that's what scares me the most; after all, who doesn't like late-night calls? Who doesn't want to hear that pause between sentences, the one that screams of passion, of hot, movie-style sex driving its way over in the middle of the night?

I tell myself I want to trim the wisteria in peace. I think that I want to host brunches by the pool. I tell myself that I want to live the little pleasures with someone decent by my side, day after day, even if that scares me deep inside. I want to have boring couple sex, and spiced-up couple sex. I'm ready to deal with dirty laundry that doesn't get put in the hamper if that means I get loved. I tell myself over and over again that I am ready for all the daily annoyances that come with true love and commitment. I'm ready for my gay Hallmark Channel Special Edition series. I am so ready I picked out the new drapes I am so sure he'll love.

In tarot you follow this Fool on a journey, and newsflash: You're always the fool, because that's part of being human. At some point you can be a wiser fool, but in your heart, you have to stay a little bit like a child, or be willing to be the first-day-on-the-job kid. As much as you've got to know the devil inside you, you've got to be willing to embrace your inner fool. Who knew?

Look, I knew that we are all on a trip with only one destination, and I knew it before I met Cheryl, but she crystallized that for me. She took all the psychology – and, let me tell you there's plenty of it – and she made it understandable. I mean, I was happy paying them psychics and readers before, because I knew I wasn't going to try and figure it out on my own.

"Tom, that one's an archetype."

"Oh, that's shitty."

"What?"

"They tell ya what to think about people."

"No, that's a stereotype."

"Oh. So, what does this do?"

"It tells you about mental states, actions and dynamics."

"Oh. That is different."

This idea that we're all on pretty much the same journey, and that everyone plays the fool at some point – Cheryl wouldn't let me forget it. There are other things you can be beside the fool, but you'd better be careful if you forget that you can always go back to being a fool; in fact, you have to expect it. You always go back to what you hid from yourself, and what you hid from others. When you go to change that thing, you're like a whole new person, taking one step in front of the other. It doesn't matter if you're wearing brand-new Nike or cheap secondhand shoes, you're going to be walking the Fool over and over again if you want to grow.

Now, with all this straight in our minds, I'm willing to tell you something I don't often just tell people. You see, the first sex I had was when I was only a kid, and the guy who did it with me, really did it *to* me. You see, he never asked for my permission, what they call "consent" these days. I'm going to tell you right now *that guy* is not why I am gay. I was born this way. But as I open and close these doors in my mind, I find he comes back to me sometimes.

The mixed messages of that experience opened some floodgates in me, and I think I'm still trying to channel those conflicted waters into something that won't make me crazy. You see, it was amazing to know that a man could want sex from another guy. It was mind-blowing to know I wasn't alone. The problem was that we didn't talk about any of this, so the whole thing made me feel more alone. You see how this shit goes?

The problem I'm sharing with you now is that this guy, cute and sweet and good-looking enough as he was – he wasn't so much offering me sex or connection as much as he was pulling me into his closet with him. No adult has the right to put that kind of silence onto some young kid, but that's the kind of shit that happens when people are repressed: they pick on the ones they know will keep quiet.

The guy who grabbed at my innocence in silence did it in a tent, and he was maybe 26 at the time, when I was barely 13. I don't always know how to feel about him. I forgive him on some level, but not on another because of that closet so strong that he didn't say a word. Somehow, I didn't think I could say a word, either – and that, my friends, is not healthy.

He knew I was gay, like all the other adults probably did, way before I understood too much about myself. So, I tell myself now that he didn't know how to ask for my consent, and I truly believe that. I remind myself he was brilliant, going on full scholarship to Colgate, where he was a straight-A student. I remember how I would feel a part of him was completely broken. He was on his way to medical school, then he all of a sudden broke. They said it was the pressure of competition, but I don't think that was it. Back amongst family and friends, among the whispering voices that said he would never bounce back, he reached out to me. I get it.

The guy who introduced me to sex never said a word while he was pushing himself close to me, onto me, and we never spoke about it. Five years later, he died, and they called my father to go identify the body, because he was that close to us as a family. Even then, I didn't say a word. I couldn't imagine it would do any good.

The night it happened I drove past the accident on my way home and saw a body on the side of the road, covered in a sheet. I got this funny feeling when I went by, like I knew the person under the sheet. My parents had company; they were playing cards in couples. They were telling jokes, smoking and having some drinks. I came in, and I was bugging out. I told everyone – my godparents, my Uncle George and Aunt Helen – how I'd been driving the truck, and I saw something on Route 37, a little past Vaughn Avenue.

"I saw a body by the side of a road, covered in a sheet. And I felt I knew the person."

"How do you know?"

"I don't know. I can feel it. I know who that was."

"That's ridiculous."

Sure enough, the call came through less than 10 minutes later, stopping everyone in their tracks.

He was younger than I am now, barely in his 30s, but he was dead. That night I had so many feelings, and I didn't share them with anyone. I didn't say a word; I didn't know if anyone would believe me, and anyway, he was on the other side. What was the point of running his name through the wringer? I knew not to push the conversation while the families were grieving. That revelation of mine could have sent sparks flying in every direction. Mostly, I figured they'd fly in my direction. I didn't see the point of setting myself up for a thousand little burns. I didn't think there was any point in watching my father go into a nuclear meltdown.

I can tell you about the closet of the devil, because people like me have been forced into it for years. I'm over that nasty closet voice, at least as a threat, but damned if I don't find it coming up in all the sexy bits of my life.

"If you tell anyone, I'll kill you." That's what guys say as you're taking them to a place they're scared to go, some uncharted territory they really enjoy but can't admit to wanting. I'm the forbidden fruit, and I know it. I've enjoyed it too, but life moves on. I am so over the sexy death threats. I mean, I wouldn't mind them in role play or something; I'm just over that feeling that the best thing about me is that I know how to be a secret.

I'm not going to make it so people think they know every part of my life by reading these stories that I have to share. What I want to talk about isn't just the sex; it's the journey of getting in touch with myself. Like I said, we all got shadow, and we all got light, and that balancing, juggling thing we do, that is the truth. So, while I've got my luggage and stories all laid out for you, I hope to God you're checking your own inventory. I'm not forcing you to put it into some book or even to write it in your own little journal where you sort out your thoughts. You decide on your own damn therapy.

What I want to talk about is how it feels to be a person – any person at all. I'm just your regular human, with hang-ups and habits and, like I might have said, routines. Some of them I could do without, like biting my nails or smoking these menthols that Cheryl begged me to quit. Some things are harder to let go of without getting snappy. I figure there are people who root for you in life, and they probably root for you after they pass. I can't imagine that the people who love us and we love back go off into the next life without leaving one eye on us. I mean, don't we all have routines? Imagine having to give them all up all at once. I just don't see it. I bet Cheryl is looking over my shoulder sending me advice that I completely miss most of the time. Signs from the other side don't always come in flashing like a traffic signal, and even when they do, we miss them and have accidents.

Anyway, Cheryl was good to me even when she was frustrated with me, sort of like a mom. In fact, I guess she was kind of my witch-mom. I was her baby *brujo* and she was my mama *bruja*.

First big witchy lesson that actually stuck is that you have to get in touch with your gut, to get past all the noise and hear something deeper. Next was a wave of available tools, and not all of those took. The cards, the rituals and spells – Cheryl had some way of improving any situation, and she took no prisoners. If she didn't have a trick up her Italian-ancestry sleeve, she borrowed it from some other lady she knew. Cheryl was good at asking questions; she did it all the time with clients while cutting their hair. Put her in a room with another witch, and the questions flew. The other witches, the working-class folks like us, I noticed, had a way with each other. Cheryl spent a lot of time with Latinas. They spoke the same language, knew all about the saints and the days and the way the church buried the old truth in their new calendar.

Anyway, Cheryl didn't teach me a lot with oils, because there just wasn't enough time. The only thing I can remember is that St. Anthony likes coconut and olive oil, but there's some incantation that charges the oil that I don't remember at all. There was a lot to learn and not enough time, just like Cheryl said. Still, what I got from her I can pass on, and that is exactly what I intend to do. Just be warned, it's more all these personal stories I can give you, not really instructions. I'm not a teacher like that. I'm more of the student who's been held back a few times. I know the ropes of surviving the program, not necessarily graduating out of the situation.

I drive between pine trees and back roads, and I think about what it's all going to look like after I'm gone. Sometimes I think back to that night I saw the body of our family friend by the side of the road. Like a flash it comes when I see other traffic accidents, even years later. I thank God to this day that I didn't have to go with my father to identify the body. It's one of those times I appreciate what a team player my sister could be.

That night, my sister went to the morgue and stood there as the oldest, witnessing the sand in his hair and the abrasions on his lifeless face. Susan saw the bruising that happens when someone hits your car and the impact takes your life, and she did it standing tall and solid. She told me they wheeled him out, and then they uncovered him, and that lifting the sheet in her presence made it worse. I don't know if there was any way that was going to be a good experience, but when they lifted the sheet, it felt all wrong, she said, like a horrible, warped version of Christmas or a surprise birthday gone wrong.

It was my sister's first ride in a police car and the first time she went to ID a body, and it was the first time I had such a strong hit of intuition. That night me and my sister were terrified for all different reasons, but still the experience gave us a bond. My father had seen enough dead people during World War II, and he took it all in without much emotion that I could see. Looking back, I wonder what that night triggered in him. He moved through the house to the car and came back again, notifying family and friends of the news with a steadiness I didn't expect.

He knew enough that night to understand that my mother couldn't have handled the morgue, and that his daughter could. It was one of those few times he wasn't trying to toughen us boys, and he left us home. It was one of those rare moments where nobody pushed each other's buttons, and it all came from him and this calm he had in the face of a young man's death. He had seen it before, but I swear, he didn't say a word about it; didn't bring up the war.

The once-promising student was gone, and the bulk of his family, who lived up north, relied on my father to make the identification and make the news official. He did it all without drama, being quick and efficient, making sure that the first call to the family happened as soon as he could manage, so they would suffer the uncertainty for the least amount of time. Then he got on the phone with any neighbors or friends who shared summers and weekends down at the shore with us. I could see my father holding the heavy receiver in his hand, dialing the numbers with an unusual patience and his usual efficiency.

My sister knew what had happened between me and this guy in that tent, and she told my father. I waited, but nothing happened as the news traveled inside our home. My parents never brought it up with me, but when I said I wasn't going to the funeral, they agreed that I could stay home. My big announcement was barely a sentence. "I am not going," I said, motioning to the car. "You don't have to go, Tommy," said my mother. That was it. Everything was swept under some rug and tucked into a closet. Writing this down is like pulling a chain and letting the light shine down on the whole experience, rug and all. What used to make me feel like I was dying inside looks a lot more like dust now. When I take a deep breath, that closet and the rug, the memories of the tent and of that body by the side of the road – it scatters. The devil has a grip, and when you look at him in the light, you realize that grip is dust.

JUDGMENT

When I grew up, we didn't hear a ton about God in some formal sense, but the family was God-fearing, and that meant there was no way to escape the uncomfortable experience that was Sunday service. Sometimes on Sundays, when my father wasn't too hungover, we would pile into the car: me, my twin, my older sister, my father and Mom. All of us were uncomfortable in our starched getups except for Mom, who looked like a proud hen at the head of her chafing brood.

We went to the simple red-brick building of the Presbyterian church, looking like all the other families hoping to better their odds of getting into heaven. With our clean ears and pressed clothes, we sat there like a team listening to a coach who was going to help us pry the gates of heaven open. The only thing we had to do was listen and follow the plan. The reverend was there to make that plan of attack abundantly clear. It was the reverend's job to do all the thinking and reading and to drill it into the rest of us.

Truth be told, I hated the starched collars and the ride over, but I loved two things about going to church. The first thing that made going to church bearable was listening to the Rev. Van Dyke speak, and the second was the building itself. The thing I hated more than anything was Sunday School. In Sunday School, they made us read from the Bible out loud, and that was torture. My jarring monotone mangled the words of God, the apostles and every prophet. In my voice, the Word of God was ADD, dyslexic and extra slowed-down by massive anxiety. In Sunday School, as I slowly tortured the word of God and it tortured me, I could hear my dad's voice echo inside my mind, *"What's wrong with you?"* Usually, I broke down the teacher halfway through, and in her Christian mercy she'd let someone else finish reading the passage. It's not like we had all weekend to get through it. Being Protestant, efficiency was next to godliness, and sometimes that worked to my benefit.

Now, unlike my tortured voice, when the Reverend spoke, God sounded real. The Reverend made all the school and starched collars worth it. All I wanted to do was sit and hear him preach after he read whatever it was he needed to read for that day. I knew enough to know that a lot of what the Reverend said was his interpretation of God's word. Some of it was perfect, I tell ya, and some of it was probably bullshit, but it all sounded so good coming out of his mouth. The best stuff he said went in most ears and out the others. I noticed that as a kid. Lip service is the big service for most, and there's no better way to tell that than to watch how the people walked and talked as soon as they got past the threshold from the Sunday service back into the real world. The kids went back to being kids, but the adults – you know they'd gather. You could see them judging each other, checking out the wife's dress or whether the husband's shirt was ironed. *"Judge not, unless you want to be judged,"* I can still hear my father's voice saying. I can hear him quoting the Reverend in all these unusual moments.

Rev. Van Dyke didn't even need a microphone. The acoustics in the sanctuary were perfect, and his voice traveled into every crevice of the room, into every part of your body. It wasn't what you think of as huge – nothing like today's mega-churches – but it held a lot of people, all of them bathed in that sound. Everyone knew when the Rev. Van Dyke was going to be there, and they packed in extra tight to hear that voice that gave them hope. The room was bare; I remember that, too; classic Protestant for the period. We had no statues, a "No idols before me" kind of arrangement, with only a large wooden cross behind the pulpit and those intricate windows along the perimeter.

There were no pictures of angels or of the Virgin Mother Mary, or any of those icons of saints. The only thing you had to hold onto was the Reverend's voice. When Van Dyke was up there, that was enough for me and the rest of the masses. We were a handful of people compared to today, a small-town congregation sitting upright and starched. Van Dyke didn't judge – at least, he didn't act like he did. He acted like we were all on a mission together and that life was OK, more or less.

The church building is now part of the Ocean County Library in Toms River because with all the subdivisions and the kids being born, the church outgrew it. The windows are still there, pointing up to God. The steeple is there, though they had to rebuild it a couple of times, thanks to lightning and termites. The bells are gone, though, maybe because the cost was too high for something no one would use, but the town was smart enough to make a recording of them. The recording plays to let you know the time. It's not the same as it was, but it sure is nice to hear.

We kids were baptized there; my parents had gotten married there, too. Now it's the coffee shop part of the library, in the back of the property. The rest of the library is modern, but the church part is there if you know where to look. When I drive to town to pay a fee or meet someone, I pass by there and remember those Sundays when Van Dyke was up there and tons of people walked in through the doors just to hear his booming voice. I remember that warning so many people fail to hear: "Judge not, unless you want to be judged."

Cheryl told me some things about Judgment through the cards, showing me different decks that depicted everything from butterflies coming out of their cocoons to the traditional images of bodies coming out of tombs. You see, there are so many ways of looking at Judgment and where it gets you. Anyway, there's the judgment we pass on each other, and then there's the judgment that belongs to God. There's a really big gap between the two – usually.

Cheryl started by saying that Judgment isn't just about that one big day at the end of time and that I needed to let that idea go. Cheryl said Judgment as a card, as an *archetype*, was about coming to points where we needed to let go of the past and start fresh.

Judgment isn't about other people telling you what you did wrong; it's about looking around and realizing you're not perfect. In the traditional cards you can see these pale bodies rising up from the graves, and a big angel making noise with a trumpet. You can see all the people with their arms lifted up in the air, and they look like they are being set free. If you really look at the card, there's no punishment anywhere, just freedom from the past. Cheryl was serious about that part.

"See that – no fire."

"Well, that's in the other card."

"But it's not in this card."

"So, what, they couldn't fit it on this one?"

"No, they're separate parts of the whole."

"So, they lied to us."

"Sometimes."

Judgment starts with being aware of the petty stuff we do that's shitty, like when you're being sarcastic or nonstop needling, you know – poking someone verbally. Judgment is about getting through the hard shit and being reborn, usually a little humbler, a little bit cleaner than you were. Judgment can be about shedding old skin and being received for who you are now. It can mean you're waking up or about to be ripped into it. The speed kind of varies, but the end result is the same: you change.

When Cheryl and I went through the cards, she would light up because she had a student, and I think she liked that the most. I wasn't always into it, and so she could get mad, too, telling me I wasn't working hard enough. Seeing as I met Cheryl just as she was starting to die, she had to take me on as a student. It was like fate picked us out for each other. It was just like a movie; except I wasn't some young clueless kid. I was older than her. I was set in my ways. This wasn't exactly "wax on, wax off," me and Cheryl working on witch stuff 24/7. I had other things I was doing, like running my businesses, managing my ADD, smoking weed and waking up every morning at sunrise. A full-moon ritual? I was all about it! But I wasn't doing it at 4 a.m.

Still, she'd joke, calling me *"Brujo,"* which I never got tired of hearing. I like Spanish; it's a pretty language. Even though I liked hearing the word, Cheryl using it made me nervous. We weren't causing no harm with those cards, and no one had ever told me not to use them, but I knew, too, that somehow this was dangerous. Funny how there were none of those public service announcements against magical thinking on TV, not like they had for drugs, and still all the kids somehow got the memo. When did we learn to be scared of our intuition? When does that happen, exactly?

As far as I could tell, the cards always had something to say about power because all the cards had flowers and angels, kings and queens, knights, and swords and diamonds, all the regular elements you need for a story. Inside the designs there were thousands of years of normal, everyday truth. That truth was bigger and longer than words, and so the cards made complex things simple. The only difference I could see between the church or the movies and the cards is that the cards were the only story you could change. The cards were all about your story, about you working with God and all God's forces, to live in the here and now. All the other stories were controlled by other people.

I grew up without so much as a single saint, and I wasn't much for knights and fantasies, so I was at a definite disadvantage when I started working with the tarot. I wasn't like the Italians, or the Greeks, or even the Irish Catholics around here who grew up calling on this saint or that one to find a lost shoe or put in a good word to the man upstairs. Technically, my grandmother on my mother's side was Irish, but none of that Catholic or Celtic iconography made it into my family's conversations on God. In my childhood, pictures were a waste of time once you grew up, and you would know an angel when you saw it in heaven, end of story.

Cheryl would laugh and say I was just like my father. She kept teaching me, no matter how stubborn I was. "You are about to be reborn, Tom! Can't you feel it?!" I'd look at her, flat as I could: "No."

I have asked myself a million times or more, where is that big love, where's that new breakout business? When will I figure out how to work less than six days a week? I mean, am I the only thing holding up this big change? I guess maybe I am, but I keep on trying. Getting out of my own way is harder than I thought it would be.

When I don't know what to do, and nobody's advice makes any sense, I go to the shower. I stand up straight and stretch myself out. I stretch my neck and my arms and stare up past the nozzle. I've got no time for the beach, not even time to swim in my pool, but at least once a day, I've got time to shower – and I guess right then I look like one of those naked people in the Judgment card.

QUEEN OF CUPS

The Queen of Hearts

Cheryl said being in water was good for the heart, and I admit, when I come out of the shower, I feel really good, like something inside me is loose, like some part of my head isn't stuck like it was. In tarot, the cups filled with water are our hearts. Those cups cards tell us about the way we work with our emotions. Emotions, like water, grow things. Being in the shower, coming out after doing all my stretches and my OCD rituals – thinking about how cleanliness is next to godliness, that's what keeps me sane while I try and figure out how to get reborn into the next big version of myself. Like I said, it's where I stretch and feel like no one is there except me and God. Still, I know I'm missing something.

Since Cheryl left, nobody has been able to read cards for me like she did. That's natural, of course, since you can't read like me and I can't read like you. We're all unique, but Cheryl … I don't think there's many people who could read like her at all. Before she died, Cheryl gave me a last spread as a gift. She wrote it down on some notebook paper, and that was supposed to last at least a year. She outlined a plan with astrology, and she used angel and fortune-telling cards. I know she had some Lenormand in there, too. She made the whole forecast by hand; Cheryl didn't have a computer.

Handwriting is like a voice; no two are the same. I hold onto that master reading because it's like holding a piece of my friend.

If I look at the pages now, labeled from 1 to 9, I can't help but see the Judgment card was in my seventh house, the one of partnerships. In there, Cheryl saw "rebirth" for me, along with a karmic connection to someone. There were other cards around that came with it: a 2 of earth, and a 7 of fire. Cheryl wrote that spread in some nice penmanship, the kind they don't even teach anymore. She wrote it with loops on the Ls and the Hs. It was one of the last things she left to this world, and she left it to me.

That year of her predictions, and more, have passed now, and whatever didn't come true is probably my own fault. I'm so past waiting for something to change that I'm actually curious at a whole other level, wondering what Cheryl saw. I want to know, to see it from the outside, because if I have more blind spots I want to see them. I want to get to the new level, so sometimes I look at the paper and read it like it's for somebody else. "Judge not, lest ye be judged" – I can hear it ringing in my ear while I'm looking over the old prediction for clues, and it sounds fine. It's not the lesson, it's how you teach it that matters the most, and Cheryl taught me everything she knew with love.

They say that all women are queens at some point in their life, because that's one of the archetypes, the pure states of life. You can't escape those. Unlike stereotypes, which are assumptions about people, archetypes are details in the game of life. Sometimes when I think about Cheryl, when I stare down at her writing, I think about her being a queen. I can't help but think of her being a lady of hearts, the queen of cups.

I can't help but think that her card would be special, that her throne would be the most beautiful barber's chair. Her outfit would be something like Gucci or maybe Dior, something that hugged her curves just enough. She'd have roses all around her, some of them the deepest color of wine, so they would almost be black. There'd be pink ones and bright yellow ones too, reflecting in the gorgeous brushes behind her. In the distance would be the ocean, sending up mist, with people washing their hair in it. And there at her feet would be sweet little animals, and in her lap would be this one very special one who looked less like a dog and more like a miniature deer.

Napoleon vs. Halston

I realize now that if I saved Napoleon, he saved me, too. Cheryl knew it would be like that, both of us anchoring each other. She saw the grief from my last dog hanging around me like a cloud, an actual wound to my fucking heart. She saw in her special way that there was this other being waiting out there who could match me, who needed me, and she blurted it out. I told her she was wrong. I pretty much laughed at her. Men could come and go, but dogs, no way — my heart would never heal, I told her.

Halston was beautiful, but I didn't name him for some fashion designer. I didn't care that much about high fashion, although I did buy that cologne with his name. I don't even know why I bought it, because I didn't read GQ or follow the styles. Somehow it happened that I bought the cologne, probably because it smelled really good to me. It wasn't cheap. Let's call it a splurge.

That first weekend I had the new puppy, and a couple of girlfriends came over to see him. One sprayed the Halston cologne on him, and the other said, "He should be called Halston!" We all looked at each other, and I said, "OK," and it was no big deal. Halston was named, and the girls were happy.

To be clear, I wanted to call the dog "Sinbad." I don't know why, but he looked like a sailor to me. But I was always a pushover for my sister, and for all my girlfriends. I did say something weak about calling him Sinbad, but I got no reaction. Not a word came out of their mouths. I got the message. The girls stayed happy. The cologne went back in its place. The puppy had his name.

Halston was going to be my trophy dog. He was a good-looking family member, with a cocker spaniel *pedigree*. I bought him with dreams of having a loyal companion, one who looked good with my outfit. I thought of his pale golden coat and traditional lines complementing my shirt and the drapes in our Christmas cards, and it made me smile.

I imagined our faithful relationship between a man and his dog, and I almost shed a tear. Those first few weeks, I believed we were headed to some point in the future where he did exactly what I asked. I would say, "Sit, Halston," and he would sit. I would say, "Lay down," and he would curl up at my feet. Soon enough, however, instead of that dream companion, what I got was a spiteful fucker who above all his other rebellions preferred to spend his days dirty, matted and smelling like the opposite of good perfume.

Nevertheless, I had him groomed faithfully, to a perfect show cut. I paid $45, every four weeks, and back then, that was a chunk of change. But he was the kind of dog you saw in an ad, the kind rich people had sitting on blankets on their genuine leather furniture. He was made to be clean and sweet and match my décor, and any goddamn day now, I told myself, he would realize his destiny and he would like it.

I had my own house, some cars, and now I had *the* dog who would be as perfectly groomed as my gutters were leaf-free and my tires were shiny. Every time he came back shampooed and blown dry, he looked and smelled like a winner. He looked like a dog that a man who cuts hair for a living would have. Together, I explained under my breath, we could look and feel like life was in order. Problem was, every single month Halston trotted into the groomer like a willing champ, but he walked out with a sneaky mutiny on his mind. Every time we went through this, I got unbalanced. Within hours the perfect dog would make himself dirty.

In hindsight, I see the problem was clear: I never learned a thing about raising anyone. What I knew about life, about being family with someone, was to dig my heels in whenever I wanted to get my way. I knew how to win and how to lose, but I never knew how to stop the battle from starting. Somehow, the dog picked up on this, and for the first year of Halston's life, we were locked in a never-ending struggle of wills.

I did everything wrong with Halston. I got him at a puppy mill, and I made him too pretty. He saw my eyes glaze over with adoration, and he would be sweet. Then later, when I least expected it, he'd use his cute dog ways to try and show me who was boss. I remember how I rolled up the local paper or whatever I had near me, to show him I was the one in control as he nipped. He might have been scared, but he never showed it. He'd use that threat as a challenge, a chance to be spiteful. Was I being spiteful? The thought never crossed my mind at first. Funny.

We went back and forth between love and hate. We barked at each other. We growled at each other. Sometimes I used words, but he didn't. It didn't matter one bit that he was a dog, less than 30 pounds, and I was standing on my two human feet at just under 185 pounds and around 6 feet tall. He wouldn't give in.

I would curse and scream at him like he was my kid, like my father did with me. And just like some creature from a movie, he barked right back at me, and damned if he didn't bare his perfect teeth at me. Look, I took it personally, the endless mats he got in his coat, the way he ended up tangled in no time at all. I took it to heart every time he chewed the furniture or peed on the carpet. I tried not to let it be that way, but it was. I'm not proud of it, but bear with me, because what I'm trying to show you is that just when you're lost, there is always hope, different than the kind you had just hours or minutes before.

Anyway, I menaced Halston, and he menaced me back. I demanded and did it all wrong, and he let me know it. Like clockwork once a month, I laid down my money, making him as pretty as could be. I'd drop him off and pay my hard-earned dollars in cash. I would ask the girl to get the knots out so he could come home and we could start all over again. He came home free of the drool, the shit, the eye crud and whatever other mystery dirt he found in his magical travels in the backyard. Every time he came home perfect, I had hope, but like I just said, it was for something that wasn't going to happen. You see, my hope was placed in the wrong place.

It was hell for both of us. We even fought about where and when he could shit. I would yell at him a lot, I realize now, telling him to hurry up. I hated standing outside with him in the winter or after a really long day at work behind the chair. I didn't even smoke back then, so I was bored out there in the cold and the dark. My ADD was undiagnosed. We didn't have smartphones. I thought it was him. You can easily imagine he hated my guts at least once a week, maybe as often as every night. You have to understand, when I'm bitchy, I'm bitchy. Halston was smart, and he went from shooting me dirty looks to extorting treats.

The first time I hit the dog, I barely noticed. It's not like it was a big deal. It was automatic, you know, like a flick of the hand. I did not for a second notice the way he must have felt insecure, like we weren't on the same team or something. I didn't notice what I must have done, but I know I must have done it because he went from being a stubborn puppy to a spiteful pain in the ass. He started screaming a silent "fuck you" at me, over and over again. The Halston rebellion, rightfully waged, started in the shape of a perfect little turd, left at my bedroom door one morning when I was out of line.

The dog figured he'd show me in very basic terms what he was thinking of my authority, with one perfect cocker spaniel-size turd every time he had a grievance. Apparently, he had a million of them. He left me the doorway turds, and then he left them for roommates or guests. He'd shit at your feet, and he'd shit at your door; a uniform-size turd, to let you know how he felt. You didn't have to act like you were going to hit him; you didn't even have to yell at him. Halston had found himself a superpower, and he used it to comment on the general situation of the house.

Stupidly, I kept yelling and picking up papers to roll up and swat at this perfect companion who had become my tormentor. I would beg the dog to be kinder as he stood with his face set in steely cocker spaniel defiance. It was messing with my head; the way he looked was the complete opposite of how he behaved. I begged him for mercy. I'd explain to him what was wrong with the way he wanted things. I explained I bought the damned food, and I gave him a house, and damned if I didn't own those papers proving his pedigree was mine. He'd look up at me, and I bet he wanted me dead. I bet he dreamed in his doggy way of what he would do to me if he hadn't been bred to have almost no defenses against a man my size. It didn't matter what he couldn't do. He shit like a master.

By the side of the bed or down the hall, close to the bathroom, a turd might be lurking. I started putting on more lights in the house. Still, he got me and got the carpeting. Imagine looking down to see each one of your toes decorating an explosion of shit. I'd sniff as I walked in the house, paranoid that it was starting to smell like one of those cat-lady homes. I'd watch his head as he walked past me in the hallway as I scrubbed the pile, his head up and trying to shake the blue bows out of his cut.

I would find a turd behind the couch. I would find one on the couch. I was sniffing and discovering and screaming and losing my mind, as I found turd after turd in what felt like strategic locations. I had no idea how he could eat so little but shit so much. Now, most people know that hitting the dog with a newspaper is not the way to do things. The dog doesn't know positive or negative attention; all it knows is whether it is getting attention, so all that stress serves no purpose. I didn't know that at the time. It was like an old-fashioned cartoon where the dog looked up and

I looked down, and I ran after him and he hid, and then later we'd make up, and then he'd shit and we would do it all again.

That dog was spiteful and controlling, and, I guess, so was I. He hated to be clean as much as I needed to clean all around me. He hated to be left alone to wait for me faithfully until the end of the day, while I needed to work and pay the mortgage. He rolled around in crap. He got tangles in every part of his coat, and one day he did it in spades. That day he tangled himself beyond all recognition was a godsend because it was so bad, I needed to take him to a groomer ahead of schedule.

That groomer was sunny and patient, one of those kids-and-animals people. I can't remember her name, but I can remember the look of horror that came over her face the day we met. You see, I had just picked Halston up from his regular groom. He came home perfect. I remember it was late spring, a perfect day for yardwork and tidying. I don't mow my lawn myself these days; haven't really in years, but back then I did it myself, religiously, like my father would have. I would get super focused on making the lines in the lawn. Back and forth – it was like therapy, cutting the lawn.

Halston looked amazing, smelled fresh, and was sporting an extra-fluffy blow-dried do. He was sitting on the deck, shining like a diamond. He was stunning, so beautiful, stretching and finally lying down right there where I wanted him. I felt for a second like I was actually happy, like I had hope. I don't know why. It's not like he had magically transformed into another dog, a different Halston, while he was getting groomed. It was my own delusion to think this moment would last.

I was in the back, mowing the lawn into lines, and then in the front, doing the same thing. The front is the smallest part of my property, and I couldn't have been out there more than ten minutes, but those ten minutes were all he needed. As the mower blade was bringing every last bit of grass into order I was reveling. My house, the dog, we were reaching a state of manicured perfection. That anticipation, of nearing perfection, of every single thing being in its place – well, it felt like a new level of peace, the ultimate screen in a video game. I had only dreamed this could exist. I was so close to the pinnacle of achievement in my life – and then, of course, it all crumbled.

While I was in the front, the dog had run for the pool. He knew he shouldn't, but he didn't give a shit. He went into the water, just to do a lap. I thought maybe I heard something, like someone was swimming, but I shrugged it off. I was coming around from the front, back to where the dog should be, and all I saw was a trail of wetness. Within seconds my joy turned to despair and anger at this trail of chaos. The dog once again went from being my beacon of hope to being an anchor of pain.

I followed the wet trail until I saw him, back on the deck, back in the same place as he had been, but now he was completely different. In a flash, he disappeared. I became anxious to a level I'd never experienced before, and I went into the house and yelled his name. I watched him shoot up the stairs at breakneck speed. The dog was some shade of black I couldn't wrap my head around, but I could see it spreading like ink all over my house.

I screamed, "You'd better not be on the couch!" As I cleared the room, I saw he had been on the couch. I screamed again, "You'd better not be on the bed!" Yep, more prints. I saw the dog running with glee as he destroyed everything in his path with strategic precision. I saw him writing his name in defiance all over my carpets, my furniture, my comforter – all over my life.

He was this monster from the land of black mulch. That's obviously what he had gotten into: the mulch I'd bought and laid down around the flower beds to keep the weeds at bay. It was bright and new, and it was stuck all over him, and it ran in drippy messes all over the house.

This dog who had been shitting relentlessly in my room, this dog who left exactly one turd around the house whenever you shut him out of a room or forgot to give him a treat – this dog had gone too far. This gorgeous dog, who had given me nothing but grief, was looking at me like he'd hit the lottery. I started to scream and went at him. I grabbed him before he could get to the guest room or get past me and back to revisit his muddy steps and get them deeper into the pile, and as soon as I grabbed him, I brought him into the tub.

The water was at full blast, and I was screaming. I didn't care if the water was hot or cold. I didn't care if it was shampoo or hand soap. I threw him in there and held him down to finally stop this madness. I had him by the neck, and I pulled back in a way that surprised me, and like a rubber band, my hand went out fast, straight for the dog's head.

My hand went forward, and it had made contact, but something was off with the picture.

Halston was looking at me, his neck still in my grasp, but the other hand, the one that almost had a mind of its own, it started to pound with pain. I could barely see what was happening, but I realized what was going on, so I looked up and focused. My hand had shot out and made contact with the cast iron tub. The dog had ducked, which was good for him. Jesus-God, my fingers wouldn't move; the pain was excruciating. If I hadn't been in so much pain, I might have started to laugh while my hand swelled up like a balloon. Instead, I made faces and shook my head, and when I could move, I decided to take the dog back to the groomer's.

Head down, I brought him back in there, half-wet, with my hand throbbing. I knew something had to give. I felt that spark of my father in me. I saw where I was, and I had no way to get out of it. I thought of my mother and how she hated violence. I was numb with knowing that I had gone over the edge, just like my old man. It was like a trigger I didn't even know I had. I didn't know if I could hate myself more, but I thought about it long and hard against a backdrop of blow dryers and running water, and voices saying "Isn't that a good doggy?" and "Oh, aren't you a sweetie?" I thought I was going to get sick while we waited, and I swear it was my mother who probably pushed my hand so I missed the dog, because that was the only way to stop what could have happened. So, I was close to weeping and thinking of Mom, and goddamn, my hand hurt, and then it was our turn.

When the lady came out, I asked to go in the back with her. No sunny smiles, no "How ya doin'?" while carrying a coffee in one hand. Nothing but me and Halston, looking like we'd been running around some military obstacle course designed especially for animals and their work with the insane. I went to the back station with that woman, and I let her in on how we were living.

I sobbed at the woman and told her I didn't know what to do with the dog. I told her about the newspapers, and how he shit all over the house. I told her I didn't know what else to do, that I'd never known what to do, and that it was all too much. I asked her if she'd kill me, please, or just take the damned dog away from me. She was holding her face in that way people do in scary movies as she realized what was standing in front of her. I couldn't help her. I couldn't make this easier.

"Take him."

"No."

"Take him, please."

"No."

"Why not?"

"I'm not taking your dog."

"One of us is going to end up dead."

"No."

"Why not?"

During the conversation, her expression went from horror to pity, and that was fine, because it felt good to get it off my chest. My pride was covered in a mixture of pool water and black mulch. She gave me a long, hard look, and said, "All right, you're not going to hit him anymore." I said, "Fine." I practically screamed it. "You're going to ignore him when he pisses you off," she practically screamed back.

That very nice lady taught me how to deny attention, a technique she called "shunning." I sat there, and I listened while she gave me directions, and from that day forward, I practiced how to shun. Now, I know shunning sounds like a shitty thing to do to a dog, but shunning was a godsend to me and Halston. The day I learned how to shun; a whole new chapter of our lives started. That groomer lady might as well have been an angel. She might as well have been sounding a trumpet. She changed me by giving me a tool, a word, a whole new language that I could hear even through the pain of my throbbing hand.

From that day forward, the love-hate relationship between me and Halston took on a whole new tone. I didn't hit him, and he didn't shit around the house just for the hell of it, unless you forgot to give him a treat when you left the house, or if you shut him out of the bedroom to have sex, but that was more for routine than anything. At the end, Halston would shit on command. I would say, "Go poopie!" and he would hunch and shit. I would tell him he was a good boy. "Who's a good boy?" Look, we were in progress, not perfect.

By the time that cocker spaniel died, he was 15 years old, and I had kept him alive as best as I could. I carried him places. I had him on meds until he died in my arms at the vet's, a long time after they thought I should put him down. This is why when Cheryl said, "You're getting a dog." I said, "No, I'm not."

"Yes, you are."

"No, I'm not."

"The dog adopts you."

"I'm not going anywhere that can happen."

"Good. Then mark my words."

I bit my tongue when she said, "Oh, look who got a dog!" I had only him a couple of weeks when it came up on Halloween. Cheryl came into the salon that day to do readings for whomever wanted one. On Halloween, Cheryl wasn't shy, and she set herself up right in the middle of the cutting area of the salon. She had a table and her reading rug and different decks of tarot. She had Lenormand and Angels and Oracles in special editions.

At that time, you couldn't even look at the new dog without him barking. But I caught him staring at Cheryl while she was staring right back at him. They were silent, just staring at each other.

"Want me to tell you what he's thinking?"

"You can tell me what that dog's thinking?"

"He just opened his soul up to me."

"Go ahead, tell me."

"His old owner was quick with his hands and treated him like a football."

"He told you all of this?"

"I told you; he opened his soul to me."

Cheryl proceeded to tell me Napoleon's whole story, quickly and smoothly. Even a story about guys in hoodies, probably teens, pounding on the door of the car once when he was in there for hours, waiting for his guy to get off work. She told me that I was this dog's road to happiness, that he was convinced I was the only one to protect him. She said, "He dreams about you." I went up to the liquor store that night and checked it all out. Did the guy have little girls? Did they have pigtails? Did he leave him in the car for hours? Yep, yes, all of it was true. Napoleon really had spilled his guts. Who knew a dog could do all that, could think all that deep or remember things for so long? Cheryl knew.

Completely loyal, with a few minor and a couple of major issues; Napoleon, does not shit indoors except on rare occasions. He will pee in the house, but mostly if it's cold outside, since his comfort zone is about 75 to 80 degrees with no humidity. I get it. He is a little guy with very little body fat, a mix of Min-Pin and Italian greyhound. With his breeding and personal history, he has drama queen tendencies. With his balls still intact Napoleon may jump like a tiny deer, and cling like a child, but he will always be looking to hustle you like a dog.

Napoleon gets in the car; he goes to a salon. He sits under a desk, wrapped in a blanket, worrying over the noises around him, but it's what he wants because he wants to be around me, all the time. Let's just call Napoleon the most anxious thing I've ever seen, so I can't stand to shun him or leave him at home. We drive from morning to night side by side, from store to store and to the restaurant, and I help him work it out. I tell him, "Napoleon, you gotta let go of the luggage. I'm not going anywhere without you."

Getting a dog who had a previous home is like any other relationship in life where you're not the first. Dogs, like people, come with their habits. Napoleon came complete with phobias, insecurity, and language skills. It's kind of remarkable to me that when I say, "Let's go," I can do it in English, Spanish or Portuguese, and the dog understands. The truth is, Napoleon's English isn't that great; his Spanish is much better. Instead of getting angry about him not doing as I say, I use my Spanish with him. My Spanish is kitchen Spanish, but me and Napoleon, we get along across these cultural divides. Cheryl was right, he is like Velcro, and we're attached at the heart because, you know, that's really all we have in common.

If my epic breakdown with Halston was a turning point in my life, then every day with Napoleon is a small adventure with lots of less-dramatic turning points. He's always with me, always reading my vibes. If I'm calm, he's OK; if I'm losing it, so is he. Instead of coming home to him for some emotional confrontation, we bicker all day 24/7, 365 days a year. It's our story.

As I went through the paperwork to make Napoleon a legitimate emotional support animal, I came up against a lot of challenges. The forms, the consultations with doctors, the office visits – I did them because if the dog was as he seemed, as desperate as Cheryl swore he was, leaving him home alone was not an option. I let that motivate me, and slowly I got through the paperwork. I talked myself into dealing with all the bureaucracy that I knew would piss me off, patiently and with a smile. I dealt with the hassle to get him the tags and the service animal jacket, which I have to admit is cute on Napoleon. He sports it like a big shot.

Napoleon did not start out with a big shot story. He lived five years in his first home, then his guy kept dropping him off with friends. Those were our mutual friends at the liquor store right around the corner from my restaurant. At first, I started to dog-sit in the back room of the store while someone ran to the bank to get change or around the corner for a sandwich or bread or something. One time, the guy left the dog at the liquor store for three weeks. It was in those weeks that the dog threw himself in my direction slowly but surely. Because of the restaurant, I was in and out of the liquor store two, maybe three times a day. I saw Napoleon all the time and thought nothing of it, but he was watching me closely.

My friend asked if I wouldn't mind taking the dog to my house because his apartment was small, and he already had Napoleon's sister. Napoleon came over for a couple of days, then he'd go back, then I'd get another call, asking if I could take him again. At one point I had the dog for eleven weeks, and when the guy called my friends from the liquor store, they told him they gave the dog away. The guy got mad and yelled; but they yelled, he wasn't getting the dog back.

"How could you give my dog away?"

"How could you leave your dog and not even call?"

It was a big deal, but it wasn't a big scene, because everyone knew the dog was happy with me. It was a bunch of calls and texts from the liquor store to me, to him, and round and round, but nothing changed; Napoleon stayed with me. In the end, I offered the guy visitation, and he only took me up on the offer a couple of times. I think he saw how happy Napoleon was with me, and he let the whole thing go. For a while he held onto the hope that Napoleon would choose him. We had to wait it out until that hope was quashed. It was inevitable, but sad. I remember how it happened.

It was all going smoothly for a while, and I felt like the dog had finally settled in with me and his new life. I left Napoleon with the guys at the liquor store and did some errands I really couldn't do with him, because he didn't have all his official therapy dog papers at the time. I opened the door to pick him up, and Napoleon was in his old master's company. I didn't know what to do, seeing them like that, side by side. He had threatened to come by, to make it so the dog could choose.

"I'm going to let the dog decide."

"Don't do it," said our friend. "You'll be disappointed."

(Staring in three directions.)

I panicked, thinking maybe he and Napoleon had patched things up and that they were going to leave together. I acted cool, but my aura was probably flashing colors of red for fear and anger, and I don't know what color for panic. I tried to stay cool. Finally, after some chit-chat, I said I was leaving. I made my way to the door, ready to walk out alone. Napoleon immediately jumped to his feet and made a beeline for the door with me, while the guy stood there, very disappointed..

I had no idea what was waiting for me at that moment, but I knew the dog was finally mine. I said I didn't want him, but at that point I did. Sure, I still didn't realize I would have to spring for top-of-the line duck treats, or that he'd bark at people just for looking our way. I had no idea the constant companion he would be, because he was playing it kind of cool. He was eating whatever I gave him, too.

When Napoleon came into my life to stay, I could barely leave him with anyone. I could leave him in the liquor store with the guys, with one of their moms and, of course, with Cheryl.

Cheryl and Napoleon had this way of being really peaceful together, and when she was sick I would find reasons to let her watch him instead of bringing him by the liquor store where the guys were busy with customers and inventory. The two of them would snuggle up and play games. The dog would get all this attention, and Cheryl would treat him like her best friend. Hanging out with Napoleon was safe for Cheryl. The dog didn't bring up the past, didn't ask her why she made her decisions the way that she did. The dog didn't bring up bills or white blood cell counts or all the other things on her mind. Napoleon was a really good sport when he hung out with Cheryl, tolerating outfits and tarot card readings where she had him walk on the deck while asking him questions.

After having kids pull at him, having actual hot milk spilt on him, plus all that abandonment from being left all over the place all the time, Napoleon came a long way. Now he borders on being too bossy like a real little emperor, not like he used to be, cringing at everything. Is that my fault? I mean, is it possible I'm a bossy fuck like him? Or that he became one by being with me? I'm not in the mood to answer that.

The first time I got that wake-up call to manage my anger, we were driving around like normal. I was driving and on a call while someone was cutting me off, and another car was speeding up behind me for absolutely no good reason. It was that feeling like all of a sudden, I was being squeezed, and I was seeing my life flashing before me. I yelled at the top of my lungs. I yelled at the driver in front of me and the guy behind me. One second, I was changing the radio station; the next, I was losing my mind.

I didn't even realize what was going on as I was honking the horn, screaming, getting out the adrenaline of all this pressure, when I noticed Napoleon was not in the passenger's seat. He wasn't in the back seat or on the floor. He was in the *way back* of the SUV just *shaking*. He was as far as away from me as he could get, pushing himself against the upholstery, looking like he might throw up. He wouldn't come sit near me for a long while, not until I was breathing deeply and calmly. When Napoleon finally came back to my side, I decided it was time to find another way of dealing with myself.

With Halston, I respected the little fucker and grew to love him. Napoleon loved me first, and that melted my heart pretty much on the spot. It happened so fast, and still there were all these steps of accepting and getting used to each other. People, dogs, things come out of nowhere asking us to make changes. We can take up those challenges, or we can hide. I never thought I could handle another dog, knowing its life would probably end before mine. I remembered Cheryl's words, and I took on Napoleon, knowing one day he will pass on, and it will hurt, knowing one day his little barks are going to stop, and a part of me will be broken. I took him on knowing I was going to have to deal with Cheryl's smug, "Mark my words" look. We make plans, and God laughs, but when all you plan is to be alone, that's not necessarily a bad thing.

Living the Sprawl

The deal is that for lots of years I felt I needed to bend straight men, because they were all you could see in most towns by me. Going to the supermarket or the gym, nobody wanted to let on they were gay or even curious. Today it's all different, because at least you have the Internet and forums; even video games where people let you know they're gay and OK with it, but for most of the 1980s I had maybe two semi-local bars where I could go without it being an ordeal.

I would have to trek to Fire Island or the city, driving hours to hit a real club. The closest I could get was North Jersey, which was not nearly as good as when I got to Studio 54 or the Limelight. Being gay got expensive with the gas and the tolls, rooms I would have to rent so I wouldn't end up driving home sleep-deprived. Locally, there wasn't much, maybe one club in the summer in this town or that, but by winter all those places emptied out. I didn't want to move to the city, because I didn't want to leave all the people I'd known my whole life, but staying around had its challenges.

Even in the '90s it wasn't that easy to find a local place that was gay, so most of the people coming at me in clubs were women in push-up bras and perms trying to get me in the sack. I've slept with women, of course, and it was fine, if not my thing. If my father hadn't died when he did, I guess I would have stayed half in the closet, too, thinking of men while sleeping with women. Who knows, maybe we would have ended up with our fists flying during a fight, or one of us turning a cold shoulder to the other. Maybe then I would have wanted to get so far away I would have moved and had a life in the middle of a gay community, but I don't know, since I like waking up to birds, not horns.

I'll never know what would have happened to me if my father hadn't died like that. All I know is that he did die, and I stayed local, and most of the people around me were living the straight life. I don't blame those babes in the bras who hit on me, though, because you know it's always flattering to some degree, and I give them an A for courage. It's not easy to get through a regular workday and then go to some bar with loud music and pricey drinks trying to find someone who doesn't look dangerous or like a total asshole. I do, I give them credit, the ladies who used to hit on me in those summertime bars; for showing up in their sunburned shoulders, their tits jacked up, their smiles trying to hide how pissed they are at the last guy who traded them in for someone cuter, younger, older, smarter, easier, whatever.

It's not easy to be the one who makes the approach, and for women it is even harder because they're vulnerable, smaller than the guys, usually, and so if they pick wrong and find themselves getting shit on or smacked around, they have that guilt to contend with, too. I understand what it's like for them, because I'm a mid-size guy, in decent shape for most of my life, but I like my men strong and built, and that means sometimes I've been pretty vulnerable, too. It's one thing when a guy goes to hit a woman; there's some part of him that knows it isn't a fair fight. But man to man, that changes things, and no matter how you might feel inside, you have to be aware that the guy you're about to hit on, he might want to fight you, especially in a bar that doesn't have some rainbow flag or something else saying, "We don't kill gays here."

I got by, taking my time, figuring out the signs of straight men who were flexible. It's the bait that matters, and I couldn't do the bra and pouty thing like the ladies, so I had to figure out something to compete. Luckily, I always felt like I knew what men really want, in a way that most of my female competition didn't. When men want sex, they want to get off with a friend, someone who seems like they're on the same page. They don't want someone getting the moment all mixed up with obligations and needs. That's the way to get them in bed, and maybe it's the way to win them for good. I'm not sure about what makes most men settle down. I should probably know this, but we all have our blind spots.

The homophobes are the most challenging and fun to bend, because they act like there is this huge difference between them and me. Right away they think I'm hitting on them just by saying hello, when reality is I'm just saying hello. Then they act condescending, like being gay means I want any guy at all. For years I've watched straight guys who let themselves go, walk into my hair-cutting chair acting like they were irresistible because they convinced some poor woman to put up with them and their elastic waistbands. I find it insulting when a sloppy guy with bad hygiene comes into my salon with his greasy hair, and he assumes I want to sleep with him just because I'm gay.

Some people can get so caught up in their stories about how I must be that they don't even realize I'm not attracted to them. The one thing I don't want, besides some guy who is sloppy, is someone who thinks I'm desperate. I have a hand, and I'll take that over a jerk or a pity hookup any day. Bending men isn't about taking any guy, it's about satisfying myself and them. Bodies and looks are a major factor, so maybe I am slightly shallow, but that's my right. Straight men think one time with me and they're automatically gay, too – well, I slept with women, and that didn't turn me straight. All I want is people to respect that nothing with sex is black and white. The truth is, the ones who were genuinely curious were the most fun to bend, because they were open with no judgment.

I like shredding people's stereotypes about gay people, because if I were a straight guy flirting with women, people would think I was macho. Because I'm gay, my sex drive scandalizes those same people. What it really means is people are paranoid about their own needs and pleasures. But honestly, it doesn't stop there. In fact, I used to be quieter about the stereotypes for most of my life, but then everyone got hung up on judging. Now everything is supposed to fit into two categories, and I'm living proof those categories aren't true.

Liberal and conservative – people fight all day about which camp you're in, but all it means is you're open or closed on some things. My pocketbook is conservative; seems like a lot of the rest of me is liberal. Ultimately, it's not the labels that matter to me. I care about people leaving each other the fuck alone, since that is supposed to be the American way. I know you thought I was going to make this all about sexuality, but I'm saying that all of this is about respecting personal preference. Two camps and two camps only? And you can't pick anything from here and mix it with something from there? My God, that sounds like a nightmare. Imagine going to shop and you could only pick from two stores, and once you went to store A you were forbidden to shop from store B.

I spent years talking straight guys down from their stereotypes, not to convert them, but to get them to play, to do something different for once. Other gay guys aren't like me, because I'm just me, not some representative of all the gay men in the world. For the record, I never wanted to get lost in gay culture because it seemed like too much of a party. When I came out, I was gay on the weekends and a regular working guy all week. I was living "out" but doing it quietly, not looking for trouble, not taking too many breaks from building up a future, just like my friends and neighbors.

My fucked-up shit, and my good traits, too – those are mine, and they don't have much to do with my being this or that as much they have to do with being Tom. I would lay it out to them, from the preps with the collared polos to the muscle guys with tiny sleeveless shirts on their big chests, that gay people are individuals. Yes, I've had a lot of sexual encounters in my life, but it really never was a free-for-all; it just looked like that to people who had nothing better to do than follow my every move like it was a reality show. Maybe it was kind of crazy, the way I was living for a while, keeping myself on the down low while splitting my date nights into shifts.

Today we live in a different world than the one I grew up in; the one I came out in. Kids today don't seem to be hung up on labels as much. It's true they have a million of these labels but after a while they all kind of feel the same to me. They feel like a language that helps them say the things I'm taking great pains to explain to you. To me, it's all the same, just people being people. On television and the internet, it seems really simple, but in real life I see young people all the time who are struggling to be themselves. It's not easy to be yourself when your parents are trying to pray the real you away. Nothing about being a real person is easy, no matter what your pronoun, abbreviation or inclinations might be.

We're all dealing with expectations and traditions we don't have any clue what to do with, and a lot of it is based on things like religion. In other parts of the country, you've got mostly Protestants, plus the Baptists and Born-Agains, all dealing with this. Here, you've got those, plus Catholics and Jews. Hindus, Muslims, we got everyone here. Every one of those groups has their gays and natural witches; all who are scared to death to come out of the closet. Even now, the curious, or mentally adventurous types keep their mouths shut, too. Sure, they could move to go in search of their "tribe" somewhere, but if they're close to their family or they like their town, it's a shitty choice to have to make.

I learned that in attracting men around here, I had to give them space to be themselves, to work that area between curiosity and action. You want to have sex and be with me, well it doesn't mean you're gay. It means you want good sex. It means you needed a break from your day, and it means I was there at the right time, to give you that. Maybe it means you liked my blue eyes or the way I stood there all cocky. Sure, I could give you exactly what you needed but what was that, exactly? Flirting. It doesn't need to be dramatic to be hot.

That's something nobody talks about much: a lot of forbidden sex, it isn't dramatic. It's actually safe from the drama you find in your regular relationships. In fact, most of the straight men I've been with have just been looking for a release, a break from the monotony of life's ups and downs. My approach in dealing with uptight guys has been to let them see that their secrets were safe with me. I wasn't walking into the grade school Christmas pageant acting like I had nailed the wise man's dad, even if I did. I wanted the ride, that feeling of hotness between us, not the auditorium.

Look, I'm a Taurus, a person who likes feeling grounded, someone who likes routine. I mean, I really like routine. Without a routine, I become unbalanced. Even though I despise time I do everything at a certain time. There begins the turmoil of my life, every day, trying to do things at a certain time and in a particular way, so I can feel relaxed for a little before I get stressed again. Secretly I hate that I'm like this, that my world hinges on these habits being played out all the time, but mostly I like that groove of stability. Just like it says in all the astrology profiles, my house makes me happy; familiar things feel good.

I can be habitual. Sometimes I can be stubborn, and I can use my surroundings like a great big bubble. Here I am, at this house on a 155-by-165 foot lot with big trees and a raised, wooden deck. When I look out along this lot, a good size around here, I remember the days with all the parties. I remember all the roommates that came and went, and I can feel how it has all gotten quieter over the years. Routines come and they go, but the act of having them is what holds me together.

Breakfast on the weekends was one of my routines. I had to get up and make something nice for my crew. I still like to make breakfast at home, and I don't mind making it just for me and Napoleon. I like to go to sleep and and make that note in my mind, adding something new to the list as I drift off to sleep. I think how I'm going to make bacon and eggs for me and the dog, and how easy that is. He has no requests, no dietary restrictions. It makes me smile.

Sure, I think of this last guy, this notch on my belt, and I smile, because it was kind of nice. It's a thing to think about, a new memory I didn't expect this week. But it doesn't make me want to have him here for breakfast, or lunch or dinner.

When I look back, in my mind's eye I can see some of those times when I watched a guy lay back and let go. It was so simple to make each one of them happy, at least for a night, especially if I knew the guy as well as I usually did. The truth is, I've never had a real one-night stand. Everyone I ever had an adventure with was someone I knew. In the sense that I never liked dealing with total strangers, I couldn't imagine not knowing some guy's name or not having some type of connection. It's how I'm built. It's been almost impossible to get me to commit since my first big heartbreak, but I swear I can't handle anonymous casual sex. Go figure.

I guess when you grow up in a smalltown way, you never really lose some of that reserve. You know, all these developments around here, , the Whatever Hollows and Fake Estate Glens – these were all farms when I was a kid. One ritzy road now, those houses were all chicken farms maybe 50 years ago. We have more people around here now than ever before, and there's just no getting away from that, but I still like to feel like I know people. In my heart this is still a place where summers mean eating real peaches picked down by the highway, and noticing your neighbor's sunburn as he takes out the garbage. Small-town old ladies ratting you out if you got fresh, phone calls being made from house to house, I feel it all.

The old nothing-fancy places around here have survived long enough to get visits from New York newspapers and food television shows. Seems like they go scouring for a story just about anywhere that still has a few wooden buildings with a fresh coat of paint. In a way, these places look good on TV, and give the reporters something to say about day trips you can take. cute old building where the food is definitely fine if not amazing, is all it takes and you've got yourself a destination. Lucille's is one good example of this kind of destination that I personally wouldn't drive hours to experience. It's th diner that put Warren Grove on the map. It even got Anthony Bourdain to come down one time, but it's nothing special to me.

We spent some time in Warren Grove as kids, going there to visit our grandparents until they took off for retirement. Before my grandparents left for Florida, they were down to a garden; having given up the farm, but there were leftovers from those real farm days for us kids to explore all over their land. On that farm there were coops more than 50 feet long, big enough for 100 chickens. There were tools and trees and patches of wild berries. Our instructions from our elders were, "Stay off the highway." It was Route 539, and back then a car came by about once an hour.

Tourists come down to eat simple food in a nothing town, and they fascinate themselves talking about legends like the Jersey Devil. The waitresses act like they care, and it's good for business. But I have to wonder who told those television people about Lucille's? Years ago, no one from New York would have cared about some place situated in a downtown of about one block long. These people here didn't care about the city that much, either, and wouldn't have greeted the strangers with all these big smiles. Times change. Someday Warren Grove might even have traffic.

As a family we never ate at Lucille's, the now-famous diner, even though my mom's name was Lucille. We were no relation, and unless we were getting a discount for the matching names, which wasn't likely, my father was not eating out on our trips to visit his parents. Grandpa, having lived through the Depression, might have screamed for an hour if he saw my father wasting the money, what with my grandmother ready and willing to cook us all a Sunday dinner. Anyway, the tourists can't believe the place is still so small and cute, but they don't know what it was like a long time ago, when it was all emptier and people had memories of lives that didn't always make them ready to smile.

No one cared much in those days for things that were flashy, at least not in places like Warren Grove, and so for Lucille's to survive the food had to match the rest of the place, serving good size portions of the same kind of food you ate or wanted to eat at home. The buildings of Warren Grove were simple, and the locals were proud to be part of the original thirteen colonies. Nobody cared for flashy cars – or worse, flashy people – and, strangely, not eating at Lucille's back then was just as much of a virtue as eating there is now.

This whole state has changed since we were kids running in the woods that stretched in three out of four directions anywhere you looked. There's barely a whiff of a dairy cow or the smell of summer peaches like you used to catch around here. The farm stands are novelties now, mostly geared to selling pies to tourists on their way to the beach or to some amusement park. The cars pass through on their way to somewhere else, stopping for a meal or a trinket. Most don't know about the military gunnery not too far from here, or the pygmy pine forest where the trees don't grow past 5 feet tall. What they see are the buildings, the new and the old ones, but they don't see the way this place was and how the people in it were. They can't see what it was like, because that takes time. Time enough to watch a field of corn grow, or to watch a cranberry bog flood with fresh rains. To see the old New Jersey, you can't be in a rush, and that's all there is here anymore, people rushing.

The farms gave way to the developments after World War II, and we grew up in one of the first ones of its kind. It was called Bayshore, and they built it in Toms River, the seat of Ocean County. We were just a few blocks away from the water there, able to run around in the summer and feel nothing but quiet and mosquitoes. The old industries and people were gone, the shipbuilders, most of the fishermen and the farmers, too. What was left was the land, lots of it, just waiting for something new to happen, and the builders and developers took care of that.

Pretty close to the house was a bridge, and it led to Seaside Heights, a strip of land between the mainland and the open ocean, and that's where families went on the weekends. It started small and gave way to improvements over the years. They even had a carousel they brought in from Coney Island, with hand-carved wooden horses with real horsehair tails. It lasted through the 1980s until someone sold off the horses one by one. They replaced the old rides with newer ones. They added more lights and games and more and more places to eat and drink. Eventually the boardwalk area grew so big with arcades and bars and hotels that concessions took over the town. Then they brought in film crews to Seaside for spring break parties and then a few years after that, for the television show Jersey Shore. That series is when they followed around a bunch of loud, foul-mouthed young tourists behaving like idiots. My father would have hated those assholes.

The property in the area was pretty cheap back when I was a kid, and so people bought some of the smaller bungalow models at Bayshore as second homes. We lived there all year, in a bigger Cape Cod house, but maybe half of Bayshore emptied out when it was time for school. In the winters it got quiet around us, with empty homes leading all the way to the river. Our cousins still lived on a farm; Grandma and Grandpa still thought like farmers, but we lived somewhere between that old stuff and the new ways. Back then, you could see where one development ended and the next began since there were trees between them. Now you've gotta look really hard to see where one ends and the next begins because that space is gone.

First, we visited Grandma and Grandpa in Warren Grove, and then we visited them in Florida, where they went to live out their retirement. My brother and I were 11 years old, and my father had just bought a new custom Country Squire station wagon by Ford. It was a splurge, but it was justified because it was a good family car, perfect for a vacation. The wagon was green, and it had an FM radio, which at the time my father didn't want. He wanted the AM-only, because it was cheaper, and asked if he could take it out to lower the price of the wagon. The salesman's jaw dropped when my father asked if he could take it out to save a few bucks. My father was brutal in his view of what mattered and what didn't.

With its woodgrain-patterned panel decals covering the sides, we headed down to North Miami Beach to see Grandma and Grandpa, these two New Jersey Pineys living in the South. In a way, it was the right place for them by then, since the land there was cheaper than it was at home, and they could get enough to keep Grandpa busy with growing and chopping things down. He could make the world in his image down there, cutting and trimming, cussing at trees that didn't get offended.

Anyway, my father, Jimmy, knew how to drive, and he took the distance to see his parents in stride. Like any red-blooded American he enjoyed roadside attractions and things that make a bang. He made sure we stopped to get a dose of our God-given right to fireworks, every trip. Wherever we headed up and down the interstates for vacation, we'd always stop along the way for fireworks. Our family road trips were pretty consistent to our regular lives, with my father calling the shots and the rest of us following orders. Every time we went toward Florida we saw these signs for "South of the Border," and there we'd arrive as a family, with Jimmy in the lead.

We would buy fireworks out of buildings big as barns. We kids had favorites, pre-approved by our parents, but we looked at everything we could before it was time to leave,

We got into the stacks of candles and crackers for a while. We brought a whole wad of them up to the counter because the small ones didn't cost that much Fireworks were this amazing thing to me. It was like you didn't have to worry about anything once you lit the fuse. Fireworks were the closest you came to feeling like a bad boy when you lit them yourself. As a family we spoke very little as we watched them light up our nights all throughout our trips. By the time we got to see Grandma and

Grandpa that one year, we knew the route. We waited for those billboards. In every little explosion, I found release. I also liked that none of us talked much while we lit them. Words in our family were a lot like dynamite.

That year, when my sister was 16 and we were still boys, the tensions ran high. All three of us kids ended up getting a sunburn like never before. The Florida sun had burnt me and my brother right through our T-shirts almost as soon as we'd crossed into the Sunshine State. It felt like those rays were trained right on us, and from our pale shoulders and exposed necks, down our backs and all the way to our fingertips, we turned pink, then bright red, before we even got out of the car. Then we hit the beach with Grandpa as soon as we got there, and that sealed our fates.

We parked the Ford wagon outside the ranch's screened-in porch and we were ready to stretch our legs and get a good night's rest. The wagon stayed there for a night. It was a typical scene. We were all tired and settling to our beds. My parents were in the living room, attempting to sleep. We were in the bedroom, hoping someone would turn on the air conditioning. We were whining for it. I was even whining in my sleep;I was so tired and so burnt. I couldn't help it, but I was whimpering I was making my parents kind of crazy. Grandpa heard us too, but he kept saying no, we kept making these pathetic noises but nothing moved him. In no time my father about lost his mind. The proverbial fuse had been lit, and finally, my father shot into action.

It went something like this: Jimmy threw some money in his father's direction then he defiantly put the air on full blast, saying he would happily pay the electric bill so he could get some rest. known to be a and or or So it happened, father and son stood there in utter silence, exchanging glares like rapid fire. They were shooting off accusations in a silence that was louder and more precise than words. Nobody made a sound. My whimpering had shut down.

At that stage in his life, Grandpa had that convenient type of hearing loss the one where he said he couldn't make out what we were saying lots of the time, but that night in the summer heat he heard everything his son said – and everything he didn't say.. That was the last straw for the time being. We gathered our things in the morning and left. Years later, one of them would die in the other's arms, but this was how they would live in the meantime. When we left that morning Grandpa had gone on so long yelling at my father that he lost sight of him. He was so taken up with rage that he didn't even seem to see us all leave. All I know is we didn't say goodbye, which was good in this case, because similar to fireworks after the fuse has lit the powder inside the wrappings, you step away.

That was the last time we pulled into North Miami Beach, Florida, to visit my grandparents on my father's side. We'd still see them, of course, but we never again drove that trip. We let my grandfather share his sunny outlook with his new neighbors. Most of them didn't speak English, and they probably thought the poor old man was raging that day because he was senile. We figured, what else could they think at an old man screaming at nothing but fruit trees.

We drove back up the interstate to New Jersey and toured all the sights along the way, so as not to ruin the whole vacation. As kids, we forgot things quickly, so we got lost in all the touristy stuff like seeing the Fountain of Youth and watching men wrestle alligators for fun. I bet my father remembered that incident every day for a while, but he never said much about it. He and Grandpa were tied to each other, but for the moment they weren't on anything close to speaking terms. We saw my aunts from time to time, and despite all the drama it seemed like nothing much had changed. Grandpa was pissed, and so was his only son, but blood was blood to them, and all the throwing of money and yelling over the air conditioner was just one more part of their story. My father kept up with the family, no matter what, using his sisters to plead his side, and delivering short but sweet hello's to his mother regularly.. Not a word between the men was said, until eventually that drama faded, and they spoke with not a word about the past. Then one day it was time for Jimmy and his father to be reunited.

Grandpa was a farmer, and when he got down to Florida, he kept up his ways, and that meant more than being too cheap to put on the air conditioning for his grandkids. He was growing mangoes, bananas, lemons, limes, grapefruits and more things I don't remember. They were big and delicious, and all of it was ripened on the tree – that, I do remember, because how couldn't I? In a way it was a perfect place to retire, with no winters to speak of and all the fruit practically growing itself. It was all going well until one day Grandpa realized some of his mangoes were disappearing. He got out his shotgun and loaded it with rock salt, and then he went looking for the thief. The rock salt he loaded into the shotgun wouldn't kill, but you would feel it, and it would teach you a lesson. Grandpa was hard with everyone.

Grandpa went walking his property and took off after this Cuban kid who was around 13 years old. He definitely had mangoes in his hands. Grandpa had fire in his eyes. It was kind of funny, and sad; definitely a little crazy, too, considering how few mangoes actually went missing. I can hear him now, saying how nobody was going to steal from him. He was too good of a shot not to be dangerous, even with rock salt, and sure enough, all hell broke loose after he went after that kid. I don't know exactly how or what happened, but that event triggered an immediate reaction on the part of my father and his youngest sister. They got the phone call regarding an "incident." They got on a flight headed south immediately.

Before anyone knew it, the house in North Miami Beach, was getting packed up. Grandpa must have been impressed with his children's efficiency even if he hated the idea of leaving his own house. He was heading back up to New Jersey to live out his days. He didn't make it exactly easy for them to move him without feeling guilty, but considering how his temper was, he didn't make it as hard on them as he could have. My grandfather had three girls and one boy, and all of them learned to shoot from him. The two who came down to bring him back north happened to be the two best shots out of the four. I don't think that was a total coincidence.

Grandpa never lost the ghost of the Great Depression. Those holdover ways caused fights with my father and made him run after a kid a fraction of his age for a couple of mangoes. Those old ways even got him to call Grandma over to share the last two spoonfuls of a bottle of cough medicine that was expiring. My aunt screamed, "You don't have a cold!" as she watched his shaking hand pour out the syrup. He snapped back, "I paid for it!" and gave her a hard stare. "I'm not wasting it."

To Grandpa, God was constantly judging, and the thing he judged most were idle hands. That's probably why I'm constantly straightening up the things in my life: my house, my car, my businesses and my napkin. I can't rest when a napkin is on my lap-I have to fiddle with it. It's like I have to busy myself and form a ritual to justify me sitting there. It's like being in the shower; it's so good to feel the water and breathe, but I have to build up all these routines, so it's also kind of a chore. With the napkin, I pull this way and that way, I run my fingers along the stitching and down to the corner as I lay the napkin down, even during business meetings. Someday I may not be like this, but for now I am. It seems like a lot of life is spent trying to let go of memories we don't even know we have.

The men in my family argued because that was what they knew best, and when I think of Grandpa these days, even when I think of my father, I laugh more than I get upset, because I don't want to judge them anymore. Before, I was angry, sick and tired of being told what I was going to do and how I was going to do it. Now I'm free to think, act my own way, to design the life I want. I don't have to worry about being ridiculed for every decision. I hope my father is happy for me now. Maybe now he sees that I am breaking the cycle, letting go of the family luggage little by little.

I know this one guy who had a wife who got sick with dementia. She lingered for years, and he took care of her every day while she suffered. He was good to her to the end, showing her respect even as he spoon-fed her and later carried her to the bathroom. When she died, and he was seen on a date with some woman a month or so after, someone had something to say about it; how it was too soon after the death for him to date like that. I couldn't understand why anyone thought they had the right to comment on his decision. He said to me that he had started mourning his wife the day she was diagnosed, and every day that she slowly got weaker. The things people tell me as they sit in my chair – those things are the truth. I can tell if they're not. That man did what he had to do, and when he buried his wife, the old life he had with her had been gone for years.

I twist up a joint for tonight and get myself going out the door. First, I need to get some clothes on. I haven't left yet, and I can't wait to get back here, to my sanctuary. I have jeans in the closet. T-shirts, socks and underwear are in the drawer. When I'm at my best, you can bet all my clothes are color-coded. I still like good jeans, but as a man over 30, I'll only pay discount, not high-fashion prices. I'm a fashion-conscious person, but instead of paying top dollar, I demand a bargain. It's the way I've built my businesses, too, offering people discount cuts and good early-bird specials at the restaurant. Maybe it's the influence of all these old people's villages. I'm all about the discount.

I pass four retirement communities on my way to work every day. They're pretty to look at, and they've got those great names with words like "harmony" and "haven" in them. Let's not kid ourselves; the names sound a lot like these people are moving into the space before heaven. The landscaping around those places makes me a little jealous, but I swear they have a smell, or something around them, that isn't made up of the flowers and shrubs. Most men might live lives of quiet desperation, but the air around these old folks' homes smells like concentrated desperation, like a parking lot full of people bargaining with God.

I'm thinking of smells, and I can't help but wonder why I didn't buy that incense I really liked in bulk when I saw it on sale. It was such a good deal. Money is easy. People are complicated, like ants and grasshoppers. I grab a polo, which is my uniform 50 percent of the time. It's been a while since I sported those designer blue jeans, the ones that make your junk stiff. I grab the slightly faded denim with the embroidered back pockets, zip up and calculate the hours until I can get back my house and stare at the rhododendrons in full bloom. I check myself in the mirror. I don't know how I feel about today's outfit, except that it hides my belly hanging slightly over my waistband, and it didn't break the bank. Like my father used to say, if you can't pay cash, you can't afford it.

We're like the bank, at my salon, and open promptly at 9 – at least, that's true when I open the place. You have to go in and turn on the lights, make sure the stations are clean and stocked. Then you have to check the register and make sure there's a sign-in sheet for the customers. It doesn't take much more than that. You check the AC, make sure that the fans are on, all that small stuff. It does not take long to get one of our salons open, but sometimes it's still too much for my staff. I manage it but I don't have kids or a spouse distracting me. Like I said, we've got all these old people around here, and they get up early. They make being on time seem late.

One old geezer comes in from time to time, making me feel guilty about having a routine, about filling my water bottle or wanting to settle the dog in his bed before I open. I mean, I understand it's not easy being old, but some of these people, they're just working you. This one guy, he'll stand there in the cold like a puppy, making you feel guilty because he can't or won't tell time.

"I open in ten minutes."

"Can't I come in, out of the cold?"

"It's not that cold out."

"Can't I come in?"

"You drove here."

"Yes."

"Can't you give me ten minutes and wait in your car?"

I don't know, some of them are just rushing to get back home to the recliner; others are shuttling between doctors' offices, some want to talk. I don't care what they need before 9 a.m., because my public drama doesn't start before then. Free will says if you don't like it, you can take your business elsewhere, and I'm fine with that. It's bad enough that most of my clients will get on the road and at some point, will be responsible for cutting me off or forgetting to signal their turn as they crawl into the off-ramp from the right lane. I don't feel guilty most mornings if the early birds shiver or sweat. We all make choices. Even old people have choices.

Cheryl used to say that at some level, even death was a choice. You have to go through it, but the way and the reason you die is tied to your story in life. She made me study the cards, made me look at all that was going on in them, even that Death card. It's number 13, enough to make you feel uneasy, right there. We were always taught 13 was unlucky, and we knew that was why no elevators in America had a 13th floor, so it made looking at the card really uncomfortable.

I can see her now, staring that card down, with her dark brown eyes, open wide. "OK, Tom... See, here Tom! You don't want to miss this!" She'd point out some little detail, and I laughed but I paid attention. I may have raised my eyebrows, but I'd be lying if I said she didn't teach me things. I could act like a bitch, but the more I helped take care of Cheryl, the more I understood things.

The thing about death, Cheryl said, is that it's a great leveler. No matter how rich or poor you are, you die. No matter how much you suffer or party, you die. It's comforting, I guess, and most of the time when you pull the Death card it just means transition. You know you're switching jobs, or you're getting a divorce or some other major transition. Sometimes, though, it actually does mean death, and when that happens, you're never fully prepared. I know Cheryl wasn't. In those last months before she passed the Death card kept popping up. I'd go over there; to this tiny little house the size of some people's garage, and she'd be pulling card after card. She got tired of pulling them for herself, so she'd pull them for me. Cheryl knew I wanted love – because, of course, who doesn't? – and she'd do these huge spreads for me. She did an especially big one for me just before she died, and she wrote down all this advice on paper with pen. It's not every day that someone does that for you.

We all make choices every day, and sometimes I make a choice to let the old geezers wait outside while I open the shop. I make stupid choices sometimes, and sometimes I make good ones. As for death, I've already decided I'm not going out like my father. I'm not going out because I tempted fate. I still do my own electrical work sometimes. I even fix my own hot tub, but I do it with the breakers off. My father of course, worked with live wires. As for other potentially dangerous situations, I sure as hell don't get involved with things like snakes or hornets. If there's a pest on my property, I call a professional.

I want to live until I'm very old. I don't care about wrinkles or how in the hell I'm going to afford living that long, I just know I have a lot to do still. That's what Cheryl said, too. She said she didn't mind the dying so much since she trusted a lot in the other side. After all, with her ability to see spirits, it's not like she was facing some abyss. Cheryl said she was dying too young because there was so much, she'd learned that she hadn't shared. I wonder why some of the nicest people end up dying without a spouse or some kind of heir. I drag on a Newport and realize I'm hovering at the same age my father was when he died. I think about quitting.

Juice vs. Cancer

Cheryl did everything she could with her diet to make herself healthier so she could beat the cancer. She took her juicing seriously. She went a solid six months of juice alone, no solid foods. She never faltered. They said she'd be dead in three months, and she was in her sixth when she decided that since she'd proven them wrong, she could have a day of solid food. Eventually she started to eat a bit more, and soon it was enough that she had a cheat day, on Sundays. That's when I would come around straight from the restaurant with an eggplant parm, or maybe a chicken francese. I was so glad when Cheryl started her cheat days, because for a while I didn't want to eat around her because I felt guilty.

I had the juice with her once to be supportive. She was packing down 32 ounces a clip using her Jack LaLanne juicer. She had some roasted vegetables for dinner, with a sweet potato being most of it. Broccoli, kale, romaine lettuce, escarole and Swiss chard – those were the staples she stuffed into that machine day after day. Cheryl told me she juiced knowing she couldn't do chemo because of her lupus. She knew she wasn't comfortable with the double mastectomy option, either. Her condition made her susceptible to never coming out of the surgery. She gave up potato chips and sour cream and all the other snacks, and I knew she missed them, but she was fighting for her life with a limited number of really good options

The day she convinced me to have the juice, Cheryl was funny.

"The least you could do is taste what I'm drinking."

"Fine."

"I knew you would!"

"It's not terrible."

"See, I told you. It's not even bitter; I didn't put that much Swiss chard in this one."

She did have some green apples in it, and I tasted those, mostly. It wasn't bad, but after drinking it three times a day for six months, with no real break, I might have lost my mind. On Sundays, I brought whatever she wanted from the restaurant, from the entrée right through to the desserts. We ate carbohydrates, and we didn't worry about nothing during our cheat meal. Cheryl would do the juice in the morning, first thing Monday and all the rest of the week, along with her veggie roasts, but Sundays were fun days. After the big meal, Cheryl would rest a little, and then she would get up, flip some cards and then make another 32 ounces of juice, to keep her pH up.

On Sundays we partied, and the meal was only half of it. We would make oils, cast some spells, practice egg divinations, and do things I did not even know existed. Cheryl would pull out a quartz rock on a chain and teach me to ask the thing questions. She warned me, though: "The pendulum is low level, Tom. It's not always true." Then she would have me hold it out at a right angle dangling from one hand, over the other, palm face-up. You would think it was so easy, but Cheryl hated the way I tried to hold it. I don't know what it was, but as a lefty, my right hand did not want to go out the way she told me it should. I couldn't understand how it made a difference, but she always corrected it, telling me the angle had to be away from my body. I tried, but I think a part of me was annoyed that it mattered.

Despite myself, I learned how to do dangle the thing and ask it "yes" or "no" questions, ones that are very precise. Ask the pendulum a general question, and you'll get a very general, almost useless answer. Ask it something focused, and you will get something useful out of it. A lot of this stuff is about how you ask, and that was easy to see after a little while. It takes more time to get where you want to go, asking the right kinds of questions, but trust me, it's worth it.

Sunday after Sunday we went through this stuff, with Cheryl teaching me things like "If you want to get a real answer, you go to the cards." Tarot was the "Grand Poobah," according to Cheryl. It was where you went for details, to get a sense of the players. I can still hear her as we looked at the cards together, "What do you see, Tom? Listen to your gut." When I really got stuck, she would look at me and say, "Tom, read the pictures," so I would read them like a little kid reads a picture book. That worked.

We would flip the cards in Cheryl's dining room area, her reading rug spread on the table with her quizzing me. Cheryl's reading rug wasn't an actual rug but a piece of cloth, a pretty shawl or something along that size, that she used to keep the energies around the cards clean. I don't always use a rug when I go to the cards, not like Cheryl did. I'm not sure why I'm not using one, though, because lots of times I get lost trying to read and I get frustrated. I don't know, pulling out the reading rug feels witchier than throwing them down on the bare table. Anyway, those were Sundays with cards being spread and flipped, and that was nothing like most Sunday dinners in my life.

I remember family dinners; the crying and the yelling, and when I think of how much Cheryl and I laughed, I can't imagine how different those worlds are, and how good I felt when we spent the night laughing. I know we did it up with the fried food and all that white sugar and cream, but none of it probably hurt her that much. Even if she was at a place where every meal, every single thing, made a difference in whether she lived or died, she needed to feel free for a few hours. That cancer was doing battle with her heart as much as her body, and the way we laughed had to count for something healthy. Sure, I know her pH took a hit during those dinners, but whatever she lost in vitamins or gained in cholesterol for those few hours had to be balanced out by the good feelings. I still believe that, and I know Cheryl went to her grave believing that, too.

While Cheryl was sick and trying to beat cancer, I drove to the health food store instead of the regular supermarkets, and lots of time delivered the groceries with our Sunday cheat meal. I became an organic, clean food hunter, reading food labels, figuring out what would make the purest type of food option. Cheryl needed things that weren't shady with preservatives or polluted with chemicals. She needed all new food for a new body to grow out of her dying one. "Cancer can't live between 7.5 and 8.5 pH" was her mantra, so that defined everything. Her food world got smaller; even her juice choices were limited. We avoided cucumbers and celery because Cheryl would get nervous about the sodium in them. On top of things like that, I had to check to make sure she wasn't getting GMO or other types of engineered food. I left the big-box stores for tiny shops with small selections, tiny aisles and signs that said things like "local" and "biodynamic."

I was at a complete loss with the brands in the natural stores. Everything I ever knew about food fell apart when I started buying the food Cheryl said would help her get healthy. Everyone around her could notice she got happier the more she juiced. As she got her body to the ideal pH, I have to admit, she started to look healthy. It took weeks and months, but pH strip after pH strip, she was changing her body. For a while, those pH test strips ruled our lives, and waiting for the results was more nerve-racking than flipping cards.

"Drink Life; Give Life." That was Cheryl's way of giving thanks to God for every juice. Cheryl was raised Catholic, and she never left that ritual stuff alone; she just expanded on it. The Church taught about the saints, but they didn't teach about the roots of them, the things that came before. That wasn't in their self-interest, to teach all the stuff that came before, but Cheryl looked for it and found out about it. Cheryl took the Catholic mysteries and compared them with Elemental Dignities, using one set of symbols to unlock the power of the other.

She looked at the St. Anthony, and she saw Oshun, and she would teach me all about him. She looked at the Sacred Heart of Jesus, and she saw the Three of Swords. She knew about saints everyone talked about, and she knew about the ones who got their saint status cancelled by whomever was in power and felt threatened by their story. She talked about the goddess and how she would show up after Christianity got popular and they all started calling her Jesus' mother. She knew all these stories of how the supernatural survived all our politics and trends. I didn't grow up Catholic, didn't know much about saints or any of that stuff, but Cheryl brought me into it, little by little.

As Cheryl said her little prayer of thanks, I couldn't help but feel a difference in how she prayed. It wasn't different just because she was raised Catholic and I was raised a staunch Protestant. It was all in her tone. When Cheryl said things like, "So mote it be" or "Drink Life; Give Life," her prayers sounded more powerful than mine. All my prayers sounded like I was doubtful, like I wasn't sure that I was worthy of anything I wanted to come true. Cheryl's prayers, on the other hand, sounded like she really believed she and God were on the same side. My sense of fear wasn't anything like her sense of awe. I figured this out through our Sundays, through all the little things we did together. Cheryl wasn't like my mother, my sister, or even my aunts, but in her tiny rented house I got this new sense of what it feels like to eat and be with family.

It was the routine of meeting, of being together meal after meal and juice after juice, that brought back memories and that feeling of family. My mother, I remembered, wasn't the greatest cook, but she faithfully cooked most nights. Like any normal person stuck in a job she didn't choose, she did her best not to show how much she hated it. I give her credit for getting that dinner done and never once throwing it at us, especially me. I may have had my charms, with my blue eyes and my slim build, but out of her three children, I was usually the one who would whine about the menu. At dinnertime this expression of my personality had the potential to transform the whole house into a full-fledged war zone.

As a conservative family, living off one salary, we did not eat out much. We ate at home as much on principle as because of budget restrictions. Those restrictions did not inspire my mother, and our dinners were a lot like Cheryl's in a way: predictable – but nowhere near as peaceful. Cheryl and I laughed at stupid things; at home, we were required to take everything around the dinner table very seriously. No matter what showed up for dinner, we had to pretend to be happy about it. I have to admit there were more than a few dishes my mother hit out of the ballpark, like her mac and cheese, meatloaf and beef stew, but those other dishes like the tuna casseroles or the organ meats were nothing short of horrendous for me.

"It's my house," my father said, in that way that men used to do. "You'll eat what's in front of you and like it." It didn't matter how he said it, exactly; it was the way he said it, letting you know that he was always in control. I get that he wanted us to appreciate the meal, but you can't command someone to like something. Life doesn't work that way. Dinner had to be on the table between 5:30-6 every night, and Mom had it there as a point of pride and a way to keep the peace. In our house deciding not to eat all of dinner was like announcing you were going to break a law. It was hard enough to choke down a plate of liver or "stick-to-your-ribs" kidneys, but it was a hundred times worse with my father looking over my shoulder. I'd see him get angry, but there wasn't much I could do about it; the food stuck in my throat. Something makes me think that as my father was breathing down my neck, watching me suffer through dinners, he was probably suffering, too. He was a much better cook than my mother, and he gave that up for a job he didn't want. The result was that he was always seething, always ready to tear anyone who dared to complain into tiny little pieces. I complained enough, and so I was torn to pieces pretty much all the time.

My father was born in a different New Jersey, one that had cranberry bogs and kids who shot guns in the woods. That New Jersey was made of people tracing their roots to the colonies of Dutch and Germans and Scots; all with die-hard Protestant roots, people who didn't have much patience for wasting food. In fact, I don't know if it was our roots or just that side of the family, but being angry and pissed off at the smallest sign of weakness or someone or something not going according to plan seemed to run in our blood. In our family we were supposed to be realistic, to the point that we accepted life was meant to be shitty most of the time. Fairytale endings were what happened in heaven, and even in there, chances were there was a reservations book without your name in it. In my father's view of things, you worked hard, and you expected very little, and your biggest triumph was passing that low expectation onto your kids.

When my father threw that money in grandpa's face that time in Florida, he had no idea that one unexpected day in his 50s he would die in his father's arms. Neither of them knew that was going to happen. The scotch, maybe a half-gallon a week, and two to three packs of cigarettes a day meant it shouldn't have been a surprise, but somehow it still was. My father had a massive heart attack at basically the same age I am now. I have a few vices, stress for sure, but overall I feel I'm doing fine. I don't have a death wish; in fact, I'd say I have a very strong will to live.

Despite the Newports and the coffee and tea I do my best to stay healthy. Whereas my father drank scotch I'm supposed to quit the coffee and tea on account of my kidneys and the gravel they've accumulated. I'm supposed to be living a very clean life, and I haven't managed it all the way. I hear that kids who grow up with smoking parents develop a special chemical relationship in their brain to nicotine, so that's a battle. As for the coffee, well, I don't know too many people who get off that one.

Traffic here starts around Exit 98 – and yes, I know, that sounds like typical New Jersey, to mark distance by exit, but at least we have infrastructure. . We all give directions based on exits and yes, we use the numbers because who has time to rattle off names? By the time you get from door to door you've crossed this old route, and that new overpass and you have barely survived with your life. We'll use our exit numbers if that's what we need to do to keep it easier.

The construction isn't that bad right now, and so I cruise to work past the signs that threaten us with fines, but nobody seems to slow down, and I have to admit I barely notice. The projects take forever, and the orange cones and the signs might as well be flowers. I don't have time to stop and smell flowers enough, and I don't have the time to take the signs too seriously, either, unless of course there are people actually working. I don't want to kill some poor guys on their grind.

The red brake lights of some mom catch my attention. She's pumping her brake like she's having sex with it. It's unconscious, of course. Maybe she is thinking about sex, but mostly I imagine she's in a state of anxiety. She's thinking about the kids, the mortgage, the interior design of her living room, maybe the gel pedicure that she can't stand anymore. There she is, just pumping that brake thinking about everything but the road, while I get annoyed. I cut to the left to get away, but it's like she knows what I'm trying to do, and she slips in front of me and then pumps that brake again, pretty much destroying the flow of traffic. I feel a tightness around my temples, like I might be getting annoyed. This lady is a clog in the artery of everything, an oblivious obstruction, and somehow, she makes me think of my father.

My father's heart just gave out one day, maybe from some similar unconscious block. He was there one minute, cruising the ocean by the inlet, surrounded by water and birds, and in the next minute he was in Grandpa's arms, the sun flooding his field of vision, while the life drained from his body. All it took was one clog to stop his heart and to change all our lives. My father was probably aggravated when he went down to use the head on the boat. He was probably thinking about everything but his heart when it stopped. Grandpa noticed his son was taking a while down there, and as he opened the cabin door to see what was going on, he saw my father gasping for air. They dragged him onto the deck of the boat, and since only my father knew how to use the radio, Grandpa and my uncle tied sheets to the outriggers and signaled to the lighthouse. All in all, my father didn't suffer long.

As for Cheryl, she suffered a while, first with the lupus, then through thirteen months of cancer. I don't know what held her back from making a full recovery, although I guess I have some clue. I know Cheryl lived for a promise that never came true, and just like my father's American dream never really materialized into happiness, Cheryl's dreams of love dropped her just short of the fairytale ending she worked so hard to make real. Hearts are muscles, but they're also places where we keep things hidden, even from ourselves. Cheryl had a man for years, and she waited while he hemmed and hawed about commitment and being there. He ran when she got sick, and there I was picking up the slack for her "real" man, another 100 percent straight guy who seemed to be meaner to the woman he said he loved than anyone else. I don't know what went on between them, so I don't judge his actions. All I know is that Cheryl ended up with a broken heart, that did not improve on her will to live, though she would have denied this.

I was there for Cheryl when she passed, just like I was there for my mom. Fate had it so that I wasn't there for my father, and it was probably better that way. He died in his own father's arms, and maybe, at some level, that was the most comforting place for him to be. All my father seemed to want was for Grandpa to show him some compassion, and probably the only thing that could have made him do it was seeing his son dying in his arms, before his very eyes. Cheryl's father couldn't be there for her, and she always made a point of mentioning that her father sent me to stand in his place. I don't know if that's true, but I know it made easier on her, to think that her father was looking out for her from the other side, so I never questioned it. Dying is one of those things that brings out the pain, and it brings out the little miracles, too.

Cheryl was a miracle for me, and the fact that I could be one for her blew my mind. I didn't want to sleep with her, but it doesn't mean I didn't love her. Honestly, lovers, in general, seem to torture one another. If that weren't the case, soap operas and sad love songs would not exist. Most of the time Mom used to fold laundry while she watched her soaps, and I could tell they kind of took her away from us. She'd have us be quiet as the dramas unfolded on the 1960s black-and-white RCA television console. Sometimes she'd just stop the folding, light up her own cigarette and blow out these huge smoke clouds while people just like us, but with bigger houses and lots of money, cried.

Mom wanted to live in the world she saw in "Guiding Light" and "Days of Our Lives." It was a place where women wore fancy clothes to have their hearts broken. We were the last people I knew to get a color television, and Mom didn't say much about it but I knew she wanted to see the colors of those outfits more than anything. She didn't say much, but she let it be known, in sideways remarks, that soon we wouldn't be able to deal without color. That kind of approval from Mom was all we needed to feel bolder, to beg and beg for a color screen, but we were stuck with that TV until my father couldn't find replacements for the bulbs in his special TV-repair shoebox. When his stock of bulbs and tubes was finally gone, we figured we were close to a breakthrough. But he sourced the little tubes in the back of the TV from similar sets he found at the dump. He could keep that RCA going until the picture tube went, and he let us know it.

By the end, it was a struggle to get through a day without the picture going fuzzy or going in and out. I swore the thing was teasing us by going right to the brink, then coming back to life for one last night. All the while, our father held onto that TV with a vengeance, acting like he could hold back all the progress of the world by keeping a black-and-white television set alive. We all knew it was a matter of time; eventually it would go, and Dad would have to deal with it.

One day, the picture tube finally went, and when the screen went dim our eyes opened wide with excitement. We weren't out of the woods, but we were closer. My father looked for weeks for a compatible set in the dump, but nothing showed up, no gem in the rough. Mom was losing patience like never before in our lives. She was missing her soaps, and no number of cigarettes were going to replace them. Things started to get rough around the house; the quality of our dinners was going down, and for the first time in our lives, Mom was picking fights. Dad found himself in uncharted territory with a grumbling wife and nothing to look at from his chair at the table. He must have sensed a mutiny was in the works, and he realized he had no choice but to head to the store for a brand-new color TV.

I dreamed of a big, beautiful set with upgraded wood paneling and speakers to match. I figured once we were there, buying a new set, that we might get one like they had in the magazines. Dad quickly explained to me that I was dreaming. The console was out, because that was too expensive new, and the screen went from 26 inches to something like 13. I was trying to get the man to upgrade, to really go for the best new TV he could get, but my father put his philosophy into perspective for me.

"It's smaller, Dad."

"It's color, ain't it?"

"Yes."

"Then, shut up."

Whining was not tolerated by my father, and the price of the color television, plus the fact that the new set was powered with transistors he didn't know how to fix, set him on edge. It was one of those few times I decided not to respond.

I enjoyed the color TV. It was harder to gather around the thing, seeing as it didn't have much of a presence in the room, but with a little maneuvering we could all watch the same show without getting in each other's way. Things were all right for Mom and us kids, but for Dad the television was an annoying reminder of how things were always moving ahead even when he wanted them to sit still.

It went from bad to worse for my father when, after about a year, the color set broke. This is back when things were expected to last at least ten years before you had to fix them. This was my father's world, and as far as he knew, no appliance had a right to do this so young. Grudgingly, he took the color set in to get it repaired by a professional. He had gotten used to the color, and they had charged him plenty for the thing at the appliance store, so he had no choice. He brought the set in, took his paper receipt, and then we all started the wait back at home, silently hoping for the best. I was scared that if the repair shop couldn't fix it, we would go back to a black-and-white set. I imagined him still looking in the dumps for one. I imagined him finding two of them and making a Frankenstein's television from parts. The longer the color set stayed in the shop, the closer we came to going backward.

The day my father went to pick up the color set, he had called the repair shop several times but gotten no answer. My brother and I got in the car with him and drove on a single-lane highway to the place in Toms River, not knowing what to expect. We pulled up at the shop, and it was obviously closed. There was no sign of life. The place had suddenly gone out of business, and the place was empty. It was like something from the western show "Bonanza," which we all watched. In this episode, cowboy Joe Cartwright, our hero, pulled into the parking lot to learn he had been screwed out of his color TV. With no other recourse, Joe, played by Jimmy Sharpe in this episode, made himself feel better by screaming, "Motherfuckers!" about a hundred times on the ride home. It was epic. I was terrified and I pushed myself as far into the seat as I could, not uttering a word. I kept reminding myself to shut up before I said a single word and it worked.

So, my father had to buy another brand-new television. A broken man at that point, he went to the appliance store immediately. He paid for the color screen while gritting his teeth, and he paid for the console because everyone was tired of the stand. He gave in to getting himself a little luxury because he had no real choice. My mother smiled from ear to ear, and she told him how nice the new set was, and somehow that seemed to make it better for him. My mother knew she was stuck as a homemaker, stuck with us kids and the same repetitive chores, and so she worked with it.

Every once in a while, you could see Mom raise her eyebrow at something, and you could see my father receive her message. She could be passive-aggressive with those brows, using them instead of words to make a point. There were plenty of times he started to pick on me when a single eyebrow raise could end the conversation. I was thankful for Mom, even if I did not for the life of me understand how she could be so calm around him. I had a long way to go in learning how women survived for generations. I had no idea at that point, never even considered she might have wanted to keep her job or exercise her mind beyond the drama of the soaps. I never dreamed she could get so tired of holding her tongue, that she eventually became a master at raising her brow.

When I was a child, my drama was focused on the house and dinners, and I watched her eyebrows shoot up and down, trying to take the cues to keep the peace. Later I learned there was a lot to the silence that I didn't get, but I tried. One thing was for sure, if my father was late for dinner she would raise one eyebrow while we waited. If it got to where she raised both eyebrows, then she would calmly load all three of us kids into the car to go look for her Jimmy. With Mom behind the wheel, acting like he could be anywhere, we all knew we were going to find him at one of a handful of bars.

We all knew that, just like those ladies on the soaps, Mom was going to pout and whine, and maybe yell at him. She might cry once she knew he was safe, depending on the day. There was only so much she could handle silently and finding him smelling of booze while her dinner waited on the table – well, that was generally her breaking point.

We were the troops in Lucille's search party, stopping at the regular joints where my father would go to quietly get sloshed. Drinks were fairly cheap back then, and my father would throw them down with other working stiffs. We had clothes on our back and food was on the table, and he almost seemed surprised on those nights when we came to get him that we wanted anything more from his life. He would get in the car after some begging by my mother, and then we would head home with each of them digging at the other. We, the troops, pretended not to watch or hear them, but we heard each word like it was spoken over a microphone.

When my father passed, I thought my mom would have more peace, but she ended up looking more lost than I thought she could. She'd sleep sitting up, or stay on the couch, waiting for me at nights. I would find her in the morning sometimes asleep on the dining room table.

"You slept in the dining room again?"

"I have no reason to go to bed. I have no husband."

She didn't have a perfect marriage or a fairytale husband, but he was all she knew. They started out in love, and they became a habit for each other, and habits are hard to break. Without her other half, Mom looked absolutely lost. At one point, my brother and I decided to make her a deck out the back of the house, to make things brighter and finally get her better access out the back to the yard. She lamented that we'd have to move the heating pipe; she worried about the glass of the doors and the bills. She was perfectly fine with walking through the breezeway and out the garage to get to the backyard.

We didn't know about Wolmanized® lumber, so we built a deck with regular planks and supports. Charlie said, "How do you build a deck?" and I said, "I don't know," but instead of asking anyone, we decided to figure it out on our own. We had joists on center and some decent squares that we built after we put down some cinder blocks. It looked good, and our mother was thrilled for a long while. The deck lasted at least fifteen years, and then one day, my mother called me up.

"You're not going to believe what happened to me today. Thank God, the phone was on the picnic table. I fell through the deck, and I reached over, and I called your sister."

(long pause) "What did she say?"

"I told her, 'I fell through the deck, and I can't get up.' "She started laughing. And then I hung up on her."

(Uncontrollable laughter)

Then Mom hung up on me, too. I couldn't help it; the whole image was just too much like a movie. I laughed with tears in my eyes. I turned red from laughing so hard. To this day if I call my sister and mention the deck, we still burst out laughing. Years have gone on, decades even and something about that moment still hits us. We knew she was fine since there she was casually talking. Who knows, maybe some part of us felt relieved since we already lost our father in seconds. We already understood that tragedy and comedy aren't just for the movies.

I can picture her falling through the deck, screaming, wearing this one dress that was "the dress." She wore that dress for years and years. It flared out, and since Mom was full-figured, it looked good on her. For years she wore it and kept mending it, even at the armpits. It was her favorite, and she'd do anything to keep wearing it, even if it made us crazy. She had other dresses, but "the dress" was green with these flowers and the full skirt, and when I got the image in my head of her falling through the deck with those flowers going up in the air, I lost it, and so did my sister.

Apparently without the pressure-treated wood, that deck was a time bomb. Without my father and us kids around, it gave Mom the most excitement she had had in a while. I'm not saying it was good for her to have the deck collapse, but I am saying she had lived through much worse. For the future, my brother and I learned to look for the Wolmanized® brand, but seeing as they load it up with chemicals, I'm not sure what's worse. 15 years isn't a bad run for a deck.

When we were kids, Mom kept the house running, and her life didn't have much traveling or wild days. She did laundry and all the chores that women of her time did. My mother took her break from 11 a.m.-2 p.m., when the soap operas came on: "Guiding Light," "As the World Turns," "Days of Our Lives." If I was home sick from school, I would get parked in the living room with her, and I would think to myself how depressing it was. She'd fold laundry like a champ, but she might not get to the dusting, especially if it was out of the radius of the television. Those were the days of dial tuning and rabbit ears, and there was only one screen in the house. I remember those not-so-wonderful days, when you'd yell down from one room to the other, all the way up to the roof to get the picture right. If you couldn't get the rabbit ears going, then someone – usually my father, of course – would have to go all the way up to the antennae. Oh, the yelling we used to have to do just to get a horizontal picture.

Back then, parenting was different, and so were lifestyles. Dad didn't really commute far, not like people do now for jobs, so he'd come home for lunch sometimes once he became a foreman on his job. The first ten years, Mom's days were probably a mystery to my father. When he started coming home during the day, Mom got my father hooked on "The Young and The Restless." He'd come home for lunch, and they'd chain smoke. I hated it the way it made the house smell, and I complained that I couldn't breathe. My parents smoked Benson & Hedges menthols. When they upped the price, Mom kept to the Benson & Hedges, but my father got into fits of rolling the cigarettes himself. He'd get the Half and Half brand loose tobacco and Zig Zag papers. For a short bit he used a rolling machine, but most of his life I remember a row of hand-twisted smokes. He'd bitch while he rolled.

I hated the Half and Half and how it woke me up in the morning. He lit up his first cigarette as he poured his Sanka, and the smell of it shot right up the stairwell. As he took his first sip of black coffee, the Half and Half made its way into my nostrils and woke me with a burning down my nose and throat.

I don't know why he picked pipe tobacco for his cigarettes. The package said it provided a lively smoke. It provided me with a headache to start the day. I didn't start smoking until I was 32, and now I can't kick it. I smoke a little less than my mother did, but I start first thing in the morning. I'm not perfect, I'm in progress.

My father was blue collar, and Mom was from a white-collar family. She went to Berkeley Secretarial School in Ridgewood, the fanciest in the area. My father was lanky, with eyes that probably looked sexy because he was fresh from the war. He was like something from a black-and-white western, and she was the girl next door. My father grew up fast and sold his restaurant when he met Mom, to try and fit the white-collar norm more, but I don't think it ever fit him. My mother loved to dance; Tommy Dorsey and Glenn Miller, those big band sounds got her on her feet with their trumpets and all sorts of other brass and swing. Times like that, even her dress, "the dress," looked glamorous. When I saw them dancing, I felt like I could catch a glimpse of their fairytale, the one that had started their real life together.

My parents danced more when they were young; they danced a lot, I think, back then. They smoked and had cocktails and some beers, and they laughed at jokes.

By the time we kids came around, my mother pretty much stuck to smoking, and my father kept up with the drinking, but dancing had moved to the edges, reserved for weddings and charity-type functions, events at my father's Masonic Lodge. My father was 22 and Mom 21 when they got married, and each of them settled into a regular life based on other people's expectations. It made them old before their time, not the marriage necessarily but doing it the way that they did.

My father got them involved in the Masons; my mother joined the Order of the Eastern Star. As we got older, my sister joined the International Order of the Rainbow for Girls, a Masonic youth organization, and my brother and I did the DeMolay International thing, which is Masons for young men. They settled in and got married and had us kids, and they raised us to be like everyone else. We looked like all the other families and did what they did. We kept our business private and our lawn trimmed, just like they did. We went to the Masonic functions, and we went to church, and everyone lived their assigned roles. From the outside, everything in our lives was in order.

My father would find scrap metal to sell on the side, and my mother always found something to keep her busy; women never seem to have a hard time with that. We kids had chores, and we got up for church and we went to our meetings. Our parents were young, but they followed the rules of society for their time, and some of it wasn't so bad. At DeMolay, which I couldn't stand because I was forced into it, we learned to honor our mothers, and we even had a ceremony about it, with carnations. They called that the "flower talk," and it was a big deal. The only problem was that there was no room for me in it, not the way I really was. I went to the meetings, and I went to church, and the more I got into it, the more I discovered I wasn't allowed to be me in those places. I could uphold all the rules and do all the rituals; I could give my mother a thousand carnations. None of it would make up for me being me, so I went through the motions realizing it was all just some kind of act.

Luckily, my father was cheap above all else so eventually we left our church and the Masons before my sexual orientation became an issue. Inflation was up, and dues were suddenly up, and my father got sticker shock. Members from the church came over one day, and my father served them coffee. Then they got to business and asked him to start giving 10 percent of his income to the church. My father went over and took the cups right out of their hands and said, "Thank you. Have a good day." He wasn't old at that point, but since he'd gotten old young, he got offended like old people can. On account of money, he started pulling out of the things that he once thought he had to do, like church, and from the things he wanted to do, like the Masons. His loss was my temporary salvation, but that doesn't mean it was good for him.

My client, Loretta; I've been cutting her hair for thirty years, and she says I never age, and I tend to agree with her. She's fantastic, Loretta; she's got a good laugh, the kind that makes you feel like a teenager, the kind that makes the laugh bust from your mouth, from the back of your throat, where it forces its way out of you with a will of its own. Loretta is Jewish, and in a way, that can be a lot like being gay, because people have their ideas about what that label means to them. Judgement is never really about you. Anyway, I love Loretta for seeing the real me, for always making me laugh, and keeping me young in that way that I don't ever want to lose. That means more to me than any label that says we're family or members in some club assigned to us at birth. Cheryl and I laughed that way. My sister and I laugh like that, sometimes at our mother's expense. You live, and you learn. You laugh, and you try not to piss off the woman who gave you life, but sometimes you do.

Lists vs. Chaos

I would drive to the health food store to get Cheryl the organic fruits and vegetables she needed. It wasn't out of the way, but it took me into towns I didn't bother with most of the time. I mean, who wants to take Main Street with all the lights and the school buses when you can take the highway and get there faster? But the detour was nice in a way, because my world got bigger by taking me to places I would buzz by normally. And let's face it, once I had the shopping list written down, I couldn't help but follow it like a sacred mission.

I had no use for the health-food store at first, even as I filled the cart with papaya or apples, greens and turmeric, because I was healthy, and the prices were sky high. I could afford to pay less and eat more chemicals. The produce was smaller and tastier than the regular produce. It reminded me of grandpa's fruit down in Florida when I was a kid. None of it was perfect on the outside, but inside it had a lot of personality. The more I got into eating organic with Cheryl, the more I appreciated the food. It made me feel fuller for longer. It was more satisfying in a way I didn't expect. The fruit with the character – that's what Cheryl wanted and that's what I got. The more I went to the store for her, the better I got at getting exactly the right ones.

North of all the hair salons, and just south of the restaurant, close by her house, I'd pull into the parking lot right on the edge of a town full of million-dollar properties. There was a post office branch, then the health-food store, and right next to it an Irish pub and packaged goods store combination. I would walk up to the door of the health store and see some old electrician or everyday guy shivering while he finished a cigarette next to the bike rack between the storefronts. The local yoga teachers and all the other hippies would walk past these guys. They'd smile at each other and make room for each other with the bikes to one side and the cigarette smell on the other. The rest of the strip was typical: a bank, a meat market that specialized in catering and bread from Brooklyn, a Chinese dry cleaner that catered to the Wall Streeters who bought these big Victorians, sometimes as second homes, and a pizzeria at the end, with regular and Sicilian slices and a can at the register for making donations to help kids fight diseases.

Disease is about being unhappy, but with kids I don't know if that's true. I feel like when kids get something serious like cancer, it's something around them that's causing it, almost like an allergy. With kids like that, you feel like maybe they were too good for the world, and fate was set up so that they didn't suffer here for too long. Those of us who aren't so allergic, we stay, and we live long enough to build up list after list of shit we wish we didn't do. We take on the grief from the world little by little instead of taking it on right away. This world can make us all cancer-level sick, because nobody's skin is so thick that you ever really feel at ease for too long. You can't feel all the shit that goes on around you and avoid making it your own. If it's not the chemicals in the water, or microscopic bath beads clogging up the works, it's the way we treat each other that puts chinks in our armor, not from the outside, but from within.

We all have these quiet fights. Unlike my mom, who had a steady man to break her heart time and again, mostly at dinnertime, Cheryl bore the blow of being outright abandoned more than once. Toward the end she ate only organic and did everything right, but nothing could fix the internal issue of being led on, and that she let him do it, too. She was sick, and she was tired, and he still wasn't into changing their set-up. Cheryl wanted a full-time partner, instead, she got me and Napoleon. We kept her as part of the pack. We drove with her to the doctor's office, everywhere she needed to stop. We drove with her to an enchantment supply shop farther away than all the others, because of something special they carried. We took it in stride. We made it an adventure, especially since this one very special place was in New Hope, a town that's so cute you feel more adorable just by being there. Napoleon jumped into the car without a growl when we got on the road with Cheryl, and he never complained about my driving when she was with us. We did a fair amount of trips as a pack. Often when we went to the health-food store, or the high-end supermarket as a group, the staff would go out of their way for her. They would get things out of the back for us when Cheryl was with me, and they asked about her when she started to disappear.

Cheryl juiced, and she meditated. She kept journals, lined composition books, where she wrote down the cards she pulled for the day. She'd pull three tarot cards each day, then she wrote down the date, the card and her thoughts about them. She'd layer her readings and have spreads that grew until they looked like tablets from Egypt. Those journals were Cheryl's own kind of list keeping. Mine are all about things I need to accomplish – who I have to meet, pay, bitch at, or beg – but Cheryl's journals were a different kind of list. Seems to me like those journals were like to-do lists for her soul, while mine were all about getting my body to points A, B, C and D.

My father always said, "You're born with a name, and you die with a reputation." Cheryl was scared to have a reputation – not in certain aspects, but in others. She didn't care if people were petty, passing judgment on superficial things that were hard to hide, but she was plenty scared of being outed as a psychic, a clairvoyant, all those things that make us think of old gypsy ladies with crystal balls. The things that break our hearts aren't just what happens to us, but the things we do to ourselves. Cheryl was scared to death of being labeled a witch, because that's a big word in our world, but you could see it without even knowing what you saw.

The housekeeping staff at the hospital whispered "Bruja" around Cheryl; because of the little things she had around her when she came to die. They knew the signs of a spiritual player. I don't think the doctors or nurses much noticed or cared, since that's how hospitals work. Anyway, Cheryl was so concerned about how people would treat her that she stayed in the closet about all the amazing things she knew and it really only came out into the light when she had nothing left to lose. I thought she might stop giving a fuck about what could go wrong if she was honest with people. I thought maybe she'd have a breakthrough, thinking of all the things that could go right if she didn't live hiding her talents. I think we got close to getting her there.

We joked about writing a book about surviving cancer. We thought about calling it "Belmar Bruja," in honor of where she lived and how she helped me. Cheryl liked "bruja" because the Spanish-speaking people were the ones who still honored the old ways – the Puerto Ricans running their botanicas, and the Mexicans, who you can't stop from having their skulls around Halloween, they seemed to understand reality. So "bruja" seemed all right to Cheryl because even though it still had some problems, it didn't conjure images of green-skinned women with warts or those horrible witch trials where lots of women were killed by their jealous pastors and local politicians. Cheryl said that she had been a Seer in lots of lives, and dealing with memories or dreams of the Inquisition was part of the reason she had a hard time expressing herself. She said she could sometimes remember the sting of the burning; the lies being told. I guess, the pain of betrayal, can live across lifetimes.

"What's the list?"

"For the juice: Swiss chard, romaine, green apples, broccoli, kale, five pounds of carrots, at least."

"OK."

"To cook: potatoes, eggplant; stuff to roast."

"For the enema: coffee; make sure you make it the rough grind, since otherwise it clogs the bag."

"OK."

"You know, after drinking all those carrots in the morning..."

"Yeah?"

"My butthole is turning orange."

"How do you know that?"

When people are sick, you say the craziest things to each other, things that might normally horrify you. Cheryl and I had some awesome text messages back and forth about how she was doing day to day. She knew I didn't care about niceties. As her world got smaller and her struggles took priority, Cheryl turned into a detective, paying attention to any new lumps, to the way she breathed, to what was coming out of her. Like lots of other people battling illness, especially aggressive illnesses, she was not above putting a mirror by her butt to see what was going on. It was all a fact-finding mission into this body that had become a mystery to her.

We made list after list and pursued our mission for her imminent success. If she had been diagnosed earlier it could have turned around for her. Getting diagnosed at Stage 4, the odds were stacked against us, but we tried. We never got to write that book together, about her beating the cancer, but the jokes we made sparked something inside me. I'm sharing all these fond memories because I wish she was here, and because I want you to wish she was, too. Sometimes I've felt lost trying to do this, even if I got some help, because people like me, regular people who work for a living, we start out from a young age being told to shut up, not to open our mouths. Writing books – that's for the world travelers, the artists from rich families, and their aristocratic lovers. It's not for a couple of haircutters from the cheapo salon in the strip mall.

If Cheryl is around now, she's probably next to me saying, "Don't be an idiot! Open your third eye! I'm standing right here, Tom." It makes me laugh, just thinking about her being around me having a fit where I can't see or hear her. They say that women who get breast cancer, that they're dying because they give too much. They give and don't know how to say "No" to the people in their lives. The affirmation for women like that is, "By saying 'No' to you, I say 'Yes' to me." I wonder sometimes if that would have helped Cheryl even more than the juicing, and meditating on the light of healing. A little self-righteous selfishness might have done her a world of good. Look, you're not going to beat cancer eating eggplant parm for every meal, and you're not going to beat it by feeling the same way about your life you've always felt. Positive thoughts are a type of magic; just like an antioxidant, they can neutralize toxins. But you can't mess around at the surface, you've got to dive into deep, sometimes stage 4 deep.

Whatever the source of the cancer, it was eating her up and coming out of her breasts; by the end it was pushing its way out like some alien. That cancer was eating through her, and as I was applying pressure and packets of WoundSeal powder along the bloody hemorrhages, I could imagine the disease slithering out of her and going to go look for a fresh victim.

My sister has had breast cancer, and so has my mother, lots of women get diagnosed, and I wonder what it is they're not getting out of their lives that makes them vulnerable to the sickness. We all get sick. We all suffer. Why we suffer in a certain way – that's not too easy to figure out. When someone makes it through and lives, you kind of forget about the "Why" and focus on the glorious path in front of them, but when they don't make it, you can't help but wonder if it was all a matter of luck. You wonder if you could have helped them get to the bottom of the mystery, or if that's taking magical thinking a step too far. You go through a lot when people don't make it.

TV commercials, they make cancer look like a walk in the park, but it's an ugly business, and when that tumor literally started coming out of her breast, I put my hands on her skin to keep her from bleeding out. Cheryl was anemic and needed every drop of her blood, and that meant I had no qualms about pushing against those wounds. She needed every bit of strength to stay out of the hospital for as long as she could, because the way things were going, we all knew if she ended up there, it was game over. Considering her diagnoses she lived longer than anyone expected but way less than she wanted to live. She had more to do, she kept saying, but some days you could tell she didn't have what it took to keep going. I would find her sometimes after days of not answering the phone, and I'd be so annoyed that she hadn't picked up, that she had shut the phone off and put it under the bed.

"Please, Tom, I can't."

"You have to answer the phone."

"My mom was calling me. She told me she can't sleep. She has no peace."

"So?"

"I can't be responsible for her anxiety right now. I have to rest."

"Keep it on and pick up when it's me."

"I'll try."

My mother's cancer also started in her breast, and then it spread all inside her. She didn't juice, and I don't know whether she would have bothered to try even if she had known about it. My mother ignored cancer like she ignored the little lies, the yelling, and the surly attitude that my father exhibited pretty much all the time. She just kept going, making dinner, folding laundry, dressing for church, planning for the holidays. If Cheryl got eaten up because of a man who wouldn't commit, then Mom must have been eaten up by what she committed to, day after day. Mom ended up with cancer running from her breast down her spine, up to her brain and back out to her legs. It was like a highway of hidden pain making itself known.

My sister is a different story. She fought her way back to being healthy, despite a first marriage that didn't work out and the normal day-to-day struggles of work and young kids. Maybe she lived for the kids or just because she's stubborn. My sister, she's the strongest woman I know. Hell, if it weren't for her, all sorts of people would be dead, including one of my employees.

SHARP

I was watching TV late one night after closing the restaurant. My phone rang, and it was one of my employees. I won't tell you her name because she would hate that.

"I did it."

"What did you do?"

"I took pills."

"You always take pills. Wait – how many did you take?"

"The whole bottle."

"Do you want to die?"

"Yes."

"Do you want me to come over and watch you die?"

"Please."

"I'll be right there."

When she told me she'd taken all her Xanax pills, the night took a turn. I only need a few hours of sleep, every night, but those hours, well – I might as well be on another planet. There I was with Napoleon on the couch, with my eyes half-closed and before I knew it I'm in the car, off to save this crazy bitch's life, With Napoleon wrapped in a blanket, I was driving fast, and shaking my head, feeling this mix of panic and anger.

I called my sister, not sure what to do, and she laid it out for me: Call the police and give them the address. I dialed the number as I pulled up to the house where this woman could be dead already, for all I knew. I got there and let myself in. She had been cutting with me for years, and she was out of her mind, begging me not to tell anyone. All I could think was, thank God I didn't walk in on a body. I talked with the 911 dispatch, and I talked with my employee, and by the time the cops walked in, I introduced this woman, with her head bobbing and tears running all over her cheeks, to "my friends." She told me not to call for help, but I did, and if it weren't for my sister, I might have been stupid enough to have gone there with no backup, trying to honor her wishes, struggling to get her into the car and off to the emergency room. She would have yelled and screamed, and it would have been horrible. I know that bitch. When the police took her in the patrol car, I signed with relief. Much later, in the early morning, I got a call, waking me up.

"Thank you."

"Are you OK?"

"I'm better now."

"Did you get that note off the dining room table?"

"No, the police took it."

"Shit. I've got some explaining to do."

My sister is still alive, and so are other people, because for whatever reason, she's a natural survivor. As for that note, it was all about feeling alone, and my employee had a hell of a time trying to explain that the pills and the note were completely unrelated. She didn't want her kids to know. You see, most of us will bury our pain because we prefer it to coming out with the simple truth. Of course, after that episode was all done, I let it go. I never called my sister to let her know how it went. She would have killed me for waking her twice in one night if the situation was already handled. We're all like that in a way: my sister, me, and my brother. We try not to get attached to the drama because it interferes with you bracing for whatever is next.

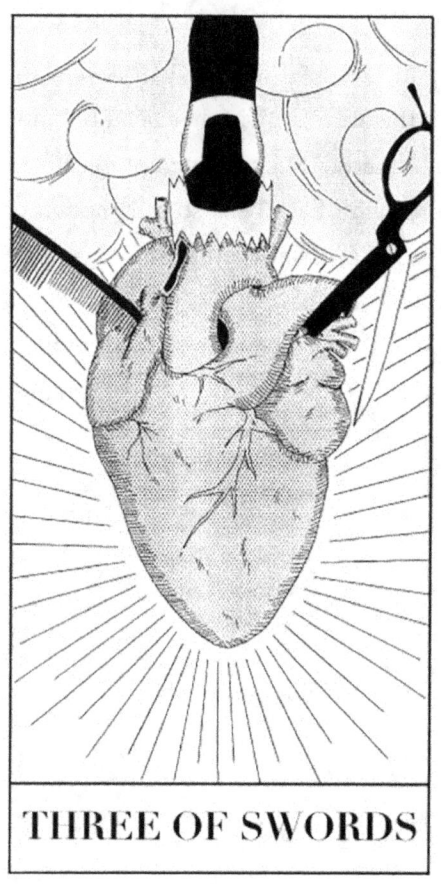

THREE OF SWORDS

Three Swords, One Heartbreak

When life gives you heartbreak, you do your best to get over it, and you try not to look back on all the details of what it was like. When it comes to the men in my life, I try not to think about the feeling I got in the gut whenever I would admit I was being used as a free place to stay or a cash machine with benefits. To get through life, we try to forget the pain while remembering enough of the details, so we don't repeat the same mistakes. When Cheryl was sick, it brought back shadows of my mother. It brought back the things I couldn't fix, when she told us kids one day in the sunroom that she had some news. I turned away from Mom that day, and I was barely there for her the first four weeks of the six she had left to live.

I was about to be abandoned by the woman who was my protector, and I was mad about it. I spent those weeks working and driving over the speed limit. I spent them on the phone with my sister learning what was up with Mom, while keeping my distance. I knew she was dying, and I couldn't bear to see it. When Cheryl came around, for some reason, I guess she reminded me of Mom, and for that year, I gave her all the things I wasn't able to give to my mother. One of them went quickly, while the other went slowly, and both of them went too quickly from my life.

Before Cheryl died, I watched her long, brown hair get brittle and saw all the shine fade away. People commented to me about how she had been a married man's mistress, about the way she was weak with lupus and now cancer. Co-workers bitched about her getting special treatment, and I bitched right back that it was none of their business. With Cheryl, I tried to avoid the truth, and so did she, until one day she couldn't see a future for herself. She shuffled her tarot decks. She pulled and pulled to find a way out, and then one day she looked at me and said, "Tom, there's no future for me." It felt like swords going through me. The moment she was sure that her time was over, Cheryl moved faster to make a brujo out of me. She gave me decks of cards, and she gave me more lessons when I stopped by the house with groceries, and she gave me a Saint Barbara statue that I keep by my front door. She gave me a pendulum for asking "yes" and "no" questions. She gave me everything she had that she thought I could use.

One day she'd get some pink back in her skin, the next, she was a kind of gray that could only be bad news. So, there I was, her brujo-in-training, holding her up, getting her food, offering her whatever I could. Sometimes Cheryl would joke that we should have sex because she was dying, but I never took the bait. I loved her so much, but there is not an ounce of bisexual in me. Sometimes I felt guilty that in between being a friend and a caregiver I still had a life, my own life.

"I don't want to break up the family."

"I don't want to break up your family, either."

I know that Cheryl must have heard those words from her man's mouth more than once. I know I've heard them myself. In my case, going after straight guys, some of them think they'll never be straight again, and the words they're saying are way too dramatic. In my kind of predatory days, the ones that lasted the better part of a decade and change, the last thing I wanted was for some guy to think I was going to be his boyfriend because of sex. I have watched more than one guy standing there after sex, looking confused. I would have to tell some of the guys how special they were, and how great it was, but it was only sex to me – not love.

"I don't want to break up the family." At the end of a quickie or a two-week affair, those words are a sign that I got him off good, but it's also a sign that he really wants my silence. People watch all these shows, and they think I'm going to pop up at the door or maybe send some crazy anonymous letter in the mail. I don't think they're actually scared of me outing them for having sex with another guy as much as they're scared of all the other stuff I know, about their real feelings on life. Once a guy hits the point of sexual release, usually most of his defenses are down, and then they start spilling their guts. That experience, by its very nature, is messy.

In between appointments and keeping up appearances, people live out these little scripts, giving into expectations bit by bit. Once I came out, I had to live life my own way and make up some of the scripts as I went along. Seriously, no bullshit, I had to figure out how to survive and by the time I figured it out, I became a control freak. I had to figure out how to get the things I wanted, and that meant I had to strive for order. For someone with as much ADD as I've got, that was an adventure.

I don't like to ask for help, not because I'm being a martyr, but because I do it the way I like it. It's like hair, for some reason, I love orderly hair. For whatever reason I want to control the things I find beautiful. I just see it as projects, as having ways to entertain myself. I don't see how my own life could be simpler with a bunch of loose flyways, or random weeds by my walking path. I don't understand how I can live without perfecting the hedging by the pool.

It's all about making a world full of physical comfort but not getting enslaved by the maintenance; that's part of the balance problem I've got. In my case it's part of being a Taurus. When the to-do list gets too long, when I have no patience, when I am working everyday like a good little guy and feel like I still don't have my financial cushion, I am not OK. Being Taurus means I can help other people handle both the temptation to give into pleasure and confront the nagging fear of losing it. If you know the torture, and can name it, then you can help others deal with it too. It's part of becoming conscious.

The last few years have been rough, and my kidney stones show it. I feel pain in there sometimes just like the Three of Swords looks. It's not my heart getting pierced, but it's both sides of my body. That card reminds me of the feeling I had when L told me he was going to marry a woman. We had just finished having sex, and he was lying on top of me. I think I couldn't have been any happier, and then he opened his mouth.

"Don't get too attached to this."

"Why?"

"Because I'm going to marry a woman."

"Why? You're gay."

"I don't want to disappoint my mother."

Then he started stealing from me and cheating on me, and I let him until he walked out the door. For six months, those blades kept ripping me up. My heartbreak was hard and sharp because of the closet. Maybe that was good, and maybe it wasn't, but it is my history. He didn't want to disappoint his mother. Those words stayed with me because a part of me understood. He pushed me away in every way possible because that was easier than staring his mother in the eye and telling her the truth. Even I had a hard time telling my mother, letting it slip out at first in pieces. If my father had been alive, I might never have said it, so I guess that's why I put up with my boyfriend's behavior. I would lash out at him, sure, but what did that accomplish? I knew he felt he had no choices. For a Puerto Rican man, there was no competition: Ma wins, Tom loses.

Days like that make you reflect on your life, and on the way no two lives are the same, or all that different. After my father's death, I would find my mother in the oddest positions, sleeping, exhausted at the dining room table, on the couch, always waiting for me way past her bedtime. She lost her mother, her sister, and her husband within the space of a year, so she waited for me in case I was dead. Before I fully came out, she still knew, and part of her staying awake was to somehow be there for me. I would yell and tell her to go to bed, that I didn't want to find her there in some contorted mess in the living or dining room. I really wanted to come home and avoid looking her in the eyes. Little by little, we worked up to the reality that I was never going to bring her a pretty, tall blonde to be her daughter-in-law.

On my birthday the year before my father died, we laid out my Aunt Edie, my mother's only sister. Aunt Edie left behind three children. The kids all went to different family homes, including my one cousin to my mother and father, because Aunt Edie's husband was also dead. She fought breast cancer, but she didn't win. Everyone liked Aunt Edie, a single mom raising three kids, and no one wanted to see her go. My father liked her, too, though when she called to announce her ex-husband's passing, he shouted at her.

"Why are you crying? He was a drunk and he beat ya."

My mother hushed him, but he kept on.

Aunt Edie had moved back to Jersey, to Lincroft, where she had become the secretary to the dean of a local college. They had divorced in Michigan, and Edie came home without a husband. She was crying because no matter what, that man was a big chunk of her life, and losing him was shattering her to pieces. My father didn't know how to say it sweetly, but he wanted her to keep going, to keep her chin up. He also hated the drama. The man was a rock. He was prickly. He was cold. Later, when her ex died and Edie did, too, my father didn't think twice about taking in my cousin. That was family; that was what you did.

I only remember a few times my father wasn't cold. One of them was when a family friend – a kid, basically – was driving out onto the highway, which they were repaving. He got on the road, and the shoulder wasn't painted in, and the boy didn't notice anything missing right away. He made the right onto the highway and hit two girls walking on what should have been the shoulder. One girl died, and when my father heard that news and realized the penalty this 18-year-old boy would pay for taking that life, my father wept, saying how he wished he could go in the younger man's place.

After that, Mom had me, my brother, my cousin and my father in the house. My cousin was a little bit younger, and he was a handful compared to us kids who were older and almost out the door ourselves. After my father died, my mother didn't have the energy and sent him to her brother. She wanted to help, and so had my father, but doing it alone was too much for her. Losing her sister, losing her mother, her husband, all within a year; the trajectory was not in her favor. The only thing that seemed to keep her going were the grandchildren.

Mom lit up when those boys were around. My youngest nephew said he saw her in the room after she had passed. My sister admitted it to me on the phone, kind of freaked out, that Matthew says he sees Grandma sometimes.

"I was cooking breakfast, and he said, 'Mommy, Grandma is here.' So, I said, 'I wish I could see her.' He said, 'She's right there,' and pointed to the air, and then his face changed."

"And??"

"He said, 'She left.'"

Kids have a way of seeing things adults can't, like spirits, you know, energy beings. Animals are like that, too. I think it's because they're so pure and don't have anyone telling them they can't or that they shouldn't. Sometimes when I talk about Cheryl, Napoleon gets funny. He might start whining or moving around like he's excited in a way that makes no sense for what's going on in the room. He can't tell me he sees her, not like children can, and that makes me crazy, because sometimes more than anything I want to know if he sees her. Then I think of my sister, and how the second my nephews pointed to my mother's spirit, she left the room. I think if you're meant to see something, you will, and if you don't, you're not ready. Love and ghosts are kind of the same; they come and go when you least expect it, and only the person who sees the ghost or feels the love can explain what it was or know that it left the room.

KNIGHT of SWORDS

Forever the Knight of Swords

When I get into the salon for the day, I get Napoleon some water and put out his blanket so he can nest in his bed. He yaps up a storm if he thinks someone is coming after me, but mostly we have a quiet routine. I live a lot of my life behind these salon chairs, working on cutting shapes out of all these heads with all their personalities, textures, and cowlicks – not like it was when I started out and it was a lot of the same people on heavy rotation. I still have loyal customers now, but my bread and butter is volume. As I do the opening, I think about the swords, and the cutting blades I work with every day, tracing back to before I had a fish tank and a Ficus tree, the car of my dreams and the kidney stones.

My brother and I are twins, but I was the one born like our father, seeing challenges and charging at them. Growing up, I was the thin one, the one with an attitude to match our last name. I was always Sharpe, always in battle. Not surprisingly I got into a profession that literally depends on blades. I loved cutting hair and putting notches on my belt. I was flirting, even when I wasn't. I was sarcastic as anyone, which counts for something in Jersey. One liners, cold stares, I could cut anyone.

After Dad died, I embraced my calling and signed up for beauty school in what felt like a minute. After I graduated from the Wilford Academy of Hair and Beauty Culture, I still worked at a nursing home most days, but nights and weekends I was driving from house to house, making calls. I used to cut this one lady's hair who was close to my mom's age. Her son was a friend of mine, which is how we started. Age didn't matter to me, and age didn't matter to her after I started blowing out her hair. She loved what I did, and in the privacy of her own home. Our bond obviously grew. When a woman lets you cut her hair, or make her up for a special night, she trusts you to prepare her for the social battlefield. Sort of like having gay sex with straight men makes them feel like they can tell you things they don't tell other people, cutting a woman's hair, especially in her house, makes her feel like you two are buddies.

She used to say I looked like Andy Gibb, but she wasn't hitting on me. Everything she did was for her Mr., and let me tell you, "I take care of my man" was her mantra. She'd say it with this serious look in her eyes, and you knew she meant it. Those two had names, but I'll keep calling them Mrs. and Mr. because to me they were some kind of ultimate couple of their time. She was always impeccable, with matched outfits and jewelry, and even though they weren't rich, they were comfortable. She worked even though the Mr. made more than enough for them to have a good life. My mother only worked a few years, until the mortgage was paid and we kids started coming. Mom's world got small that way, but the Mrs. kept her world as big as possible, and I liked that part of her. I did her hair for years, and we were real friends – so close we could even fight, though it didn't happen often.

She was a role model for me, having a husband who adored her. She knew she had it, all right, and she put in a lot of effort to look good for him. The Mrs. prided herself on satisfying her man, and that kept some part of them young. She told me how one time Mr. came home and had bills sticking out of his pants. He said, "Baby, I won $10,000 at the casino," and she looked up at him and smiled while she pulled bills out of his waistband with her mouth. He played craps, and that night was good, she said. Anything Mrs. wanted done around the house, he did it with no complaints, and when those two had sex it was until death did them part all over again. I couldn't imagine Mom telling me a story like that, and I couldn't imagine my father winning it big, either.

As my parents took their final exits from my life, Mr. And Mrs. entered the picture, giving me a feeling of stability. I would drive over to Mr. and Mrs.' house ready to start the weekend laughing and getting annoyed at Mrs. not knowing what she wanted to do with her hair. She was always switching it up, and she made me crazy trying to figure out what she wanted and how we were going to make it happen. Not every hairstyle is for every type of hair, but she didn't want to hear about that.

Back then I was already driving a Corvette, showing up in less than fifteen minutes, door to door. I was in my twenties and driving the kind of car that made people notice. Sure enough the state troopers were no exception, pulling up behind me, flashing their lights. Back then, I would defend myself as quickly as I drove, coming up with a defense, never giving in.

"Why are you stopping me?"

"I clocked you at 100 miles an hour."

"You clocked the Mercedes, not me."

"No, I clocked you."

I told him he could get in the car with me and hit "Resume" on the cruise control, and it would go to 75. Instead, he walked back to his car and came back with a ticket for doing 75mph. It wasn't exactly a win, but it wasn't a total loss.

I decided not to keep tempting fate and the state troopers with my cream-colored dream come true. I bought that car, a 1981 model, in 1982, and sold it in 1985, with 32 points on my license. I drive as part of my living, and suspension after suspension, I felt I had no choice but to make a tough decision. I hated the tickets and how the cops picked me out of the crowd. I would challenge the cops just like I challenged my dad, and the consequences were getting excruciatingly real. By the end of owning that car I had to drive 5 mph under the speed limit, just like my mother, mostly because I wasn't supposed to be behind the wheel at all.

By the time I bought the blue BMW, we were in the heart of the '80s; Jordache or Z. Cavaricci jeans were our local style. I wore those designer jeans and, after I lost weight, my favorite parachute pants, which I had in two colors, light gray and dark blue. I was down to a 30-inch waist after bulking up for a while from the grief of being dumped by a boyfriend and losing my mother. I was doing better, and even though I missed the Corvette, I chalked it up to experience, remembering how I used to miss the Mustang, too. That car ended in an actual disaster, with me slamming it into some trees. I escaped with no problem, freaking out that the car might explode. I was terrified of a fiery death.

Visiting my Mrs. friend was a highlight of the week, and we laughed so much, it would always calm me down. I would pull into their driveway and make sure that not a hair was out of place. I had probably spent too much time picking out my shoes and a belt, showing up dressed to impress. I wore a dress shirt, fresh from the cleaners, always. This was when Mom was leaving us, and I focused on style to distract myself. I sparkled on my way into that house, and we sparkled together until I left. I had a good time there, and the cash I made didn't hurt. We talked windbreakers and leather, and dirty jokes I couldn't imagine sharing with most women my mother's age. Mrs. loved her weekly blowout, and I loved her energy, and we both liked feeling glamorous.

Everyone should have a client like Mrs. in their life, someone who makes them feel special, someone who makes you want to do your job at its highest level. I was heartbroken when Mrs. got sick, too – cancer, of course, in her lungs. I had done her hair for so long, and she always had a cigarette, but I never thought much of it. She gave me hell when I started smoking, too, but mostly because I was starting so late. By then, at age 32, I'd been cutting her hair for a decade. Time flies no matter what you do, and people end up dying in ways you don't see coming. Even when you can see it coming, that doesn't mean you can change it.

They say when you get sick in the lungs it's because of grief that you've buried. For a woman who laughed so much and had sex into her 60s and never had to worry about money, I don't know if that's true, but maybe it was. Some people smoke all their lives and never lose their lungs or their breasts, and some people never smoke and get it worse than anyone. So maybe it was something nobody knew about that made her lungs into an Achilles heel. I don't know, and I can't ask her now, but the older I get, the more I know we all have hidden hurts. It's not always your business why somebody dies.

My days behind the chair in her house were over the moment Mrs. got diagnosed. She knew me when my mother got sick, and so she told me not to come anymore. Mrs. knew we kept the house after my mother passed and that I would go over there all the time, fixing things, walking between the rooms, sweeping and tidying. She knew I did that for about a year until my sister finally said it was time to sell the house. When Mrs. died, her kids told me she wanted to spare me seeing her in that condition because of all those memories. All the years of up-dos, dye jobs, and blowouts, and then suddenly she was gone. Before I knew it, she was laid out. It wasn't the Louise I knew, not that spitfire Mrs. That was one of the only things that made it bearable, that body didn't look like the friend I knew. Yeah, her name was Louise.

I never knew what being a haircutter was going to mean to my life. I knew it was a way to make money, and I knew I liked the idea of making people transform. I realized after seeing my father laid out in his own casket that I had to come up with something to do with my life. I remember standing at that casket and feeling all of this responsibility of being an adult, and I remember just as much this sneaking feeling coming over me. It was slow at first, but then it came on strong as I stood there looking at him in his last suit and tie. I was free. As terrible and terrifying as losing him was, that initial feeling of freedom, from the yelling, especially – that was electric. There was a similar feeling when I saw Louise like that, but with a huge difference. With my father passing, I was still too young to feel like my day would come. It wasn't until one of my first, most loyal clients was laid out, that I became aware that one day people would comment on how I looked at my funeral.

Just after my father's death, my mother asked me, "What do you want to do with your life?" I said, "I want to cut hair." She was happy that I had a direction, and later I think she liked that cutting hair let me be social. When my father died, it was in August; when I started classes at Wilford Academy, it was October. It's been some years since I thought of Mrs. and how much fun we had, and how I was back then, when I was just young enough to think death only came for other people.

These days I get my jeans from discount stores, and my shirts aren't wrinkled but they're not dress shirts from the cleaners. I cut people's hair all the time, but it's usually at one of my salons where even the regulars are walk-ins because we don't bother with appointments. I like most of my clients, and I know them pretty well, but nothing feels like those days when I was young and drunk off my first taste of freedom driving to houses and making cash to build my dreams and pay for weekends. Nothing feels like those days when I was sure that the best was yet to come with every cut and color. You get to a point in life when you realize no matter the highs or the lows, no matter what shoes you're wearing, the things that matter are small. You can take any path you want in life; it's what you do on that path that makes the story.

KING *of* SWORDS

Dad wouldn't have hated my career choice. Barbers were good people in his book. An honest living was what mattered to my father, and looking neat and clean was part of that whole package. It might have annoyed him that I was working cutting men and women. He might have been surprised because if there was one thing my father and I argued over, it was my hair.

The battles we had over the way I looked raged up until the day he died. Today, I get kids who come in and the parents ask them, "What do you want?" and I'm still amazed. The only words I remember my father saying when he took us to the barber were "Boy's regular haircut, short." Nowadays they call that a "Brooklyn fade," which sounds cool, but at the time, that hair made me a nerd. I especially hated it because it was the cut I got against my will.

I wanted the designer haircuts; my father wanted me to go to the barber. I wanted to live in color and he wanted me to live in the black-and-white world of "Leave It to Beaver." It was the '70s, and the world was changing, but my father was hell bent on it staying the '50s. It was my father who wanted Mom at home, and for my sister to marry a good provider, and for us boys to look squeaky clean like him. I hated it. I resisted all the control over my life, just the way he would have. Sometimes, when we clashed, it was epic, and to remember it was over the length of my hair is still kind of ridiculous.

The second my hair grew long enough to touch the tops of my ears; the old man was on the case. When we were young, he would bring it up to our mother first, that the boys needed a haircut. As we got older, the comments were directed toward her and us. He would menace me sometimes across the dinner table, saying that he could just cut my hair himself. It was an actual threat, and we all knew it, because he had done it before. He had taken control of our hair enough times when we were little that my mother wouldn't let him do it himself anymore. She said we looked like cancer patients. She would scream, "Cancer! Cancer!" and look at me and my brother and our identical heads, and she would wail. I would end up crying, too, because that was my mother, and I hated seeing her cry.

As the years went on and we were becoming men, it had to be obvious to the old man that I was gay. My parents would try and set me up on dates. They would force me to call up a girl and ask her out to the movies or something. Things were different back then, so growing up gay was a kind of mysterious thing. I didn't really get it myself, and I would do what they told me. I called up this one girl – I must have been 14 – and asked her out. We went on a date, and another, and since our families knew each other, I started to go by the house to visit some weekend afternoons. She was pleasant, maybe a little thick for my taste, but I really didn't know what to do with her, so it was all kind of innocent and fine. I really liked her brother, too, and so we would hang out like kids. The brother dressed all right and had a nice laugh, better than his sister's.

I ended up at their house one afternoon and this girl was about to go shopping with her mother. They were going to buy her a pretty outfit, and her mother probably had ideas that she would come home and model it for me. Instead of being obsessed with her daughter, while they were out, I was focused on the family living room. I looked around with nothing much to do and wondered aloud about the furniture, and out of nowhere me and my girlfriend's brother started rearranging the furniture. We got so into it, moving the couches, adjusting the coffee table, that time flew. By the time this poor girl and her mother got home we two were sweating and smiling while his mother looked at us, horrified. Her mother's smile faded, and then so did her daughter's. An excuse was made, and I was asked to leave; the new dress went up in her room, still in the bag. Calls were made between mothers, and although I don't know what they said, I was never asked to come to the house again. I never wanted to date this girl anyway, but I really missed hanging out with her brother.

These kinds of things happened to me all the time. Just as I would find someone or something I really liked; it would be taken away from me. It happened again when one of my father's sisters got rid of this horse I loved. As long as I could remember, I would go to my aunt's farm, and as I got taller and stronger, she would invite me to visit on my own and stay. She had a son and a daughter, but there was room for one more, especially one with all this extra energy that she could put to work. My aunt was tough, and she would have a list of chores for me a mile long, but I didn't mind. In some ways, she was way tougher than my father, but she didn't drink and that was an improvement.

I appreciated the way she had a method for everything. It felt like some kind of biological insanity, that we should bond over being meticulous, but it was true. I was in awe of her, and a little bit terrified, because all she needed was a toothbrush, some vinegar, a vacuum nozzle and some newspaper, and she could clean anything. From sunup to sundown, she did her best to clean everything that didn't shine. I was her willing assistant, even if I had an attitude – pretty much the same attitude she had. I remember complaining that she cleaned the windows from inside the house, where the air was cooler and the sun wasn't beating on her, while I was stuck cleaning them from outside in the heat. She didn't care, not a drop. Each window took a while to finish; the sashes, even the tiniest bit of plastic had to be scrubbed. The glass had to be wiped over and over until my aunt finally nodded her head instead of pointing her finger to the almost-invisible spots.

A couple of times while working with my aunt, I thought she must have been a real, honest-to-goodness slave owner in a previous life. She once said to me, "Let's sickle the field," which I thought meant getting out the big tractor to cut the field down to make hay for the horses. I thought we were going to work with some baler, with a setup that would collect everything we cut down. What it meant in this case was the small tractor, with my aunt sitting and driving while I walked behind collecting the freshly cut hay and putting it into an attached cart.

My aunt did take some pity on me when she saw that my summer-red face had turned a pale white. I was pretty much ready to pass out, dressed in full gear, moving fast o keep up with that machine. She geared down to first speed and motioned for me to have a seat. Then she took out a cigarette and baled the hay herself for the time it took to smoke it down to the end. After that, I was off the tractor seat and back behind the rig, with the cart running ahead of me on high gear. That was how it was, learning to work like a farmer from the daughter of a farmer who lived through the Depression.

My father and his sisters grew up on a farm with chickens, ducks, pigs, horses, you name it, but by the time they were older there wasn't as much need for that, since you could buy a lot of meat for cheaper than it took to raise the animals yourself.

153

My aunt and uncle kept up with their farm because my uncle had a heating and air conditioning company that took care of the bills in a way that a farm couldn't. My aunt had cats and dogs running around, but her thing was horses and her vegetable garden. The vegetable garden always produced enough to justify itself. The money they made on the horses was another story.

My aunt loved her horses and kept anywhere from ten to thirteen of them at any given time, treating them more softly than any human alive. It was plenty of work to keep them fed and groomed, and I didn't mind because I liked being busy and I wanted to ride them. Nothing came for free in our family, especially not on my father's side, and my aunt worked me so hard that my cousin would make little remarks about me being my aunt's "boy." I didn't care because I kept thinking that there was going to be a payoff, but when you're the odd kid in a conservative family, that is not always true.

I worked with those horses for a few summers, pitching hay and wiping them down. I worked and sweated because I liked it, but I was hoping for a payoff, too. There was one horse my aunt had I really liked, and his name was Cody's Heartbreak. He was a gorgeous horse, with a dark, shiny coat and eyes that really looked at you. I was in awe of that horse. Every time I would wash Cody's Heartbreak down, I washed him like he was going to show that day. Going to show meant everything.

I would brush him for as long as possible, until his coat was shiny like a mirror. The horse loved the attention and the treats I kept for him, and he would always come by the fence when he saw me outside. That horse and I had a bond, and something in my aunt couldn't let me have that. I felt for that horse because he was beautiful and smart, the way he seemed to notice it all. It didn't occur to me to care or hide the way I felt about this horse. I hadn't ever met an animal like that. He was cautious, but he wasn't skittish. He made observations. I wondered to myself if that was because his mother had died when Cody's Heartbreak was barely a year old.

I didn't know I should act colder while washing him down and brushing his coat until it outshined all the other horses. I didn't realize that talking about his mother dying while she was out being bred again was going to upset the adults. I didn't realize I was highlighting the unthinking attitude that led them to take her out to breed too soon. The more I doted on him for losing his mama, the more my aunt seemed irritated. I don't know if either of us understood the struggle we were in, but finally it was clear to me. One day, after countless chores and hours of work nobody else wanted to do, I wanted my chance to start riding.

After summers of being a faithful, abused farmhand, my cousins slyly stood up for me. They tortured their mother with comments, letting me hear them. *She'll never let him ride.* I worked and kept my part of the deal, but it was never clear when I would get a chance to ride. Maybe she thought I needed to grow up because I wasn't even 15. Maybe she felt I needed to ask for, or demand, the right to ride, and stand up for myself. Becoming an adult in our family was a gauntlet of people raising their eyebrows, giving you a challenging look. You had to speak up to get every inch but you had to do it the right way, or else there was hell to pay. Eventually, it became clear that I wanted to ride and deserved to ride. My aunt was willing to give in somewhat grudgingly but she did not, despite all my hard work, give me my choice of horse. She would decide.

The horse she chose for me was not Cody's Heartbreak, the mysterious, young horse I trusted, but Chip, a horse who hated men. I mean, this horse was known for trying to throw any man who rode him, and my aunt put me on him. Like some kind of lesson or test or maybe even a joke, she chose the horse most likely to kill me. Chip was a quarter horse, too, bigger and older than Cody's Heartbreak. He could sprint, and he could stop on a dime from terrifying speeds, and he would do it to you just to show he was in charge. Chip pretty much knew his power as my aunt's favorite, and he damned well knew the strength of his weight and height. Chip looked at me coming near him, and I knew I was toast. He only listened to women, and I realized by one glance at Chip's face that I did not pass.

That quarter horse was playing like he wanted to kill me from before I got on him. True to form, he kicked his hips almost immediately, signaling he was ready to buck. We started to move, then he stopped fast and looked at me from the side like he was saying, "Are you scared yet?" Not being stupid, I was terrified. I didn't give up at first, but old Chip was merciless and finally I had to stop. Around fifteen to twenty minutes into my big ride, it was over. I can still see my cousin telling her mother about all the other horses I could try and ride. My aunt ignored her and looked at me hard but didn't have much to say. I stayed there, humiliated until my feet would move. I went to see Cody's Heartbreak, even though I didn't dare ride him. I couldn't figure out what I had done to make things go this way, but I figured with time, my aunt might give in, and I would get to ride a horse, any horse that wasn't Chip.

Within a few weeks of my near-death by Chip, a trailer rolled up to the house, and with barely a word, my aunt walked out and started directing Cody's Heartbreak to his new owner, loading him into their rig. At least, that's how I imagine that part; I wasn't there that weekend. Most of the horses didn't leave my aunt's quickly. She said they were all up for sale, but only the one I really cared about left young.

When I found out a shock came over me. Later, I cried and I yelled out of frustration. I knew not to say too much under my aunt's roof, because if I crossed her, I would pay for it twice: right there, and when I got home. Not too long after my aunt sold Cody's Heartbreak, the new owners sold him again because the lady couldn't ride him outside the ring. We never finished training him, and although it was made clear that he was a work in progress, the people took on too much, so they sold the horse. Just like that, Cody's Heartbreak was sold out from under me, sold out again and again.

My cousins felt sorry for me, but they didn't say much after Cody's Heartbreak was sold, since my feelings weren't going to move their mother any more than they would have moved my father. Talking things out would lead to an argument, so you learned to pick your battles wisely. Slowly I stopped going by the farm. Cody's mother was gone, and now so was he. I hoped the horse would end up with someone who noticed how he looked at the world, but I wasn't sure it would happen.

My cousin died suddenly when he was in his 50s. He was driving somewhere around Atlantic City on roads that weren't exactly rural but nowhere near busy city streets. He was at the intersection, stopped at a stop sign, minding his own business. Out of nowhere a driver hit him from behind, and as his car was pushed into the intersection, another car, coming from the opposite direction, ran the stop sign. My cousin, my aunt's only son, died just like that, in a driving accident where he was completely stopped. My cousins were good to me, and when he died it felt like part of us all went with him.

I remember now how quiet it could get at that farm, except for the wind chimes that my aunt had along the porch. I remembered the stillness of the land when I went to see my cousin laid out so young. I noticed it as we went by the house. It was quiet except for those chimes. Seeing my aunt lose her only son didn't bring me any joy. Passing his casket, seeing her look torn apart, I didn't have that self-righteousness that kind of runs in my family. My aunt did all the things the Protestants are supposed to do, and God took her only son. I mean, if that wasn't the hand of God, or fate, whatever you want to call it, I don't know what could be. And that kind of thing, well, you can't control or make comments. You can't even begin to judge.

No parent deserves to bury a child, let alone bury two, but that was what happened to my aunt. First her Faith, and then Ricky at the stop sign. There was nothing I could do that would bring them back and nothing I could say that would console her, I was sure. Sometimes, the best thing you can offer is your silence. When I got home from the funeral, I stood in the back of my home, smoking a cigarette, listening to the wind chimes I put up all around the place year after year. I thought about my generation, and the ones that came before us, my father and his sister, about my grandfather. I took a deep inhale and heard the word "heartbreak." I heard it over and over again.

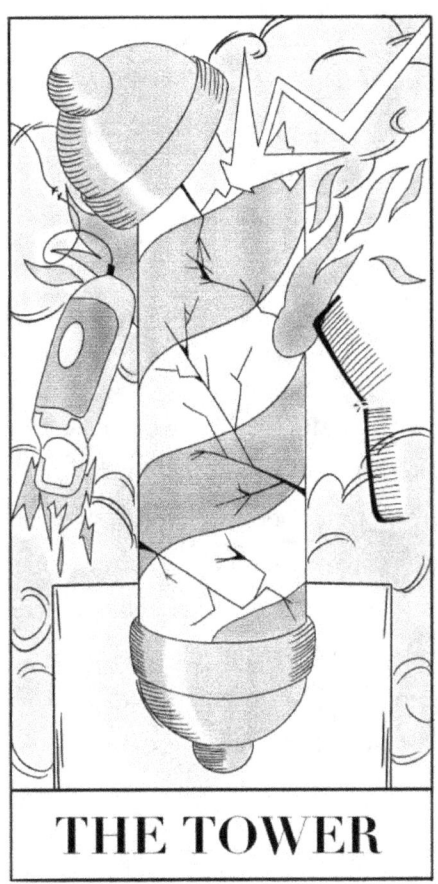

THE TOWER

The problem with heartbreak is that you can't avoid it, no matter how hard you try. Heartbreak finds you at least once in life, usually more. No matter whether you talk about the situation, or keep it quiet, heartbreak can turn you numb for a minute or years. It can make you so numb you hold your tongue, because nothing will change the situation. The problem with silence is that it hides all the heartbreaks without erasing them. The next thing you know, one day, during the tiniest situation, everything starts moving at the speed of all that unspoken heartbreak.

I think about the stares. In my family, authority was king and everyone was expected to stick to their role. When I was a child, order was everything. You took your life into your own hands if you challenged an adult – and I did it a lot. Somehow, I survived, but I didn't get out of it without some scars, some of them serious, some of them not so bad. I'm lucky; they give me something I like to think of as personality or better still, experience.

My father wanted to control us, and maybe me the most, because he saw something inside me that he couldn't control. He wanted to change who I was on the inside by making sure I did my chores, stood up straight, said the right things, knew the right rules. There's nothing wrong with any of that, except none of it was good enough, because nothing could change me being different. To make up for the flaw he couldn't quite name, my father became like an inspector of tiny little details. I didn't mind being pressed and clean. I didn't mind growing up like I was in some kind of military. The only thing I did mind was the hair.

To this day, hair is a trigger for me, and I really like men who go bald willingly. Any guy sporting that kind of hair has an advantage with me. It's like the thing I feared is attractive in others. Give me that tapered cut that can go down to a shadow, and before you know it, I'm helpless. My time opens up, my wallet opens up, the house opens up, and sometimes my heart opens up along with all of it. On the flip side of the attraction is a power play relationship.

Cheryl and I used to joke sometimes, "If you don't shut up, I'll cut your client's hair!" Cheryl knew how much loyalty and hair meant to me. She knew what I did for a living and my power struggle relationship with my father. She felt that my freak-outs over who got their hair cut without me was part of my father's legacy. Cheryl understood this control thing before I did, and she never made me feel like a jerk about it. She teased me about it, but she never pushed me into that space where I would panic. Little by little, she helped me see things about myself that I didn't know existed. That was part of her magic, and it didn't have much to do with spells, but it did have a lot to do with our sense of humor.

Work is a habit. Driving fast, flossing, going to church every Sunday – we do lots of things out of habit. You can see it when you pay attention. It's like people on the road. Some drivers cut off the other drivers when they have plenty of room, when there's absolutely no traffic, just because they're used to it.

There are habits, and then there are habits and working with the public, I've seen a lot of them. I have argued with the woman who will never part her hair to the other side, so her hair stays the same for twenty years. I have dealt with the guy who will never give up his comb-over. I have looked in the mirror, staring down a customer, holding up a few stringy hairs, knowing that habit is stronger than reason. I have pleaded and raised my eyebrows. I have let out huge, somewhat passive-aggressive "The customer is always right" sighs, and I have watched them dry up against the power of habit, the power of the familiar.

The way we look, what we eat and drink – a lot of it comes down to habit. I smoke; that's a habit, and it's at least half of what keeps me smoking, way more than the nicotine. When I blow out that first inhale, it's like I'm blowing away worries. On the exhale, my to-do list gets pushed back, and I don't care about nothing. By the time I get to the second inhale, it all floods back, but that first breath – that's something.

Habits come in all shapes and sizes just like people, and even though we all have them, some are harder to break than others. When I was younger, I tried to be careful about trying hard drugs, the kind that you found at bars. These days, I'm careful about prescription drugs, including antidepressants. Around here, where I'm writing, I look around and I see your standard America, just with better access to nail salons, delis, and some of the best heroin on the market.

In between the cul-de-sacs of these developments is a series of highways running an underground pipeline between New York and North Jersey, where the stuff gets shipped in, heading all the way down to Atlantic City and Philadelphia. It goes from those hubs onto all the well-connected streets, and it jumps into gated communities as well as the ghettos.

Drugs really took root here, and sort of like the wisteria in the front of my house, nobody has been able to keep it from spreading. You name the kind of person you think would never do this or that drug, and chances are I've dealt with at least one person like that in here, looking strung out. I have seen them nodding off or wasting away in between haircuts. I have watched them start with the pain pills and move onto the powders. I have seen stable employment thrown away for a feeling, into a bottomless hole that sometimes includes stealing and always includes lies.

People will come into the salon, sit in my chair and tell me all about how one day they turned around and realized that what started as a bad back was now a fifteen–year-plus pain pill habit. I'm used to it now, this "opioid crisis," as they say on TV. I accept it and deal with it, in the veteran haircutter who one day starts stealing, or the new hire who can't seem to get their money right. I don't bat an eye at some customer who looks right past you, barely getting simple words out of their mouth. I don't feel superior when they're itching their arms or coming up with weird lies for no reason. Oh, your mom who died is having surgery? It's all good by me.

The gossip about Cheryl was that it was drugs, not lupus, that got her acting funny and definitely not the cancer. Cheryl knew what they were thinking, and she could see their energy. She would smile and shake her head at the stupid, bitchy comments. She would let it go, saying "Tom, I don't give a fuck," and she meant it. I learned from that, because I wanted to rage for her, and she wouldn't let me. She knew what people were saying, and when she looked at their auras, she took it with a grain of salt. I'm not saying it didn't hurt her; I'm just saying she could put it into perspective.

There are all types of addictions and habits, but sometimes you look at people around you, scratching their arms or rubbing their hands together, and you see them waiting for their haircuts, and you wonder if all addictions are created equally. One person sticks to coffee and drinks ten cups a day, and that's bad, contributes to some health problems, but it won't usually land them in massive debt or dead in the gutter. I have wondered a lot if some of these people are going to live to see their kids grow up standing there, that kind of hollow look in their eyesThey had no clue what they were in for.

I know I make it sound dramatic, but it's not. People live and die around here just like anyplace else. I know how it goes: you figure you'll flirt with danger because your life is kind of boring but if you mess with it a lot you can pull a tower of hurt and instability into your life. Of course, if you manage to rebuild, you'll know how to do it better. I mean, maybe you won't build another tower at all, at least not this exact kind. I am not judging people because I almost went down that exact road myself, because I had never felt something so strong. I hit a crack pipe once, and then I hit it for a month. Fast as fuck, life got strange.

I have that same stubborn nature as my father had, and when it came to quitting freebase, that really worked in my favor. I thought crack was no big deal, something to try, like a drink I'd never had, or a food I'd never eaten. I had no idea something I put in my body could take over, find its way inside my dreams. In that month, I learned that addiction could come out of nowhere, that in a way we all have the capacity to be addicts. One minute you've never tried something, didn't know its smell or taste, and the next minute you're thinking, "How do I get more?"

Some things we do are habits, and others are addictions, and the difference between them is usually hard to figure. The difference doesn't really matter, because the line is moving constantly. It's a million little things and no one can make sense of it. It doesn't matter what gets you there; it's what keeps you there that matters. Life is about making mistakes; the trick to surviving is to not stay stuck inside them.

Addictions and habits will take you down the Tower in a second, and so can a sickness or some other thing you never expected. One minute you're going through life just fine, and then you end up feeling something you never felt before, maybe you faint, or you notice blood somewhere it shouldn't be. It's that second when you first feel something go wrong in a totally novel way, that reminds me of the Tower card. You realize you're falling; you are seeing it happen, but you are powerless to stop the crash.

The Tower is what it felt like when I looked in my pocket after a month of freebasing and realized that I had spent all my extra money on a drug. I looked into the mirror and asked myself if that feeling the pipe gave me was worth my security in the world. I decided it wasn't, and so I quit. I did it for a month, and I wouldn't touch it again for nothing. The Tower is the thing you didn't count on, and it feels like a car ignoring a stop sign and sailing right toward you. When your life is stuck, and you see the Tower get ready: this crisis is going to suck, but it is going to free you from what no longer serves you. If there's anything I can say about the crack episode, it's that it humbled me. In some ways, I was proud of my self-discipline. In other ways, I felt more for the dope heads, and felt more for my father and his drinking.

Cheryl always said that the Tower on its own meant a big change was coming, and you can't do a damned thing about it, but it was all the others cards around it that told you the details. When Cheryl saw it for herself, she accepted that things beyond her control were in motion. She couldn't tell right away if she was going to live or die, but she knew she was in for a ride. I drew the card about my love life; she got it about her health. Some people get the Tower about a divorce, a job, maybe a drop in the stock market, if you're into that, and the numbers really change your life. The Tower can be an affair, a runaway child, a sick parent; something or someone you know is falling down around you, and for whatever reason, you can't save it. You can't even pretend to save yourself by saving it. The Tower asks us to roll with change or basically be crushed by it. It's not pretty, but it's real, like an old industrial road that gets you to where you want to go faster than the new one with landscaping and tolls.

I had another client who came to me through his grandparents. First, I cut their hair, then they brought him in, and eventually his dad came to me, too. The kid was half-Greek, and his family was overbearing. His background was Spartan, and I could see it a mile away when the dad came in, with this strut. In no way am I saying he was a bad guy, but he had that kind of pride that comes across as arrogance sometimes. I didn't care how many Spartans killed how many enemies back, how many thousands of years ago, but I cared about this kid, who looked sad to be alive. The father was sick with terminal cancer, but I didn't know it, and he always talked about his opinions. Over those weeks that they came in, I was smack in the middle of their lives, all three generations, including the grandparents who were Irish Baptists. I liked the grandmother a lot because she was this cute little old lady. I would always dry her hair with a flip, and she would smile beneath layers of strawberry blond.

"Talk to my grandson. He likes talking to you."

"Sure."

I had an intuition things would get interesting when she said that, because it had that feeling like there was something more to it. The first time the grandson was sitting in the chair, I noticed he had an orange tongue, the kind you get from taking lithium. I had seen it before, figured they diagnosed him bipolar. Honestly, the kid seemed fine whenever I'd been around him, but now the kid in my chair was medicated and not ok. I know a haircut once a month isn't a lot of face time, but this kid just never once struck me as being on the edge. Eventually he got the whole smorgasbord of antidepressants and chemical equalizers, and he sat there, month after month getting that pudgy look and losing his feelings.

His cotton T-shirt rubbed up on the nylon of the protective smock, and I could barely stand to look in his eyes, he seemed so old. As I shortened and re-layered his hippie look, I told him that I saw a diamond inside him. I told him I saw brightness that didn't seem lost like it does in a crazy person. I told the kid about the last person I knew who acted like this. She went from this therapy to that hospital, always threatening to throw herself off a bridge, any bridge she could find. Then she went deep inside and got real with herself. Next thing we know, we all got a message: she was gay and happy. The message to the kids wasn't, "Hey, you're gay, because I'm the expert on you, and I know it." The message I was sending and maybe receiving was more like, "Hey, you have to be free to express yourself." I wanted him to know, you can't live for other people's expectations.

He was so scared of being the wrong thing that all his life was squeezing out of him. For a young man to lose all his curiosity because he's scared of making the right choice – now, that's a problem. I saw him look at me both scared and relieved in the mirror.

All I was saying was that whoever he was, or needed to be, he had to be it. See, sometimes people will make you crazy without even knowing. Sometimes it's up to you to be the surprise, to stand up for yourself about things that nobody even knows are bothering you. You might bring some worlds crashing down when you do that, but it is not your problem.

The Tower is not my favorite card because it means things in life are going to start moving fast, and that, more than holding onto some fantasy, challenges my need for control, my sense of safety. I know control is an illusion, but I like pretending I have it as much as the next person. We can't control the winds of fate or how much they leave us looking disheveled. At some point, we're going to lose in love or business, in health or in failing to be what others want us to be. When that happens there is nothing left to do but sit up and look at what's left in the dust that was your life.

Behind the Chair

Knowing how you think about things is the key to success. It's like the law of attraction; think about things in a certain way, and that's what you'll get. The trick is figuring out what part of your life is luck and what part is what you're attracting based on the messages you're putting out there. I attract good -looking men, but I don't necessarily attract ones who want to commit. Maybe that's my luck, but maybe it has something to do with what I've been putting out there. Maybe there's a part of me that doesn't trust being part of a couple after all, I've only seen one or two relationships that I have truly admired, and I've seen maybe a handful more that seem like any fun.

I think about this, and I remember watching one day as someone pulled into the parking lot of one of the salons. It was a perfectly fine day, no rain or snow, not even a cloud, but this car was acting like it couldn't figure out where the hell to park as it floated between the lines over and over. I turned my head to get a look at what was going on inside the car as it moved back and forth, left and right. It could have been anybody, a screaming mom, a guy on the phone, someone on drugs, and I needed to know.

I looked over, and there was a couple in there, some really old-looking guy and his wife, probably snowbirds who just came back from spending the winter in Florida. If I were driving behind these two, I would have been losing my mind, but I was just standing there, cutting hair, when they pulled up.

I was watching them in this big, old car, the husband in the passenger seat with the wife driving. She pulls into a spot, then she pulls back. Then she pulls in, then pulls out again. It's head-in parking, with plenty of empty spaces all around, but it takes maybe 15 minutes from beginning to end for the couple to park. Then, when the car was parked, he got out of the passenger seat and opened the door behind him. He took out a walker. Then, ever so slowly, he made it to the driver's side. Then he opened the driver's side door and the backseat driver's side door and proceeded to get out another walker. Then he closed the door and put that walker in front of his wife. After what seemed like an eternity, she finally stood up. In what seemed like forever, they turned around and walkered their way toward the salon.

Me and everyone else in the salon, from the operators to the customers, were all watching. In and out, trying to get it right, while there's absolutely nothing around them. The way they kept hitting the little curb every time they pulled up made it a small miracle that they managed to come inside. When they came in the salon and sat down for their cuts, they barely had a full head of hair between the two of them. I laughed because them going to get their hair cut was the big outing of the day, and they could have helped each other out with a pair of scissors instead of paying someone else to trim a lost situation. Then I thought, at least they have each other. We were laughing at how determined they were, and we laughed at whoever was going to get them in their chair. You have to laugh at the insanity of those two driving; otherwise, their sweetness would make you feel like they were the luckiest two people in the room, and it's hard as hell to reconcile yourself with the idea that two old farts who rely on walkers have won life's lottery in a way that you haven't. When luck fails, you can always laugh. It might be a bitter laugh, but it's better than nothing.

One thing I learned about cutting hair is that people either want you to laugh or to cry with them, and depending on the day, both. Most people want a little entertainment or some therapy when they get their hair cut, and I try to deliver. I don't spend a lot of time with people who get in these chairs, but I know people expect some kind of emotional attachment. I'm making rent on offering a service that people on a budget can afford, so I have to be quick, but I have to give them some kind of feeling or they won't come back. This is real haircutting for real life, and people need us in a way that fancy places don't cut it. We're like a walk-in clinic, offering self-confidence for the thrifty or strapped. We are here for the mother with five boys who shudders at the thought of giving that many haircuts. We are here for the old people who could accidentally kill each other with a pair of scissors and some shaky hands. We roll our eyes, and we shake our heads yes and no. We talk about the weather, and we let people talk about shows we've never seen. The cuts are only part of the work; the rest is based on personality.

Cheryl was a good haircutter, and that was part of why I liked her so much from the start. She wasn't too bitchy, but she wasn't going to take anyone's shit, and that's important when you're dealing with the public. After all, you have to know how to deal with so many personalities and all sorts of drama that people bring with them. You can almost tell what they're going to want or if they're going to like your cut before you even start, just by the way they sit down. Cheryl was good and fast, and unless she was sick, she would always show up for her shifts. That reliability she had at her core meant a lot. The worst is when people call out because it's slow and they know they're not going to make a ton of money, and then I have to try and hustle in myself or find a replacement. I pretty much work seven days a week and having to go in on my off hours – not my off days, but my off hours – is enough to get that bitter laugh going.

Cutting hair, no matter how precision or simple a cut you do, is a brutal job. It's physical, and we don't really have a lot of space for sick days or "working from home" like office people. This exposes everyone to our moods as much as it exposes us to theirs. I know I don't have a lot of space for my aching shoulder or my tired legs, but I know nobody wants to hear me bitch about it. When you pass from 20 to 30, and from 40 to 50, and so on, you can Botox, peel, lift, staple, whatever you want on the outside, but on the inside, you feel it. You stand on your feet long enough, and eventually you'll be able to feel every strand of hair underneath them. Do that for years and you'll start to get a certain kind of intuition that only comes from behind the chair.

For a while, one of the biggest problems I had at the salon was when Cheryl first started calling out sick. Everyone bitched at me, and some of the other haircutters started to hate her, not because it was personal, necessarily, but because it's literally a pain when you have to work those extra hours.

If the cutting is good, you're making money, so you don't notice as much, but when it's slow, that shift can be torture, and then you really want to let someone have it. For a while dealing with Cheryl's sickness gave me an amazing headache, but mostly because of the bitching and moaning from her co-workers. Don't get me wrong; none of them are horrible people. It's just, like I said, we're all fucking tired. We stand there talking about the TV or the weather, but we are fighting for dollars, standing on our legs for hours, with our arms in the air. I don't know if it's what I expected when I got to the Wilfred Academy, but then again, I was young and naive, and that was before the Internet, so I was that level of clueless.

For a while after Cheryl's death, I was pretty harsh with people, even harsher than I had been in the past. Even though I had been out for years, I came across as straight a lot of the time, because I didn't want people to define me by their prejudices. Lots of times I just didn't want to be bothered sharing my private life with other people all day. I didn't give a shit about keeping up appearances on that or playing it safe because I didn't want to upset some old woman or some pastor.

I was so tired of people acting like all the other gay people were freaks but I was "different" than the rest of them. I was beyond livid when people started talking about things in the Bible. I started asking them if they condoned owning slaves and believed in stoning people for things like planting their crops in a particular direction. I couldn't take the hypocrisy of people being literal only when it served their bigotry, and suddenly I went from being a guy with subtle rainbow flags to this defiant man defending my rights. For a while, my chair offered shock therapy, and everyone said I needed a vacation. I wasn't sure what they meant by that, so I stayed with my usual routine.

I was losing it because I lost someone who accepted me completely, someone who never felt it was safe to be herself, either. Now all her tarot cards and her life were a done deal, and I was supposed to be OK with it. I had very little patience with everyone, and I found myself getting a kick out of it when karma was kicking people in the teeth for stupid shit. I smiled when one lady told me that she moved to get away from her gay neighbors, and then lo and behold, fate moved her next door to a lesbian couple. I mean, I actually laughed in her face through the mirror. She was so frustrated with herself that when I laughed, she just sat there.

I got into it with people instead of talking about their bills or what they were going to fix for dinner. I got into it hard with some of them talking about love and humanity. The woman with the neighbors wasn't the only one – oh no, there were plenty more. I started to ask the smug ones, especially, more serious questions.

"Doesn't your child live nearby?"

"Not anymore."

"Did he get married?"

"Not yet."

"Is he seeing anyone?"

"Not that I know of."

(Silence with eye contact.)

I looked at that face in the mirror, and then I gave her an extra great haircut. Maybe her kid isn't gay, but he is not on the marriage track. And if he is, he might decide to have an intermarriage of some kind. Maybe he'll marry a witch or, at the very least, an astrologer. I wasn't trying to make the woman hate her son, but I was planting a seed of doubt. I was asking this lady if she really was willing to hate her child because of what she was picking and choosing out of "the book."

Finally, my business partner made me take a vacation because I was tearing people new assholes about everything from oppressing their kids to the state of politics and the way we all need to get a grip and start being kinder. Once those floodgates of grief and truth-telling were open, I could just as easily be yelling about compassion as I was at the idiot who took up two parking spaces. I said "fuck" around old people and probably children, too, because I just didn't give one. I didn't give myself a heart attack, but I'm pretty sure I got close.

If Cheryl had been there, able to speak to me while I was raging over life, she would probably mention the moon and she'd laugh. She would probably just sit there, right in that chair where she liked to work, and talk about these wild things like Venus in retrograde, and she would say that means old flames might come back now. She would wink and make me laugh, distracting me from myself. But she isn't here, and getting used to that was harder than you would have thought had you looked at it all on paper. We didn't sleep together, and we didn't know each other for long. We weren't blood-related, and we didn't grow up in the same place, but we had a soul level relationship, and when I lost her, a part of me was torn.

That summer when Cheryl was sick, we went through a roller coaster of good days and bad days, of boyfriends, no boyfriends, of her being able to get out of bed, and her not picking up the phone because she needed the silence. It was a lot of time running between salons and the restaurant, and so many talks about life. With most people you talk about what happened today, what went on with getting from here to there, and what people said and all that, but with Cheryl, we talked about that and more. She had a way of talking about life that made it all sound a little bit like reality was just this fairytale you tried to put together. She made living sound like fun, using the cards and her sixth sense.

"Tom, you're my brujo."

"Your what?"

"You're a male witch."

"I am?"

"Yes."

"What does that really mean?"

"It means I can trust you."

"Well, yeah."

"You're in my coven."

"OK."

"So, I have to protect you."

(Silence with eye contact)

Cheryl kept telling me I had a good feel for stories and for what motivated people, and she said I could use that in reading the cards like her. I always thought that being a witch was something women did; I never thought I would be able to read at the same level. I'd come to see her in this little white house she was renting, a place so tiny you could practically spit out the back window from the front room, and I would humor her. She gave me my own cards, and I collected them after a while, too. I could read for others, but I understood I couldn't really read for myself. It's like your mind plays tricks on your intuition when you do that – at least, at my level that's what happens. Anyway, I got into it.

The good tarot spreads were awesome. They made me feel like I was about to be living in a movie on the Hallmark Channel, like everything was magical and worked out in the end. Bad spreads or cards made me feel like my life would soon become a horror show. The more we gossiped and flipped cards, the more we made fun of our lives and our bad luck, the more it made life seem all right despite the shit. When I would pack up Napoleon and head back toward home, I would feel better for the time together, even if another part of me was freaking out about getting this close only to lose her. I wasn't going to be a witch like Cheryl no matter how much I flipped the cards. She saw stuff that I never saw, felt things I didn't even know how to feel.

Cheryl had sixth sense, but she still talked trash, and she had a pretty wicked laugh that was awesome. She was the kind of sexy that was a little dark and goofy at the same time. When I look back on it, you could tell she had levels, and that's what some people didn't like about her. She was complicated and she knew it, and she knew that everyone else is complicated, too. She was like the Empress card sometimes: innocent but showing her boobs. Or she could be like the High Priestess, completely covered up with secret knowledge. When she was feeling herself, she was full of what it meant to be a real woman, not some doll. She had this kind of smile or a mysteriously hard look that let you know Cheryl knew things, and for a second she was going to let you see it. In those moments, Cheryl had power.

As Cheryl got sicker, the veil got thinner, and her psychic powers got even stronger. Whether she was strong or too weak to say much, you could see her eyes shift around things that to me looked like air. The better she felt, the more she could tell you about it. If she was weak and keeping to herself, you got a feeling like she was half there, paying more attention to whatever was going on in the psychic plane. I could see it: She would be shooting the shit, maybe with a client, something normal would be happening, and then you'd see that look in her eye. I knew then that she just saw someone's grandma or their lost dog, or a dead lover. Sometimes the person in the chair would be talking about some funeral or a wedding ring that was handed down, and Cheryl would get that same look. That's the look I try to remember when I'm having a panic attack or a meltdown, because that look was all about Cheryl holding all her levels together, not getting carried away by them. Like, I said, in those moments, Cheryl had power.

THE MAGICIAN

Lots of things happen in a haircutter's chair. It does not matter if the salon is high end or discount, made for men or women or unisex. The haircutter's chair has its own kind of magic, the one where you transform. The hair chair is where your public look meets your private terrors. It's the place where you have to negotiate your curls or your bald spot in earshot of strangers. By bringing that part of yourself into the open, in that chair, everything is up for grabs in terms of conversation. If Cheryl had talked more about dead people, who knows? She might have lost us all the customers, but then again, maybe she would have increased her following. I know what people pay for psychics, and I know how talking about that stuff can freak people out, so I respected that she kept that stuff to herself lots of times. But I still think she could have made some serious money from it.

She separated her hair-cutting from her psychic self because that was safe for her, but if she had lived, she might have gone the other way, getting more open about it. I feel I saw her coming out of her own closet, her witch closet, the whole time I knew her, and watching that potential get cut short felt unfair. The couple of times she did offer readings to the other cutters and even to the customers, I was over the moon about it. Of course, not everyone was thrilled about it. One cutter who had been working with me for a long time, she looked at the cards with this look of disgust.

"You don't want me to read for you?"

"No."

"Because you don't want anyone to know who you really are."

"You got it."

Some people, they're scared of that stuff because of the church, and some people don't like it because they don't let nobody close. The talent and passion Cheryl had for helping people was so deep that I really could see her doing that kind of work every day. It seemed like a shame she wasn't, especially as she spent some days so beat up from lupus. Being behind the chair must have been the worst on those days when she could barely move her legs or raise her arms without pain. Cheryl was content cutting hair because she was comfortable with the chair and the lifestyle. She was OK with working weekends and evenings and holiday rushes, but I didn't really know how to tell her I didn't think it was the best thing for her at that point. How do you tell someone to stop being who they are without it sounding like you don't believe in them?

She liked the way being a haircutter let her control the conversation. Cheryl pretty much cut hair listening, not talking. You would think that being around people all the time, you leave a bit of yourself with everyone, revealing all your secrets, instead you end up perfecting the art of saying something and revealing almost nothing. Cheryl knew how to do it, and so do I. Every person behind the chair knows how to do it.

So as much as I flirted at the salon, or as much as I talked about this or that, I might have had sex in the chair only once, maybe twice. The truth is I didn't flirt hardly ever but I would sometimes troll, like a fisherman at sea.

If I had sex at work, it was mostly in the office, not in the chair, since the windows out to the street are huge.

It happened once or twice, though, and when it did it was memorable. I remember being at work, and the salon was closed. This cute guy came by one night, and I got charged at the sight of him. I was glad I had stayed late. The day had started strong, kept up like that for hours, but by the end of the day it was dead. I could have left early. He was standing there, trying to get a last-minute haircut and all I was thinking was how he was a loyal customer. His hair was pretty grown out, and he sat down, like a gift, asking me, "Can you shave it all on a one?" Did he know that a voluntarily bald head was maybe the sexiest thing in the world to me? I had to control myself because this had levels, like a regular haircut and a fantasy all at once.

I always start on the sides, and despite my excitement, I did that, just in case he started to see it all going off and decided at the last second to keep a little at the top. He was wearing his Carhartt's, another thing I find hot. I cut his hair slowly, like I had all the time in the world. I was not missing a hair or risking even the tiniest divot. Then I outlined him and shaped him up from top to bottom and side to side. When I looked at him, and he looked at himself, he was transformed. He went from this shaggy, hot worker guy to this clean-headed idol, shining with confidence. He was really happy with the cut.

"How can I thank you enough?"

I shot him a look.

"You really want it that bad?"

"You have no clue."

"All right, I'll give it to you."

"But?"

"But you never tell a soul."

He unbuttoned his pants. Unzipped his fly. Said to me, "That's as far as I'm going. You have to do the rest." I had set out bait in this guy's direction for months, never sure he would bite.

I wordlessly agreed to that. I wanted to give him the memory of a lifetime, because whether he knew it or not, he had already given me one of my all-time fantasies. "If you were in a movie right now," I asked myself, "how would you make it a blockbuster?" I spun the chair around and came up on his navel. I put my mouth right where I knew I could tease him. Working that movie magic, I thought, "This is where I give a kiss and a nip," then I had to discreetly take a smell. I couldn't believe we were good. He was clean, almost like he was fresh from a shower. I carefully undid the boxer shorts, then I bit at his package, watched it grow. I didn't rush things. I didn't know if this would ever happen again, and I wanted it to last. From there I built him up, kissed all around his special piece (because every piece is special) before going in for it. I decided as I looked at him, getting more and more turned on, that I was going to let him feel appreciated, not just wanted.

He was manscaped like something out of a catalogue. His sack was shaved smooth, and I thought to God, "Thank You, I couldn't ask for better." I was so excited, I pulled out all the stops doing what I know feels good, giving him the head I know I would want to receive. I got down there and I worshiped him, just like something out of an adult film. I meant it, though, because we had flirted for months, and each of us was crossing some invisible line. I was having sex at my place of work, and he was having sex with a man.

I gave him oral sex for the ages, with his legs shaking like they had thunderbolts inside them, until finally he came with an upsurge so hard it pulled his whole body sharp. He went tight from his feet through to the top of his neck, where his chin pushed up against the air like a statue. When I finished with him, after he stopped shaking, and after his eyes opened wide, he said, "Thank you." After that, he said, "Oh my God, is it like this every time?" and I said, "It could be," and he said, "You're amazing." This movie was a blockbuster. I could hear the audience clapping. There were men in tears touching themselves; there were women taking notes. I was so happy; I did not even think of charging him for the haircut.

He came around a bit after that, for an encore and then some. I wasn't sure if he would, but most men who bend with me have come around again for a second round. I become this adventure; a local representative of a world they didn't know existed. The power of pleasure and being treated like a God by somebody with the same equipment, the same knowledge as you, can be amazing, really freeing. Even if you prefer to be with women, it can be nice to change things up.

After a few times, I think his curiosity was filled, and that was perfect. I was clear I didn't want him getting any ideas, and he didn't. I wanted to keep him as a customer, and I was glad for the encounter we shared, but I had boundaries. I never wanted anyone to feel like they owned me or that I owed them an explanation. I wanted to transform men, yes, but not into boyfriends. You can't say too much up front in situations like that because you risk hurting people's feelings and drama, too. It stays a game of seeing where things will lead. Lots of times I was the biggest secret the man had in his life. It sounds kind of flattering, but it became annoying.

These guys were brag-worthy notches on my belt, but I couldn't mention the belt almost anywhere. One summer I was juggling five independent "adventures." One night I had three of them come by my house for a quick encounter. That was a "I can't believe that just happened" kind of a moment, but I kept it together despite the incredible pressure. I was managing things like someone from a movie, living "the dream." Maybe I was setting myself up to be forever single, but you can't anticipate that kind of thing when you're so busy.

My phone is not buzzing right now and so it's like heaven, no distractions except for my regular ADD ones. I'm getting green lights down the whole strip of highway by the mall, thinking about that night and all those days when it looked like I could have anything I wanted. I learned after my early heartbreaks. You can't help but want to be part of a magic story beyond your wildest dreams, but you have to be realistic when you're staring at your guy as he leaves across the strip mall parking lot, already texting his wife. You catch a glimpse of his silhouette, and his fade is perfect against the security lights.

I could never stay in the right lane and let people pass me, but on days like today I don't feel so competitive, either. I feel like if there was a center lane here, I would take it. All those guys had wives or girlfriends; all of them kept me like their little secret. A lot of them saw me as their teacher. I wasn't teaching them to be gay, though. I think I was teaching a lot of those guys that nothing is as black and white as it seems.

The weather is nice, so people are driving extra unconsciously, if that's even possible. I'm keeping my distance and continue to sail through the details of my most successful seductions. I am moving along with the flow while going as fast as I can, finding that sweet spot in the traffic pattern. I'm not sure why suddenly I'm getting all these greens, but I find myself feeling lucky. It's like some angels are giving me extra time to appreciate all the great head I've given.

Cheryl would talk about Venus now, if we were driving like this. She would be flying through her own tangents while I was flying through traffic. My driving made her nervous even though she drove just like me. When she was behind the wheel, Cheryl thought nothing of driving her car on the shoulder to pass you.

I pull the Caddy through some potential clusterfuck led by a grandma who can barely see over her steering wheel and an Orthodox Jew with a van and I-don't-know-how-many people in it, and I just keep going without a curse or a swear.

The phone beeps, and I ignore it, to keep the feeling of the green lights and the good sex and because I'm right by the plaza where the cops like to hide. I move from lane to lane like I'm totally in charge of this vehicle, and even that feels like an illusion. If just one person slams down their brake, all hell could break loose. Cheryl would get all lit up, if she saw me driving like this, and she'd try to keep up her thoughts to completely ignore my driving. As long as we talked about things she knew and liked, Cheryl might be nervous but she would let me drive without a comment.

She had her favorite tarot cards, her favorite decks, and the more I drove, the more she talked about them. "The Empress is Venus, and sometimes she means pregnancy, but not always. She is feminine, Tom, but the Magician is about making things happen. He's like, you know, a man. I mean he can be a woman, but the energy is masculine." Cheryl would talk about the cards like they were people. It was like we were all at some party together and the cards that came up were our friends, some acquaintances, a few definite frenemies.

She would get annoyed at my repeat questions, forgetting I was paying attention while one car was tailgating me bad and another was pumping his brakes. As she lit up talking about mystical things, she would forget about how I was driving, and judged my comprehension as if I were just another passenger. Of course, she was paying attention, and if I was doing something particularly shady, I would ask her more questions so she would stay on that topic.

I swear some of those rides were some of the healthiest, prettiest times for Cheryl, because right there in the car, even with the glow of the brake lights hitting her cheeks, she was safe. In a world full of people dying to judge you for every little thing you say, the car can feel like one of the safest places, its own little world.

So, here I am, almost talking to myself, suddenly behind one old woman with a Kia and a fucking love affair with her brake pedal, thinking about Cheryl and Venus and how death takes people. I think about the Magician, and how he stands there with his wand out, acting like he's got all the answers, but that's not actually true. Half the time the Magician is faking it, just like the rest of us, and the rest of the time he's trusting in something bigger than himself. When it works, it works, and when it doesn't, it can be a spectacular failure.

I can almost hear her talking some more as I think about it. The Magician? Oooooo, he's ruled by Mercury! When I pulled that card, Cheryl would say, "See, you need me; I have to cast a spell." She's not here right now, though, so it's up to me to make my own magic. Sometimes the Magician can mean someone is helping you from the other side, like a family member, but you got to use the other cards to know if that's the case. Right now, I think about all the times I worked my magic flirting, and I look around wondering if you can lose your taste for magic, for whatever power you've got. You conquer some goal, maybe get what you want enough times, and then you don't even want it anymore. I'm not saying I won't take the sex when it comes my way, but the game, it used to be so much better.

When I pull up into the salons these days, or even sometimes when I pull into the driveway at home, I think of the cars I was excited to see in the past: that Jag with the hottie, or that certain pickup truck in the parking lot after hours, coming to see me, saving me from another night of masturbation in a huge bed by myself. I think about all the things I was willing to do to get men to bend to my will, and how I hated thinking they would get into my head and control me. "Venus in retrograde" – by now it's burned into my head that this is when old flames can come back to be rekindled. Now, whether you still want them, that's up to you.

Whether you're good to lovers or make them secretly pay for the shit they put you through, that's also up to you. See, you don't have to do spells to be a magician, you don't even need a wand. Words are magic if you put enough intention behind them. You can move heaven and earth with your words if you just believe. The other part of that is seeing what you want, making it happen first in your mind, so it can show up in your life.

I try to let my mind wander so it can show me what I really want. My mind goes back over my history, and I find myself entering another level, like in a dream, but all this happens while I'm awake. I can find myself floating on clouds, and walking in fields, with cliffs and an ocean down below. Sometimes I notice how sharp and far the fall to the ocean is. Sometimes I walk alone, and sometimes I find someone else there and we walk together.

The times I am with someone we are so deep into each other that there is no doubt for me that I can have the relationship of my dreams, the one that exists past all my luggage, my issues. It is the most amazing pure union of two soulmates with arms and backs and legs. When I come out of those meditations, I feel like love can happen. You have to be able to imagine it first, and then you have to allow for it emotionally, too. The pictures show up in my mind, and then they leave, and by the end of it all, I am not anxious anymore. For the first ten minutes after the meditation, maybe longer, I don't think about my to-do list or anything else, and that right there is a Holy F***ing miracle.

THE LOVERS

I used to get so excited when the Lovers card came up in my spreads. I would get lost, thinking that it meant I was going to get sex, because sometimes that is exactly what that card means. I would get happy just thinking about how it was going to go down, how it was going to be hot and unexpected even though I was totally expecting it. I would drive around after a card like that thinking I was going to get it all – sex, love, someone who understood me and who I could trust – and it would be a done deal within days, if not hours. Problem is, I don't really trust, at least not when it comes to my heart.

I went from being a kid who didn't know he was different from all the straight boys to a first sexual encounter that was confusing as hell. I had all these mixed signals about what I could expect from other people and from sex. I figured there were better ways, and better love stories, than the ones I had known, but none of them had materialized. I figured I needed to get to the bottom of this situation. I started talking to myself about the nature of love. The conversation is what we might call, ongoing.

The Lovers card is all about twin flames, all about Gemini energy. After a while, when the story never ended up with "happily ever after," I felt my reaction to The Lovers changing. Cheryl always said, "Look at the pictures. What do you see?" At first, I saw the angel and the tree of life. I saw the serpent and the blue skies. Most of all, I saw the two lovers ready to join hands, with the sun shining on them.

Eventually, I didn't trust the angel anymore. Then I noticed that the woman in the picture was never looking at her man. That card went from being one where I was sure of everything to being one that left me a little confused. I was in the middle of one of those times when I let down my guard, and I felt like my heart was being crushed. The Lovers card came up, and I felt doomed. Looking at these twins under the angel of God, knowing that all my twin flame stories were not the stuff of fairytales, made me think about everything. It even made me think of my twin brother and how we sold each other out so many times as kids. If these Gemini twins were anything like real twins, I was in trouble.

Given the chance, we twin boys threw each other under the bus as often as possible. I guess that was what we did to survive the family dynamic. Siblings teach you about survival of the fittest, so the cards showed me that maybe when he teased me, he was only surviving. That helped the pictures on the card fit a little bit better, but it didn't make it all fit perfectly. It's about twins but it's not called the Twins, so I focused on the meaning of love.

God is love and the angel represents God, so I started to think about this. Outside of God, there is no guarantee anyone else will love you. Reality is, even when someone loves you, they'll never love you perfectly. That's why the lady looks up at the angel, because when things get rough, she has to look up for guidance, for strength. When she looks up to the angel, she's maybe praying for something very specific, or maybe she's just in a mood. No matter what, she realizes that her best friend in this picture is not her lover. In fact, he's looking at her for an answer. To be honest the guy looks clueless.

Everyone says The Lovers is a good card, and it can be, but it doesn't guarantee you anything. There are two sides to every story and two sides to every coin, and when a relationship fails, there are two sides to that, too. When you look to your lover you have to trust that they are doing what they need to do for themselves and if you're lucky that coincides with what you need them to do. Your lover is your mirror, but sometimes they mirror the thing you don't want to see in yourself. Sometimes they mirror some hidden facts. Lovers, twins, whoever is next to you, most close to you, that's the person that is going to help you see your flaws.

I remember my mother screaming in sheer despair about how me and my twin were treating each other. She would beg us to get along, and a few times we really brought her to the edge with our side comments. At the time I didn't have any idea how it can tear a mother up if her kids hate or hurt each other like that. No matter what she said, it didn't stop us.

"Twins are meant to be inseparable! To protect each other, to love each other, and all youse do is fight!"

It was like the moment after our birth we started to fight for no good reason. Who knows, maybe the reason was as simple as one of us was on Dad's side and the other was on Mom's. Maybe we were meant to be our parents' wake up call, but it didn't happen like that – at least, not while they were alive. Anyway, they dressed us the same and cut our hair the same, hoping that we would start acting like other twins. The more they tried, the more we hated it. To be honest, if there's anything I can tell people about being a twin, it's that trying to be exactly the same is hell. Now that I think about it, maybe that's another part of why lovers break up; it's that constant wanting to make two into one. It's not actually natural to be twinning all the time.

Now, my mother was not the cook in the family, as I already noted, and this is not to say the woman didn't try. It just wasn't her thing, and seeing how she was stuck in this role of homemaker, I get it. I also get it that my father really loved cooking, and owned his own restaurant, just like I do now. My father had a knack for cooking. It might have even saved his life, because if they didn't have potatoes for him to peel back in the Navy, they wouldn't have known what to do with him. If the military would have kicked him out, then maybe he would have come home with no future, landing right back into the hands of his father. So maybe the kitchen felt safe deep down somewhere in his mind, and that's why he loved to cook. Anyway, he was good at it and the worst thing you could say about him in the kitchen is that he used every single pot and pan.

Upon declaring his love for my mother and asking for her hand in marriage, my father sold his restaurant and got a regular job with benefits, and for the next 30 years or so he went to it, working for bosses, hating it as much I would have. He traded in the thing he loved to do for what was expected of him, and so did my mother. We suffered through shitty food, they suffered through jobs they both hated, and everyone tried to pretend that was what happy looked like, but that's not what it looks like, and as we got older it wasn't too hard to see neither of them was satisfied with life. People doing what is expected of them instead of what they love to, does not lead to happiness.

I can't pretend to understand what made my parents tick. Sure, it was the times, people didn't get divorced so much, but still my mother never packed us up to leave him in a fit. She never took us over to her parents' or got herself another man on the side to make him jealous. There was a stable quality to them even for those times, even with the tensions of his daily drinking threatening to overturn everything. They call that "codependence" now, but I don't think it was as simple as that. I think the thing that made them stay together wasn't just stability or her hoping someday he would change. I think, as much as I don't understand it, that they loved each other at the start, and that sealed their fate to be together. They had, once upon a time, been in love like those two people on the Lovers card, and no matter what, the memory of that spark kept my mother and father together.

Their life together was predictable. He would be a dick, and she would correct him. He would say something vicious to me, and she would stare him down. Instead of taking us away from him, my mother packed us into the car to go find him at bars. That was her man, and she would bring him home instead of worrying all night. At the bar, he stopped his drunk flirting at the sight of her and without question, got in the car with his wife. They were devoted to each other, down to their cores, even when all logic would say they should split up. That devotion, even if it was dysfunctional, had its own beauty to it, like a dark Norman Rockwell scene where the family wagon idles outside the bar, and a woman goes in for her man while the kids squirm in the back.

Matched sets come in all shapes and sizes, and just like me and my twin brother, my parents were that kind of normal matched-up couple: not perfect, not terrible. Fate had them meet for whatever reason. She worked as a secretary to the mayor, and he had his restaurant right around the corner, and that was how they met. It must have been at a lavish Thanksgiving feast, where the young, single version of my father gave out his famous cream puffs and pies to all the town. It's safe to say my mother probably fell for my father because of his skills as a pastry chef. It makes them both seem kind of innocent when I think about it. All the yelling and screaming that came seemed sadder for them as a couple, not just for me as the kid he liked to mercilessly pick on, who she had to save.

You don't choose family, and no matter if you leave or stay around them, there is always a connection. Each generation has to make peace with both sides of their upbringing, and with what they inherit. Sometimes you get older and stare in the mirror like I do, because you look a lot like your father, and you're around his age when he died. You look a little harder because you're at that same age when his heart went into shock and suddenly stopped. There are all sorts of ways to die, and some are neater and cleaner than others. Lots of times you can't see how one thing connects to another but in my father's case, it was easy. My father was stung when a rake hit a tree, by accident, rousing a nest of hornets. The rake slipped from where it was propped, and Jimmy wasn't quick enough to stop it.

In a way, my father and I were our own matched set, and when he passed, I felt it down to my bones. A lot happened to me between 13 and 17, and one of the big things was being attacked by bees. I was in the backyard clearing the weeds when I heard something in the barrel where we burnt leaves and that kind of trash. I banged it once, and I hit it again. I wasn't thinking at all about the noise. I was thinking, "What's in there?" I had my father's way about me, and instead of looking in or tilting it, or walking away, I slammed that can hard. I happened to hit the can, startling the bumblebees who were hiding from the sun. Before I knew it, they were all over me.

I ran for the house, screaming for my life. My mother found me running for the door and met me with the flyswatter. She beat me with it as fast as she could. My brother ran out, too, with a rolled-up newspaper. There were so many they didn't know where to hit me. From my head to my socks, I was being attacked. They beat at me like that for five, maybe ten frantic minutes, and when it was done my mother brought me to the couch. I was trembling from shock, from the adrenaline of all the stings. When my father came home, there was hell to pay.

"Your son got stung by bees. I told you to get rid of that burning barrel." He came over to me and asked, "Are you all right?" and I weakly said, "Yeah," and nodded my head. Then my father went outside, threw some gasoline in the barrel, lit a cigarette with a match and tossed the match into the barrel. The flames went up, and he took a few drags. Then he came inside and announced, "The bees are gone."

That was a brush with death, and I knew it. I did not whine about it because I had provoked them. I knew, maybe for the first time in my life outside of when I rode that man-hating horse of my aunt's, that it wasn't just my dad that could kill me. Maybe more than anything I learned that it wasn't something big and strong, but something small, something I could barely see, that could change or take my life in an instant.

A few years went on, and things settled down, as they generally do. I got stronger, and smarter, but I wasn't about to take off on the family. I don't think it ever occurred to me to actually leave, even if I wanted to sometimes. Maybe I would have eventually, if things kept going the way that they had been, but then fate stepped in. The year that I turned 21, my father left this earth. In April, I was celebrating a milestone birthday, but by August, I was a son in mourning. In the middle of the heat and on one of his vacation days, my father left us. What got him were those stingers that almost got me.

I grabbed the phone and called the hospital. I asked them if he was there, and it got silent. Then a doctor came on and said, "The family has already been notified." My aunt was pulling in the driveway to tell my grandmother the news, as I was sliding down to the floor. It felt like the world was dropping from under my feet. I was breathless, felt like I was drowning, as relatives kept coming to the door and it became undeniable that he was gone.

I tried to hide in the bathroom, my room of refuge, but this time I wasn't crying; saying how I wished he were dead, or wishing that I were. I was in there, up above the whispering that was louder than it wanted to be, crying for the loss of my soul. A part of me felt responsible, for all the times I had wished my father would disappear, never to hurt me again. I wasn't out there when my father went. I had nothing to do with it. Still, I was crying from guilt. That day I felt a panic I never imagined, and it stayed with me until we brought my father to his final resting place. My mother was a zombie during it all and watching her felt like my greatest punishment. My mother's pain at losing her husband tore me apart, and I can still feel that bottomless despair if I think about those moments too hard.

North or South

New Jersey is a highly divided state. It's not a political thing or something in dispute, everyone here knows it. From the north to the south, there are two different parts of the state and that is not up for debate. I grew up in the southern part of the state and that meant we had lots of trees, and people we knew had actual farms. In Cheryl's, there were highways and factories, and semi-industrial wetlands that lead you out to Manhattan. In Cheryl's world, people went in and out of New York to window shop or to work on a regular basis. New York City was less than 20 miles away for Cheryl, whereas for me, we're talking 80 miles.

I grew up around the Pinelands, with its pygmy-size scrub pines, and Cheryl grew up around the bridges and tunnels. In my world we dressed in what was dependable and regular-looking. In her world, people knew about trends. In my world, we went to the woods to do our underage drinking, and in Cheryl's, everyone got their fake IDs so they could go to the clubs anywhere from Hasbrouck Heights to the cute Irish bars in the West Village, or maybe the punk spots on the East Side. The biggest difference in how we grew up didn't have much to do with clothes and trends, or all the other things between the north and the south. The difference between us was that Cheryl was never physically scared of one of her parents. When my father died, my pain was half guilt; hers was pure loss.

Cheryl missed her father in a way I couldn't. No one in Cheryl's house was an alcoholic. Nobody went from happy to furious in the blink of an eye. She was spared a certain type of insanity that happens when you find yourself trying to reason with a person whose blood type is temporarily set to S for scotch. Cheryl's father had died slowly, from the complications of Parkinson's, and so her grief went on for years. She didn't have any guilt about her father passing. She never had that mix of love and fear well up inside, confusing her.

In our house there was way more hollering and tension, lots more nights where we were balancing between the most intense silence and straight-up chaos. Cheryl and me, we talked all about what it was like growing up as kids, laughing at all those superficial differences. Things I never knew bothered me came popping up to the surface. All the terrifying stories were somehow almost funny when I told them to her. If you want to survive in a dysfunctional family setting you have to have a sense of humor about it.

In my family, my sister was the cool one, the one who picked up surfing in high school. My brother was the one who would say and do anything to keep people out of his curly hair. I was the lightning rod twin, the one who defied his father. In our family, I was special, but not in the best way. I loved listening to her stories because they were always so nice.

When Cheryl was 5, her aunt died. Cheryl's mother had company over, and little Cheryl walked over to her.

"Mom, Aunt So and So said she's OK, not to worry."

"No, she's not. She's in the hospital."

"She just came to me in the bedroom, to tell you."

A few minutes later the phone rang, and Cheryl's uncle was on the other end of the line, telling her mother that their sister, whose name I can't remember, had passed. That blew her mother's mind, not so much that it happened, but because Cheryl was so young. In the world at large, Cheryl was exceptional because of her psychic abilities, in her family though, she wasn't that strange. They all had these sensitive natures and they could feel things that didn't always make sense to others. Amongst themselves the channels were open and they swapped their stories of strange dreams and dead relatives without a blink of the eye.

Reality is. most of us have those channels, then we lose them, and then much later, we try and open them back up. Cheryl's channel was always open and she never got told to close them. She loved living in a world that was full of extra layers. Following those different layers and connecting their threads was like keeping track of fashion trends. She approached it a little like she was a stylist. She'd pull coincidences together and see the story. Cheryl thought it was sad that people shut down that creative part of themselves. To her someone shutting down their intuition was like refusing to smell a flower or turning your back on a rainbow. It was like choosing to see, smell and wear nothing but gray instead of embracing life.

Closing that psychic channel down made no sense to Cheryl but she knew sense didn't have a lot to do with why people shut themselves down like that. It had everything to do with emotion and fear even though people swore it was all about logic. You never know what makes someone shut down just like we don't know what makes some people open up. Who knows, maybe Cheryl was on the cusp of closing that channel, too, but her aunt's passing message gave little Cheryl a reason to stay open.

We were coming up on the ninth month of fighting the cancer when Cheryl was doing really well, and then it turned. Within weeks she went from looking kind of vibrant and testing well on the pH strips to looking like she was going hollow. The pH tests proved what we were seeing, that something was changing in the bigger picture. "At 7.5, cancer dies," she said, in between shakes and enemas. She had said it countless times as she packed the juicer. She had lived past the three months they had predicated, and she managed to stay away from the doctors the entire time. Now, finally in the sixth month after her diagnosis, Cheryl's sister insisted she go. When Cheryl walked into that office, she was getting weaker, but she still looked amazing. The doctor was shocked. Cheryl was anxious as hell, but she hid it. When I asked how it went, she was cagey.

"Fuck them, they already told me I'm dead."

Then she flipped her hair.

"I'm a North Jersey girl, Tom."

She flipped her hair in a clear sign of a crucial victory. Suddenly she was her 17-year-old self, the girl who dressed like Madonna, and flirted with the muscle car guys. She was the girl with the perfectly lined Wet 'n Wild lip gloss and the shiniest, bounciest, softly waved hair getting you into the hottest clubs. In this case, she was a cancer patient scoring herself discounted healthcare, all with that one timeless move.

When the old Cheryl showed through, she and I would laugh for hours. We would bitch about the kids today, how they were so skinny, while we were spreading out in our middle-aged bodies. It was like they were showing off all the time, we would say. Then we would practically howl at our own jokes. That was back when we were in the salons together. Cheryl wasn't heavy at all, but she had these tits that could make her look bigger, and that bitch had an appetite. She had curves since she was 13 and they had always looked good on her.

"Look how thin I am."

"Yeah, you got no butt."

"How could you say that to me?"

"You don't say that to a woman."

(More silence.)

"Oh my God, Tom."

That was obviously a big mistake. Sometimes my mouth can get me in trouble, even with Cheryl. When she stopped coming to the salons, we would still talk about growing up, and we would pity the kids today because of all the drugs and the pressure to look camera-ready. We would snack and laugh. God blessed Cheryl, and she ate right up to the end. She kept her pooch and managed to keep her sense of humor most of the time, right until there was nothing left to do but start her crossing.

Cheryl looked gravely ill if you knew her, but if you didn't, you saw a full person, a curvy, womanly person, not a sick person. It took until the very end for the sickness to show, and I think that's because her spirit covered up the situation. My comment about losing her butt – well, never again did I make a stupid remark like that.

We would eat and talk about whatever. We would eat in between throwing cards. We would talk about life and growing up, and I pull up all these forgotten memories. Then we would be exhausted and need to eat some more, especially Cheryl's ultimate favorite snack –potato chips and sour cream.

Neither me nor Cheryl would consider ourselves thin, but we weren't fat, just normal. We just weren't teenagers who could eat without consequences, and that was annoying. I never thought about going back in time, never wanted to relive the years when I was under my father's roof, but talking about life, looking back at it with Cheryl, I could handle it better.

"Your father is going to help you sell that restaurant."

"Why is my father going to help me?"

"Because he has to make amends for what he did to you here."

When Cheryl made those kinds of statements, they would somehow pull memories out of me.

I remember telling her this story of how when I was 18, I went hunting with this guy, Greg, from my high school. I had been taught to hunt, but I hadn't really tried it alone. I had a gun, and it had a matching one, a complementary gun. I had both of them with me because they were my grandfather's, and when I received them, I was told you don't separate sister guns, not ever. I'm not sure if I took that too literally, but Greg and I went out into the woods, and I had them.

We were in the woods for a while and I saw a spike buck, with just about 3-inch antlers. I shot him, and I felt a little relieved, since it felt like Greg was depending on me. Then I realized I shot the deer in the leg instead of the chest. I had broken the leg, and the deer was stumbling. I sat there, in the tree where I was, stunned for a second.

This was horrible, for the deer and for me. I had been raised to be a good shot, a damned good shot, and now the deer was suffering. I did hit him like Greg needed me to, but I hadn't hit him well enough to take him down. The deer made a huge pivot and leapt, and the second shot I took missed him. Then he ran, and I got down from the stand and ran after him, and then he fell. I looked at Greg and asked him, "What should I do?" He said, "Shoot it." It seems a weird question to ask, but in that second, I was still reeling from the surprise.

I pulled the trigger on that long-barrel gun, wishing I had my .22 pistol, because buckshot was messier and way less exact. I knew this buck's brain and blood were about to be all over the rocks, splattered in every direction. The mess was making this even worse. I squeezed down, firing at the head of the buck, finally putting him out of his misery. The four pellets pushed through the buck's skull, making his eye bulge. The life passed from him like a backward bolt of lightning. He was done, and so was I, horrified.

Seeing his life leave him, instantly, was different for me, even though I grew up hunting. It wasn't like watching pheasants or rabbits die. The worst mess I'd witnessed up until that day was this other time, when I was with Greg and he snapped the neck of a pheasant too hard, separating the head from the body. That was nothing compared to the sound and visuals of an animal bigger and faster than you, falling in a bloody, suffering mess. Greg and I stood there a minute, catching our breath, not having any good words for such an amateur death scene. There was blood splattered on trees, and the buck's corpse had a look of pain etched on his face. My pride was shot, too. It wasn't Greg's fault, but together we made the day a failure. That day marked the end of my hunting career.

We hauled the animal out, and I brought it to my father, who dressed it. He showed me where the scent glands were, so I could cut them out on my own when I got another deer. I kept my mouth shut about my decision to never go hunting again. He hung the animal and skinned it, then let it hang for three days. Then he butchered it for our dinners. When he butchered the deer, my father shifted into a quiet state, almost like a meditation. Every move he made was intentional, careful, patient. In no time, the deer was neatly packed and wrapped in brown paper bags, layered with aluminum foil for protecting each piece. When it came to the old ways of surviving there wasn't anything my father couldn't do.

I don't know how many animals my father butchered in his time, but it was a lot. He even arranged with the local cops so that they would call him if there was a deer that was hit or injured somewhere. He would get the call, and then he would go to the spot where the deer was seen ducking into the woods. He would take his .22 and track the deer, then shoot it in the cleanest shot he could manage. Then he would haul the deer out and bring it home. Then he would go through the ritual of hanging it and cutting it into food. Then he would pack the meat and donate it to families who were hungry.

My father was a damned good shot, but killing for no reason would never have occurred to him. Giving the meat away made sense. That was something good that came from my Dad's side, the country side that farmed and hunted and wasted nothing. They all knew what to do with a gun, and they never wasted a shot on anything just to hurt it. My aunt surprised me one day by shooting a turtle in the head. With a single shot from a .22 rifle, she took the head right off. I asked how she learned to shoot like that, and she said, "Your father taught me." Apparently turtle soup used to be a thing.

My mother, who grew up in a city with a salesman father, did not have those shooting skills, and she hated cooking game even more than regular cooking. We only got halfway through eating that buck I killed before my mother decided the freezer needed to be defrosted. I came home to half the deer in the trash. There was no end to my shame with that animal, and there was no way my mother understood how badly she compounded it. She didn't know what it was like to pull a trigger and play God. She didn't know how it could make you feel to know that you had looked into the eyes of that rack of ribs.

The day the deer defrosted, I realized that even my mother and I weren't always going to see eye to eye one hundred percent of the time. No one is exactly like another person, and nobody lives or dies in the same way. Nobody is a perfect friend or ally. No one is a perfect twin. We all have agendas and histories, and we can not take it too personally when someone else acts like an individual. Defrosting a fridge is no big deal, but sometimes it is.

I haven't shot either of those two sister guns since the day with that deer. They sit like decorations in my house, and sometimes I think about selling them, but so far, the price in money isn't worth the memories. If the price went up high enough, I might get rid of them.

Some twins look matched, like we expect them to, like me and my twin brother or that pair of guns. Lots of times those matched sets don't look like each other at all on the surface. When it comes to looking a twin or a soulmate in the eye, you have to accept that you might not always like what you see, but at least you can learn from the reflection. Cheryl and I came from similar but different places. We didn't look alike or talk alike, but we were family on the inside, and it didn't seem right when fate took her. It felt like God took a sloppy shot, and instead of hitting me direct and clean like he meant to, he got one of my twins.

The Forever Swordfight

No decision is still a decision. No commitment is a comfortable way to live most of the time. The problem is when a disruption finally comes driving by your house on a random afternoon, your reflexes might take over. That challenge to your daily routine might come cruising along in his truck while you're dangling on the roof, cleaning your gutters, and you could do something stupid, like wave. Then you realize that the change you've been keeping at bay has washboard abs and this sweet smile. You invite the whole package in, but you keep your guard up, and this mixed signal causes hell later.

"Hey, I didn't see you there."

"Oh, I was on the roof."

"Can I get a haircut?"

"Sure."

In the back of my head, I was thinking, "Why would he come looking for me?" We went downstairs into the basement, where in one big rec room I had the hot tub, a sitting area and, just off to the side, a barber's chair with a mirror and a full station of tools and products. In the salons we don't sell products because inventory is a bitch and people like to steal and I've got enough goddamn stress, but at home I've got all sorts of great stuff, laid out just like I want it.

He sat down in my private chair, and I got myself ready to give him a beautiful fade. I set my mind to it just like an athlete on the starting block, a driver at the track. I checked the clippers, straightened the cape and adjusted the chair. I took a good long look at him from every angle before I let myself feel the blades of the clipper as they made their way through the strands. I focused on the perfect cut for him, making my way round his head like he was a god. Then I felt him relax while still trying not to shift his head too much. I knew he could feel my attention, knew he had never felt me quite like that when I cut him at the salon.

Just as I finished shaping that overgrown head of hair into the manicured crown of my dream man, a girl I cut showed up for her appointment. I was always happy to see her, but she felt early.

Everyone said "Hi" and smiled at each other, and we were about two seconds away from it getting awkward. He bummed a cigarette, and while she got her hair layered and trimmed to the shoulder, he smoked. He wasn't rushing away. He got comfortable on the other side of the room, in the sitting area by the woodstove. As I cut the girl's hair, I kept sneaking glances at him, watching the cigarette go down. He was watching me, too, every move.

My roommate came through and went, and the girl eventually left, looking at him while she checked her hair and rifled for things in her purse. He paid her no mind, and when she got out the door, he looked around. I was cleaning up, tidying a little here on the floor, arranging bottles there on the shelf. Finally, as we heard her car pull away, he piped up from 20 feet away.

"When's your roommate coming back?"

"20 minutes."

"You feel like …?"

(Looks down at himself)

"All the time."

He went from the couch to the recliner, still right by the stove. Then he pulled the lever, making it into a lounger. By the time I walked over, his pants were at his ankles. Time was of the essence. Freaking out on the inside, thinking, "How am I going to pull this off?", I tried to focus. I was checking the clock while trying to build up excitement. I was trying to juggle reality while getting lost in a fantasy. This one, I had been watching him, felt pulled to him for his sweet disposition. That smile, those abs and the eyes didn't hurt, either.

I never thought it would happen, that this day would come. The thing about straight guys, or guys living straight while curious, is that they never really make a plan, never show up when you want or when you expect them. That was a rough afternoon to take a break. I still had to finish cleaning those gutters.

I made my way down his body as quick as I could, scared like hell. I had lied. There was no telling if my roommate would come back early. Still, I'm me, and I am OCD about personal hygiene, so I gave him the usual manscape test, which he passed with flying colors. For a second, I felt weak in my knees because of all the pressure. The rest I can't explain in too much detail because it happened so fast. The deal was done in about three minutes. The pace was quick, but the pleasure was real.

"How did you do that?"

"If I had known you were going to go like that, I would have gone easier."

I could feel it in my bones that I wanted this to happen again, more than anything else, but I played it cool. He left wanting more, and I finished cleaning the basement. I stared at the fire, and for the first time in a long time, I felt really alone. The dog was there, whining for duck treats. My roommate came home, and we talked about random things and taunted each other. I even finished cleaning the gutters, the top thing on my to-do list that day, but nothing made me feel better.

Cheryl said to me, "When you touched him, he felt it through every cell of his body," and I would ask, "Then why doesn't he do something about it?" Her answer was always the same: "Fear."

I would have her read for me over and over again, looking for some key to unlock the situation and move it forward. She looked up at me one day, tired but steady. "Tom, if he's not the one, I'll find you something better when I'm on the other side." That was not the answer I wanted to hear. I wanted the spells to work, the potions to make a difference. I wanted parties on the back deck with this guy by the pool, his abs getting tan, and I wanted all my best friends alive for it. Instead, I got the two of swords.

In the tarot, a two can be about coming into partnership or juggling demands, striking a balance of some kind, just like a seesaw. In the Two of Swords, the back and forth can be about trust, about protecting your heart now because you got hurt in the past. All you need to do is look at the card and imagine yourself in it. You're seated, and your hands are aching from holding these two heavy swords. Your eyes are covered. You're holding weapons against threats that you can't see. It doesn't mean the threats aren't there, but it means some part of the situation is purely mental.

You have to give yourself over to your heart and give your mind a rest to get out of the situation signified by the Two of Swords. You might need to give up some control in your life and examine your choices from the inside, it says. It teases you by pointing out that you can sit with a blindfold on, and nothing can get to you, except for that fight rising up on the inside of you. Quietly tearing you between this path and that one, the two of swords pushes you to decide on something new. For me it was all about being hurt. For him, well, maybe the day in my barber's chair was the best day of life, but was it enough to get him to change. Maybe my chair was the chair in the picture. You never can tell but it sure did seem like it.

After that day all I wanted was to see him, to be with him. After that day, we saw each other again and sometimes – well, sometimes it was hotter than anything I ever knew. I would sit there comparing all these other lovers, and over and over this felt different. Typical situation, I acted cool, but I hated seeing him leave. I sent mixed signals and caused fights. He got bold, then scared, and he ran away as far as he could, into other relationships that were safer than ours. On the outside he gave out nothing but smiles and puppy dog eyes, but we both knew those were a cover. We also knew that if he stayed with me, he'd have to stop drinking, and more than anything, maybe that was what made him scared.

That situation came and it went, and I regretted every fight, but I never regretted trying because some feelings are worth the effort. The hot tub is gone from the basement now, but the rest of it is still pretty much the same. That girl from our first big day, she still comes over sometimes for a haircut, and we gossip and then she leaves as per routine. I look over at the recliner sometimes when I am down there and give it a nod. I remember the excitement that turned into pure release and then panic. Then I think about insulating the room better because I want to cut down on my energy bills. You need to keep those thoughts moving if you want to survive some feelings.

Bees and Spiders

Some people ask, "Why me?" I've gotten to the point where I say, "Why not?" Why not lose people I love the most when I feel I need them the most? Why not drive my car through a puddle and discover a design flaw that causes the engine of my car to flood and seize? Why not get screwed by insurance so the policy I got covers maybe one-tenth of what they said it would? It works for me, this way of looking at things. Like when I accepted that every year, I am going to lose some fish in the pond. There's a loon in the neighborhood, and he doesn't miss a thing. The loon started coming over all at once, and within two visits he took them all. Now I have a net over the pond, but if I take it off for any reason, I can count on that loon showing up. When you embrace the fact that you are part of the world, not its center, you gain more than you lose.

For example, I have that pond filled with comets, and they're pretty. They're goldfish just like the shubunkins were, sort of like koi, too. The comets are way cheaper, and that's fine, because otherwise I would be a nervous wreck worrying if the loon would come. I know he will, so now I'm prepared. There is one comet in there that I can never find, because his almost-black body matches the pond liner. I got into this habit of pulling the lilies and looking for that shadow fish. Sometimes I end up in a panic, thinking another bird got one of my fish. Mark off another win for the grim reaper. Then I would spot the missing fish eventually, and somewhere between bitching at him and the lilies that clog the drain I would think about life, and how no one gets out of here alive.

I would go through the list, thinking about people passed, friends, and clients, about people I knew who were looking kind of thin all of a sudden. I would think about the ones I hadn't seen in a while, wondering who I should ask if they were OK.

Years before Cheryl passed, my cousin Faith also died young. My mother was still alive; I was only 32 and three years away from losing her, but I didn't know that.

Faith committed suicide one day in early July, just before her 40th birthday. She always made me laugh, and we'd get scolded, "You two are too silly!", as if that was possible. Faith was divorced, and she hadn't had children. She was dying from self-judgment. Her struggle was one of those silent ones, where almost nobody knew how rough of a seesaw her days were, until one day she wasn't there anymore.

At the end, she sat in the car and wrote letters that she would line up along the dashboard. She had put towels in the cracks under the doors that led to the house, to make sure no one else got hurt. She left behind a poem that pulled my guts out. She was unhappy over her ex-husband and the gay roommate who didn't love her back. She was worn out by pain and emotions. When I went to the service, I was in and out quickly, doing only what I knew I had to do. She chose her next level, and I tried to respect that, but I was angry that she didn't ask for help. If she did, I didn't hear her, and that bothered me, too.

I've never been OK with death, and I guess that is a natural reaction, one that goes deep in each of us. Early in my working life I worked at a nursing home, and that made me hate death even more. I wish I could forget working at the home because it brought out this coldness in me. I started out in the kitchen, and eventually I ran it. During my time there, I got every little bit of motivation I needed to start building my own businesses. I wanted no part of the booming senior-living industry that was taking over all the old farms. I wanted no part of dealing with the old people who got left behind by their families, or who were too hard to deal with at home. Some people live so long and get so weak that no one can take care of them, even if they wanted to.

At the home, I watched people drool and pee themselves, and I watched them sit there, day after day, waiting for kids or grandkids to visit, passing their time. I hated it, because most people would hate being part of a last-stop situation, some holding area for people about to transition. Sure, some people are born like angels to that kind of work, and they think nothing of making a senile person laugh, or of cleaning up vomit and shit. They don't even seem to mind that smell of slow death, the one we think of as old-people smell – but me, I was terrified. The only way I survived was to pretend I didn't care. I tried to avoid feeling anything for their shriveled-up bodies, and I got pretty good at it for a while. Then one day I broke, realizing I didn't really care anymore about any of them. I was starting to sound like my father, saying cruel shit under my breath, sometimes saying it audibly.

I didn't have a lot of self-confidence back then – still don't, to be honest – but I had a job that felt like hell on earth to motivate me. I kept cutting hair, and I used the kitchen experience to get myself ready to open my own restaurant. Every day I plotted my escape from that smell, away from a world of adult diapers and pureed food.

I couldn't handle death in the home, because people were alone, spending their last days and months tied to their drips and oxygen, some of them oblivious, others panicking. At least when you're born, God provides someone to greet you, but when you die, there are no guarantees. You can go out lonely and sad no matter how good you were in life. You can pass in your sleep or get a pain so bad it wakes you up just to kill you. Wide awake, clutching your blanket, or out to sea on a drip of morphine – the ones in the home were on the losing end of things, and everyone knew it. I couldn't handle wheeling them around, watching while no relatives came. I couldn't handle the cries and the whining, sometimes for people and things that didn't exist anymore.

It takes strength to go after your dreams, even if they are modest ones. I never dreamed I could be a top cutter, touring the world with my scissors. All I ever thought about was doing something I liked, something that would keep me out of a desk but wouldn't break my back. Cheryl said she had to protect me, that despite my hard exterior, I was, energetically speaking, a pushover. She would tell me how I had to get tougher, how even though I was yelling and screaming it wasn't me being tough. The funny thing about spirit people like Cheryl, the ones who can see things and feel things the rest of us can't, is that they see through all the layers. I always thought I was born to be bitchy, but apparently that's my defense mechanism, not my nature. Maybe, it's a little bit of both, because how can you separate what you are from what you learn when you're young? It's hard.

When my father passed, I knew I'd have to have more strength than ever before in my life. We all have it inside us, but sometimes we do better than others and have to be strong for each other. We had to go see his body before we could have the wake and the services. We went in as a family, and as we got closer to the casket, everyone's jaws dropped. It didn't look like him at all. My mother could barely say a word. I went back in there alone while the rest of them stood in the front room. I went in there and worked with the mortician, who didn't have a picture to work from. I tried to figure out how to make his body look more like the man we all knew. I made a few comments and watched the mortician as he filled my father's lips with cotton. He was trying to make him look more lifelike by bringing up the volume along his gums. It's hard when you didn't know the person in life to recreate their essence. There was no way to make his dead body look exactly like his living one, but there are some things that made all the difference. After he fixed the mouth, I had him comb my father's hair with a better part and the pompadour, and then like magic, there was Jimmy.

They listed the heart attack as the cause of death, but we knew it was all those stings he got the day before that put him over the edge. One thing working in the home taught me is that death isn't cut and dried like we want it to be. The doctors couldn't or wouldn't put it all together, that the stings he got caused a reaction that killed him. I got annoyed none of the medical professionals would talk about all that adrenaline that was released into his system. All the details that were important to us as a family did not make the doctors blink. I was a little obsessed with explaining how hornets are what got him, and those stings are worse than regular bees. I don't know what I thought, complaining about the inaccuracy of it all – probably it was grief. My father was still this powerful figure in my life, and it was like no one outside the family noticed that this huge figure had left the planet. To the hospital, he was just a regular guy passing on, another name or toe tag to get through before lunch. Had they looked at his liver, or looked at his actual life, they might have listed chronic anger as the cause of death, but I didn't really think about that at the time. Anyway, my mother got a nice check from his employers at the public work's office, and so maybe their lack of precision on the death certificate was all for the best.

The mortician did all right with some help. When the rest of the family came back in, they could stand to look at him. He looked like my mother's Jimmy, like our daddy, and that made getting through the rest of it easier. I stared at his face this time like I was staring at a puzzle. I centered myself on recreating his look, and realized that was most of what I knew about my father. I felt like I could breathe a little better without the threat of him, but I felt something else, too. I felt like I was shallow, like I was completely immature. Staring down into the casket, I felt lost, so I focused on the good job I had done with the look of his corpse. This was some kind of transition for all of us.

I learned some useful things that day, and one of them was to always give the funeral home a picture of your loved one. With my mother, with Cheryl, we gave them a photo right away so they knew what they were working with, and each time it made all the difference in the world. The other thing I guess I learned is that life is all about illusions. People can handle anything if you dress it up for them with nice words or a pressed suit, or in this case more cotton and some foundation and rouge.

I also learned that almost everything has two sides, if not more, and that uncovering whatever sits beyond the surface is the only path to peace.

As I dealt with my guilt, I also accepted the fact that I finally had freedom. The man who ruled me was gone, and his life became this story from the past, and I was starting to see through it, like a child seeing through Santa Claus. That day was the first time I started to pull apart the myth of who he was to me, and who he was in the world. I watched the rest of the family come in, my grandparents, my aunts, and I started to see that my father was so much more than my tormentor. I still had the guilt, and I would keep it for a while, but that sense of freedom started to take over. I had no one to fear anymore and that made it easier to breathe and think in a whole new way.

Even though my father managed to get himself a steady paycheck after selling the restaurant, he fell short in life no matter what he did, and it was mostly because he never really did what he wanted. If you had asked me about him when I was young, I would have said he didn't give a fuck and did exactly whatever he wanted to do, but now I see that was only on the surface.

My father died with an office job, but for most of his life he operated a bulldozer and other machinery for the township. Down at the township offices, they didn't like my father as much as they tolerated him. He showed up on time and did his job, and it was hard to fire him. In fact, most days he showed up early, usually a whole hour before his shift, just in case he had a flat tire or something happened along the way. He knew too much about the way things worked, and his technical record was impeccable, so they had to keep him. He eventually managed to become a foreman when I was a teenager, and all things considered, that was amazing. Of course, it didn't come from them liking him as much as from Jimmy holding their paper-pushing fingers to the fire.

My father siphoned gas from the company car pretty much all the time, and that's what brought him around on strange hours to the job site. He came around during an off day, because to keep the siphon from going noticed he had to keep the fuel levels regular. If they went up too much and then down really quickly, someone would notice. Grift is a tangled web, and it has its own discipline.

Through dumb luck and his self-discipline, my father arrived on site and saw all those barrels, and the petty part of him got excited. Jimmy knew the suits were on the take way more than he ever could be, and now he knew enough to start asking some questions and making sideways comments. I doubt he knew much, but he probably knew enough to make them nervous. He wasn't going to blow some whistle and mess up his paycheck, but he was going to use the opportunity to make ends meet a little easier. Of course, I always assumed it was in his nature to play a little dirty, but the older I get, the more I realize I didn't have a clue who Jimmy really was. Sure, I knew some of the stories, and I lived with the man, but I never thought about how conflicted he was. He tried to uphold church and country and family, but he was scratching to survive, so he lived in the real world where all those things were never as clear as they seemed.

My father's first name was Bernhard, but everyone called him "Jimmy," and everyone knew that Jimmy was fast to grow up. During World War II, he wanted out of the house so badly that he ran right into the arms of the U.S. Navy and into the heart of the war. First, he tried at 16 to sign up, and they rejected him because he didn't have his parents' permission. The next year, when he turned 17, he did manage to get in, and even though he was discharged honorably four years later, it was not with honors. When Jimmy Sharpe left the military, he was still an ensign, the lowest rank there is in the Navy. He showed up polished and ready for duty without fail. He was up on time, willing and able, but he kept sliding up and then down in the ranks because of what his father taught him by example. Jimmy Sharpe left a house of punches and mean words, and when the scrappy but scrawny kid showed up in the Navy, he was ready to fight everyone, not just the enemy.

My father swabbed the decks, he worked in the kitchen, and he basically did every shitty job the Navy had. Over and over again, just as he had a chance to go somewhere, my father blew his chances and ended up cleaning the head or peeling potatoes, his mechanical skills and all the other talents he had were going to waste. In some ways, it worked out for him because he learned how to cook there in the military, being stuck in the kitchen a lot. In other ways it didn't work out for him, because nothing could get through to him. No matter what happened, it was because of some other asshole, some SOB with an attitude.

No matter what, he was still just a kid running from that upbringing of closed-fist punches. They make movies about kids like him, but in the movies the kid meets a mentor who breaks through the pain and gets the kid to see life differently. My father was not living in a movie like that where redemption is easy and fast. He was living in a regular story, where no one could get through to him, not through punishment, not even through mountains of potatoes.

In spite of his bad attitude, the officers made him a gunner, at least part-time. He was such a good shot that the officers would call during battles, pulling him out of the kitchen and putting him on deck to shoot. He must have loved that moment when he could tear off the apron and run up the ladders and into the pit behind that fast-launching gun. He must have lived for those moments when he knew his target, and he knew his role. In those moments, the world he grew up in made sense, and Jimmy sprayed those bullets into the air in a way that would have made his old man proud. That wasn't killing, it was protecting his family and his country, and so Ensign Sharpe, for once in his life, had free reign to be himself, to aim, shoot and do it again. Who knows what he was thinking when he did it, but I'm sure he wasn't feeling any pity.

Jimmy grabbed hold of that loud, fast, powerful machine, and in the heat of the battle my father was living out what he lived in his mind every day. The world was always on fire for my father. As a kid, he lived scared of not eating, and scared of his father beating the hell out of him. He lived scared of God, and when he gunned like that, I bet he felt like he was taking part in the natural order of a world run by an ultimate Father, one who lived to throw you in a fiery pit for the smallest screw-up. When my father was gunning, the world on the outside matched the world he knew on the inside.

The battles didn't last, though, and where the other soldiers wanted to turn down the pressure after blasting at the enemy, my father just couldn't. One day in the kitchen, some guy challenged my father to put out a finger on the work table. I have no idea what led up to this event, but I'm pretty sure it was all ego games. My father took the challenge, pulled out his left hand and put it down. I don't know who the guy was, but in the end, he was pretty stupid in my book. Baiting my father was like yanking the chain of a junkyard dog. The guy looked at my father's hand, lifted his cleaver, and slammed it flat side down, splitting the finger.

Months went by, and Ensign Sharpe did not and could not forget about his finger, which still showed the split. Sure enough, the day came when my father told the same guy to put his finger on the table. I don't know if he bullied the guy or blackmailed him or what was said, but somehow the guy put that finger down. My father pulled back the cleaver and slammed it, with the blade straight down. In one fast and accurate cut, my father sealed his fate in the Navy. He chopped with the precision that made him a damn fine gunner, and he took that other soldier's finger off at the first knuckle. I don't think my father flinched, and I doubt he backed down when he stood in front of the commanding officer to explain himself. He grew up too rough for young Jimmy to do anything but take his lumps. He would rather die a potato peeler than give that other guy an inch, and there was no smart way to justify that lapse in self-control, so he didn't even try.

I can still remember my father hollering, with his neck tight, the fucking veins in his neck bulging "I never hit you with a closed fist!" At the time when he said that, I was too young and too hot-tempered to understand what that meant to my father, and I was 17 going on 18, and I was still scared of being hit even though I regularly mouthed off. I could see that glare coming up in his eye, and I knew we were pushing on what I called nuclear-level fallout. You had to watch out for him, because the old man did not forget, and it was proven he was not one for forgiving.

I didn't know how he felt growing up and didn't really have time to think about it because every day together felt like I was in my own personal war zone. All I really knew was that the man had a mangled finger, and I could get a close-up view of it as his hand came sailing at me, open-palmed. Jimmy came out of the military believing in doing things the right way, the respectable way, but not necessarily the nice way. And his get-out-of-jail-free card was that this, this was life. Life was not pretty, according to Jimmy.

After Jimmy was out of the military with his honorable discharge, he went back to normal life. One night when he was fresh from the war and not yet living on his own, he decided to go out bowling with his parents. They were barely settled in their lane when Grandpa started being rough on Grandma. He was starting to push her around over something stupid, and my father the veteran stood up to the bully. My grandfather went on the attack and took a swing at his disrespectful son, close-fisted of course, in the bowling alley. My father, now a man of the world, decided not to take it anymore, and he hit Grandpa back. Ensign Sharpe returned fire with his own closed fist, and all hell broke loose. The hit landed hard, and there was hollering and curses, and then it was over in a flash. Then Ensign Sharpe took his mother and said, "Let's go." He left his father at the alley with people gawking at him.

My father wasn't one for drawn-out speeches or showering you with kind words, but his father was worse. My Grandpa was cold, and he didn't spare his wife or his kids from a rage that seemingly had no end. He never went after us grandkids, but you could feel not to push him. There are lots of things you can sense as a child that you can't put into words, and Grandpa's way of looking at you told you to watch your step. That was probably why when Grandma asked you to do things, she expected them done. It was like a deal you made with her, and you knew part of the deal was she put distance between you and Grandpa. She told us stories, she stuffed us with food and spoiled us with special things she made, but Grandma Sharpe did not tolerate self-pity or disobedience. She hated it if you cried. In fact, tears were the one thing I remember making her angry.

I never once thought that Grandma was tough because she had to be. I never thought about things that way, but sometimes I know that I felt it. My brother and I, we must have been about 5 years old, and our parents had somewhere to go. Our sister was off being older, and we were there at our grandparents' house. We didn't go there very often, and I don't remember being there alone before that day.

Grandma looked at me hard as I whined over being left, and she said, "What are you crying for?", and the question felt very intense. In hindsight, I realize that in that moment, I was seeing with my father's eyes. I was seeing some kind of invisible lines that stretched across all our lives. I was feeling the web of time and space, feeling the sticky strength of family ties, the ones that don't get advertised.

That day, nothing Grandma did could make us, especially me, relax. For all I know, we were feeling the echoes of old beatings or the ricochet of angry words still bouncing across the room like phantom bullets. Maybe I caught a glimpse of Grandpa's stare and the thin line stretching between his bad attitude and Grandma's impatience with me. His fist became somehow obvious to me as part of the scene. I caught a glimpse of the thin, invisible line that separated who our grandfather was to us and who he was to his children and wife, and I started to feel it pull tighter. After a time, I calmed down enough to give back into Grandma's direction to just relax.

Grandma made the best of her situation and put her energy into other things. She worked at her own survival quietly. We just thought of her as crafty, making things all the time. Now I think of her as an artist, pouring all her life's dreams and probably all of those uncried tears into her projects. I can see her now, trying to make the perfect pastel flower out of clay, putting all she had into it. I can see her perfecting the flower, doing it over and over like a type of prayer. Grandma made bowls. Grandma made plates. She made all these pleasant dishes decorated in the happiest colors and the most delicate flowers. All those happy, delicate things she made had to pass through the fire of her kiln. I can imagine her staring at the clay, then into the fire, getting satisfaction from the process of making something seemingly delicate into something durable.

After watching her children wake up to broken toys at Christmas, after all the other tragedies that never got named or noticed, Grandma would go to work with her pottery. She molded life out of clay, day after day, year after year. The kiln was a part of Grandma, and it even went with her to Miami Beach when she and Grandpa retired. Eventually they sold it, because Parkinson's got a hold of Grandma, and her plates became deformed. They weren't pretty or useful in that condition, and Grandma had no use for that kiln once all it could do was collect dust.

Grandpa stayed harsh until the day he died, and when he passed everybody showed respect, but nobody shed a tear. When they lowered him down, Grandma looked like a prize fighter who had stayed in the ring and won by decision. She stood and prayed, she bowed her head and asked God to receive her dead husband's soul, but she did every bit of it with completely dry eyes. The reprieve of her husband's death came late for Grandma, and it came after her only son, Jimmy, was gone from this world. To me, my father was a persecutor, a raging and angry man; to her he was her baby boy, a forever ray of hope in her world. She cried for her son like I never heard her cry before or again. It was as if she poured forth every tear she'd held back. That day, and only that one, I can imagine Grandma transformed by her sorrow.

Gone is the hard shell of survival, and all that remains is this majestic, soft, woman inside. I guess she would be this amazing crone Queen of Cups, but I don't know if crones and queens co-exist. I never saw cards like that, where the powerful woman was older than middle age. Anyway, I can see it now if I think back to that day. I can paint my old memory of her with something more than the confusion I had at 20.

I can use that knowledge to admit that my father did all right in many ways, without glossing over the dark shit he did. I mean, he never got rough with my mother. I can note, in hindsight, that there was some improvement from one generation to the next, but that doesn't fix it all. Jimmy died throwing tantrums and blaming everyone else for his rage. He never walked away from the family, but he never walked away from the rage, so his progress was kind of a wash. My father was an example of how family can be a double-edged sword, and it's generally where we get hung up on ourselves. Jimmy was proof that family is where you learn to love, and it is where you learn to associate love with pain. I am trying very hard to not follow that track.

My father inherited a bunch of bad habits and expectations of what makes a boy into a man, and the more I broke those expectations without even trying, the more furious he got at me. He never questioned authority publicly, never really stood up to the things he didn't like, so it made him extra-sensitive to all the things I did wrong. I mean, he hated the fact that I always had to make the question known. My father never managed to walk away from anything he didn't like. He never shouted a word against the system. He muttered under his breath with this cynical attitude that sucked the life out of every joy. He lived in that constant fear he had since childhood. Even when my father made you laugh, it was cynical and cold, like the humor you would find in a prison. I think there's a lot of truth to that kind of laugh, even if you don't want to admit it.

Time goes on, and you learn to forget the fear and the anguish. You forget what it was like to cling to the edges of the bathtub, hiding while crying that everything you did was wrong. Eventually you laugh about even some of the horrible moments, because you can't believe you survived it. Part of moving on is forgiving, and the other part is about letting go of how it felt to cry tears in a family where crying was seen as the ultimate weakness. I think about these things from time to time, mostly after talking to my sister and sharing a good laugh, because she and I don't need to bury things. Instead of forgetting the tears I had to hide, now I can think about how good the cold water felt on my face. You can't change how you grew up, but you can be proud of surviving.

As far as burying things went, that's what my father did for a living for most of his life. When it snowed, he worked the plows, clearing the roads and the storm drains for the cars, making sure it was meticulously free of snow and ice. When the weather was decent, he moved and buried trash into the dump with the same meticulous attention. He drove that dozer all day, digging massive holes that then became slowly filled-in layers, until they became huge mountains. Then he drove to another spot and repeated the whole process.

He used to narrow his eyes sometimes and say that the dump held "a multitude of sins," while he looked into the distance. I thought it was dead bodies he was talking about, like something out of a movie. Later on, I realized I was kinda right, except the bodies that were piling up weren't there in the dump. The sins my father talked about came in the shape of industrial barrels, delivered at odd times by haulers that traveled in unmarked rigs. Those barrel-shape sins did get into the ground and the water, and eventually people got sick from them, but the bodies ended up in the cemetery, and the causes of death got written down as different types of cancer. The sins were buried in a way that was quieter than what I expected.

Jimmy Sharpe hadn't gone to college or gotten very far in the military, but it didn't mean he wasn't smart. He was always on the frontline, looking for a way to improve his situation, and he had his eyes and ears peeled for little ways to work the system and its secrets. He didn't think he could beat the system, so he would never risk his job, but he would make those bosses know he could see through them. There were other people in the world who made a living from making sure industrial waste went where it should, so he didn't seem to worry about being a whistleblower.

His only job was to do what they told him: move piles and maintain his equipment by making daily repairs, basically staying out of the bosses' way. He filed their sins in his memory and kept his mouth mostly shut just like he was taught. If my father was horrified by what he saw at work, he never let on about it. He muttered under his breath and showed up on time for the job he never wanted, to learn things he didn't want to know.

My father focused on making sure we kids did as we were told, because he did more or less as he was told. He gave up on his dreams because of what people told him he should do. He may have seduced my mother with cream puffs, but that was no way to win a pension, according to her father. A restaurant would keep him too busy and away from the family on holidays and weekends. It was no life at all, said the future in-laws. Maybe he could have respectfully declined the suggestion, but in my father's world, despite all that swagger, that wasn't an actual possibility. Once someone put it in his head that what he was doing wasn't stable, I imagine he just panicked. I doubt you could see it on that hard face of his, but nothing else makes much sense.

In his world you either gave in completely, or you put up a fight; there was no middle ground. He gave up cooking because his father-in-law thought it was more stable to have an employer, and that might have been the fatal choice of my father's entire life, the very thing he shouldn't have done. No one can tell now, but it makes me think about the things we do to minimize life's surprises and harsh realities. The check my mother got from my father's passing set her up financially for the rest of her life. Too bad all mom wanted was to have her man back, and all the money did was make it easier for her to get mired in the sadness of losing him. That was her Jimmy, her mate, and no matter what she thought of him when he sneered or when he smelled like a scotch bottle, a part of her was still fully wrapped up in him and the dreams they had when they started out together. As far as my parents go, I really do believe they loved each other.

My mother had her grief, and I had my own sadness. For me, the guilt of wishing to be free of my father lived on, like a ghost haunting me. All his sayings, all the good and the bad that he did – it rattled around in the back of my head the way the statue of Holy Death rattled around in the back of my Cadillac for a bunch of these months after Cheryl's death. I got freedom when my father died, but it came at a price. Everything in life has a price, and only some of it is paid for in money. A lot of the cost is paid in letting go of the past and moving on. If you can truly forgive, that's the big prize, because then you don't feel hostile inside.

I went by our old house not too long ago, and it was peaceful. The current owners had moved out, and no one had bid at the asking price the bank wanted. There was no furniture, nothing inside, and the bright sun made it look happier than I remembered it. I liked seeing sunlight fill the corners of the breezeway where my mother passed, and the dining room I dreaded. The house was quiet and calm in this way that made the screaming matches feel like this dream from another life. A golden light was shining in the spot where Mom told us she was dying and later passed from cancer . A few feet away, the place where I was interrogated and called names had that same glow, like angels could be sitting there. I really remembered all the good times in that room. The dinners faded away, and they were left with laughs from when my father shot a skunk and the smell got inside the house. We all complained, and, looking back, it was hilarious.

I don't think our father-son story would have gotten much better if my father had lived to a ripe old age, because I had long forgotten. I think we would have dug in our heels and said even more mean things to each other. I think at one point I would have realized I had grown strong, and he was older and weaker, and it would have gotten to be just like it was in the bowling alley years ago. The story would have been a little different, but the outcome would have been mostly the same, with me pulling my arm back to take a good shot at him. It could have played out in the house or somewhere else, but I think that day of reckoning would have come, and the cycle of brute force between father and son would have continued.

When I called the hospital and realized my father was dead, I went numb. When I heard my grandmother sobbing for her only son, I felt like I had to be the worst person in the world for all the things I had thought about him. I felt weak and shitty for wishing my father would stop being mean and spiteful, not really caring how that happened. To me he was a merciless judge and jury; to Grandma, he was her sweet boy. When I visited the house, it all came back to me, like I was stepping through time, but I wasn't that young son anymore. I was looking back at it through double-glazed windows, almost like I was on a tour. I remembered the television and the dishes, and as I went to answer a text, I remembered the phone. Back then, phones had cords and heavy handles, and when you put them back on the cradle, you could hear a thud, like the sound of a gavel.

My father lost his life on the boat he loved, on a perfect day. He could have done worse. He could have been at work that day, surrounded by trash piles. The day I got the news that my father passed; I didn't understand that he was actually pretty lucky. Death struck him like lightning strikes a rod in a storm. It was the kind of death he had hoped for. He really did say, "I want to die on my boat," and he didn't even fish. He probably didn't expect to go so soon, but he got what he asked for. I guess God had a soft spot for my father, after all.

He was at Barnegat Inlet, on the 32-foot Chris-Craft, his wooden boat. It was polished and ready for the water. I have to admit it looked amazing. He probably smiled that day when he went out and made some half-jokes about us not doing the worst job with the hull. He might have shown something bordering on pride that day. Despite the stings from the day before, he woke up ready to enjoy himself.

He wouldn't take that prized possession out of Manasquan, or even Point Pleasant inlet; those would be a mess, with traffic and current. The bay was a smooth ride on most days, and that boat only got the best. The Chris-Craft was a beauty to my father, but to me it was a nightmare, a chore machine. Every year my brother and I got under all 32 feet, scraping off barnacles and slime, while my father pointed out all the flaws in our work.

Every year when this monster boat was pulled into the driveway, my father got us under the hull as soon as the days were warm enough to caulk, putty and paint. We had to work with these little hammers and chisels, to pull out the cotton that goes in between the wood slats, and then we put fresh materials back in. When it came to that boat, we did things the traditional way, and that meant my brother and I had work for weeks.

I hated working on that boat. I resented it from when we started to the very finish. The only thing I liked about it was when we went out to see the fireworks for the Fourth of July and the one or two times a summer, we could convince our mother to come out crabbing with us. When our mother came with us, we knew the bait wasn't going to be mixed up with our food in the same cooler. That means three or four good trips on it, in exchange for days and days of work and critiques.

He wouldn't let either of us twins drive that boat, no matter how much work we put into it – at least, not at first. My father was a stickler for earning your way and doing it by competition. He said my brother would crash it, and that I would turn it into – well, I won't repeat him exactly, but let's just say he said I would probably use it to fuck. I don't know if either of us knew exactly what was up with me at that point, but maybe he knew I was going to have a huge sexual appetite. Maybe he had that same high drive, and he saw it in me as well. I wanted to cruise the bay. He wanted to crawl on it.

fter years of work, he eventually did let us get behind the wheel, with him in the boat, of course. I don't know; I wanted to get to the ocean as fast as I could, and he wanted that scenic route still. I really don't know why he didn't throw me overboard. I would get on top of the command bridge, and I would start to kick the engine just a little faster and faster, until I got the weight down to a tight stream. My father liked to leave behind a wide full, deep wake, the water ploughing away from the bow. I wanted the hull to cut the water high, with the bow on top of the water, at almost a glide. For whatever reason, I wouldn't drive his way, so my father would have to give me that look, and I would kick it back down. We went like that the entire time, with me kicking it up and him making me kick it back down. It must have been like training a horse, a stubborn one, but one that he got. He kept me onboard because I was his son, and because no one else would go fishing with him because he went all day and never got nothing.

When Time Stands Still

The day my father passed was the first day I felt the presence of God as an adult. Before my loss, my relief and my guilt, I felt this deep power come out of nowhere. It didn't have a face or make any sound, but it filled the room, the halls, and the entire house.

It wasn't shock, because I felt that, too, and that was different, number, and it came with the emotions. This thing didn't feel like it was coming from inside me; in fact, I felt like a witness. It was something all around me, something I was in, if that makes any sense.

All the thoughts in my head stopped, and I was completely, 100 percent, in the moment. I didn't have worries. I didn't have a bunch of ideas. All I had was this presence so powerful that it felt like time stopped, like time didn't exist at all.

I didn't even know how to begin to describe it to anyone. In a way, I tried to pretend it didn't happen, because there didn't seem to be any point. Maybe God only showed up to take you away, or maybe he was there all the time and we were just too busy to notice, but it didn't bother me much. I shoved it out of my mind with work and saving money for my house and for cars. There was no point in talking about it, until of course, I realized there was no escaping it. As a kid in church, God was this judge and jury, an angry old man, and even though I knew better than that, it still seemed like God was too important and faraway to show up in my world. It took a few more times of feeling that presence to understand I was being stupid or stubborn or both.

"Inflammatory breast cancer," Cheryl said to me. OK, breast cancer I thought; people survive that all the time now. "Inflammatory breast cancer," she said again, and then she started explaining, it's not like the regular kind. This breast cancer was rare and aggressive as fuck. It blocked her lymph nodes and sickened her whole immune system, not just her breasts. They gave her three months, and that was it. "I'll show them." she said. Her treatment options started as double mastectomy and chemotherapy. Cheryl was staring down a loaded gun, and she knew it, and I was being naive. She had those big boobs her whole life, and she knew that after all the comments and catcalls she endured because of them, all the guys who couldn't get past them, those things were finally going to kill her.

Because of her lupus, the surgery alone could kill her. The chemo wasn't much of a choice, either. Single, with no real money, no kids, a lot of people would have understood if she just gave up on life, but Cheryl dug in. That's why the juice was so important; it was the reason for the enemas and all the organic labels. She saw no chemo or surgery option for herself, and every day she stayed alive it was like she was proving how strong one person could be. If she could turn it around, she got to live, but more than that, it would help her give others hope. She knew there would be extra suffering and pain the longer she lived, but Cheryl knew that if she could manage to stay alive, she could teach others how to do it. She was a warrior like that.

Three months passed, and when Cheryl was still alive, we had her favorite cannoli cake to celebrate. It was a small win, and we knew it, but it didn't matter. That cannoli cake was her hands-down favorite.. She'd see a box tied with that string from the bakery around the corner, and her eyes would light up. I would tell her how the landlord and his family sent their best, and how everyone said they were praying for her. She would say thank you and other nice things while she focused on seeing what goodies were in there. Cheryl was German with some Scandinavian blood, and some Native American, too, but her stomach belonged to the Italians. She would lie and tell you she had some Italian in her, but she didn't. I thought it was funny when her mother told me the truth. I guess she just really liked their food.

One thing I can say, if you love Italian food and you can't be born in Italy, then you might as well be born in Jersey.

In the bakery they had the typical statues and prayer cards, things that Cheryl knew, having grown up Catholic. I didn't grow up with any of that, but I never minded it. Some people collect Star Wars figures and talk about the light and the dark forces; some people line up Padre Pio and St. Anthony and talk about the same shit. I don't mind it, because it gives people hope and helps them feel like they can make sense of the world. Cheryl said it was all real, and that the best saints went all the way back to Africa and voodoo religions and that it didn't matter so much what you called them as it did that you learned respect. Now that I think about it, she really did sound Italian. Anyway, we had lots of deep conversations about all of this stuff, and Cheryl did both her Catholic and not-so-Catholic praying and meditating as she was doing this battle with death. It's a good thing we didn't get hung up on total success, because just when it looked like she had sent the cancer backward, it came back with a vengeance.

If my father died from those stings that gave him the cardiac arrest, then Cheryl died from a cancer that looked like she had deadly spiders taking over her breast tissue, and by the end the spiders were everywhere. As her situation went from a little bit better to way worse in a hurry, part of my visits included dressing the wounds that circled her breasts. The tissue got dark, and masses took shape. I wanted to cut one of those tumors out, but it had this purple and white look to it – I mean, it was nasty. If I looked closely, some of the spots got so dark they were almost black. "Like spiders' legs," she would say. She would point to herself like she was pointing to a map. When it started taking her over, she could literally track the lines running from under her armpits to her nipples. Enemas and orange buttholes were funny when we had hope, but this was like tracking a hurricane, or, in Cheryl's mind, an invasion of tangled-up spiders. No matter how it looked, the result was not good.

Cheryl would look over the pastries, because of course there were extras, so she could enjoy having a choice, maybe pick out the prettiest slice or have the traditional cannoli or one of the ones dipped in chocolate. Sometimes we'd pig out and eat them all, but lots of times the pastries were too good and too rich for us to eat them all, and she would have one for the next day. She would be dressed like normal, and we would laugh and complain about life. The dog would be needy, and I would roll my eyes, and she laughed even more.

As my hands moved around to swab against infection, sometimes I would catch the beat of her heart. It was covered by these fine lines of invaded tissue, but I could sense underneath she was still pretty strong. A little later on, when I had to apply a lot of pressure to stop the bleeding, I would feel her heart even more. I realized while I was pressing up against this skin that was getting thicker and stranger, that this was real, and she was not going to make it. It is one thing to know someone is sick, It's another thing to see parts of them slowly dissolve.

Cheryl was on her way out, but barring any accidents, I was still here and healthy. I had love potions to cast and bitches to compete with. I had things to distract me, and telling her about all my drama distracted her, too. She pulled cards to help me with my boyfriends, my friends and my obsessions. She kept tabs on everything and everyone I loved, including Napoleon, who was always by my side, and my first godchild, the only other person I would visit every week. When that baby girl came shooting out of her mother, I was in the delivery room. The doctor was saying, "Push," and her mother, who is always in shape, did. It was like nothing I had ever seen before; even the doctor looked surprised at how fast she got that baby down the birth canal. Things got really confused, and I ended up cutting the umbilical cord. I know it sounds crazy, but her birth is a book all on its own. All I know is that day in that room, time stood still.

We celebrated every week that Cheryl lived, and we flipped cards like crazy while eating our cakes. You will participate in life-changing decisions; that's what the cards said around the time Cheryl took a turn for the worse. When you flip a lot, you can see some of the same cards for a while. They become like familiar faces. It can be frustrating, like you are stuck in a loop, but it can be worse when the cards all of a sudden change. It's like walking into a room full of strangers, which can be intense. They gave Cheryl three months, but she lived 13 more, right up to the number on the Death card. For a long time, the cards saw the same stories, then Cheryl started to panic. She would point to a spread, and she would say, "Tom, I don't see a future."

Cheryl was born a Catholic, and she stayed one, sort of like the Italians, sometimes more like the Mexicans. Besides the Holy Death, which she gave tequila and smokes, Cheryl's favorite altar was built around her St. Barbara. She loved everything about this pagan rich girl who became a Christian saint all because she rejected her father's pick for her husband. He put her in isolation for following Jesus, for refusing the marriage deal he had made and for just pushing his buttons. He got the authorities involved at some point, too, because his daughter kept praying and performing miracles, and he couldn't do anything about it. He had her tortured, he locked her away, but Barbara just kept pushing his buttons by promising her love and her future to this Jesus.

St. Barbara pissed off her father, this rich Greek pagan named Dioscorus, by doing what she pleased. Barbara was supposedly very beautiful, and after her mother's death when she was still a child, her father had dedicated his life to her. When she became a Christian, she ruined everything for her father; all his plans. So, he set her up in this isolated tower, and while he was away doing business, she decided to have three windows put in around her bathroom. This isn't a tiny place, of course – she was a real princess – so she told the workmen to put in three windows above the luxurious prison she was meant to spend her time in.

The windows were meant to mark the holy trinity, and even though they didn't have any pictures on them, Dioscorus knew what they meant. He flew into a self-righteous rage and tried to kill his beloved Barbara. He followed her into the woods; he brought her to a judge. They tried to burn her, but the flames went out. They tried to torture, kill and shame her, but mostly St. Barbara came out smelling like a rose, and this made her father even crazier. Finally, Dioscorus managed to behead his daughter. The story ended with lightning coming out of nowhere and striking him dead pretty much as soon as he did it.

Cheryl was walking a tightrope between knowing she didn't have much time and hoping for the best. She did that thing dying people do; she started giving away her possessions. She gave me the St. Barbara statue because, she said, I "wasn't going to just stick her in a corner and forget about her." I actually did end up putting her in a corner, but it's right by the front door, and I don't forget about her. I keep her dusted, and she has water in her cup as an offering. It doesn't take much effort, honestly, and being an anal, OCD cleaner, it's just another thing to add to my to-do list. That thing is big, though, around the size of a decent lawn ornament. "I got her when I had money," Cheryl said, as she heaved her my way.

To me, St. Barbara is kind of a badass. She is a saint for children who rebel against their parents to be who they want to be. She is the patron saint of wind and storms, and of course she will protect you against lightning. She's still honored with shrines in mines and by artillery units all over the world. Anywhere they use gunpowder, you'll probably find a St. Barbara hidden somewhere by someone. It doesn't surprise me that Cheryl loved her, because she was that same kind of badass woman in her heart. Like I said, this kind of stuff was not something I grew up with, but seeing as how Barbara managed to stick up for herself against her father, I like her.

We stopped the constant juicing maybe a week before the hospital. Instead of three times a day, it was down to just once. She stopped the enemas and the detox, and my trips to the health-food store got faster, and the bags got lighter. Cancer had thickened her skin and taken over her insides; it was even popping out from under her arms. I did not turn away the whole time. I was working out some stuff leftover from how I treated my mother, how I tried to run from her bout with cancer, I know that, but sticking by Cheryl's side wasn't just about dealing with that guilt. On the way to losing my mother I got a lot stronger, even if at first I didn't want to face it, even if I had to have my sister and brother help me watch her toward the very end. Maybe I ran from my mother at first, but when I did step up to the plate, I learned how to face death, and that is something nobody could take away from me.

People talk about reincarnation. Some people think it's stupid, but even if you believe in heaven, then you believe in a soul that goes somewhere. It doesn't matter how many years or lifetimes it takes; you can get to heaven. My idea is that when you get those wings, you never have to come back here again, and that's the real prize. Years ago, I went with another longtime friend to the type of spiritual healer you can afford only ever so often. I got lost on the way, somewhere up north, off the Turnpike. I had to call my girl, and she helped me find my way. But first she told me to call the healer and let her know I would be late. Then it was back to the directions, to get me through to Hackensack.

"Go over Plank Road."

"OK."

"Then go one, two, three streets, and make a right at the fourth one."

"OK."

"I don't know the name of the third street."

"I'm crossing it now."

"What's the name?"

"OMG. There's no sign."

"That's why I don't know the name!"

We burst out laughing, and I pulled into the driveway only ten minutes late. The healer greeted me, and I apologized. "No problem," she said. "Your father was here already. He's gone now." I looked at her, not sure what to ask. Then she added, "He stormed out," and after a few more minutes, "He's a feisty spirit." At that moment, I knew my father had been there.

When you get insecure or worried, you get out of alignment, and just like a chiropractor or an acupuncturist can realign some part of you, so can a spiritual healer. She billed herself as a "faith healer," and I was feeling better already. Going to see someone like that helps to shut up the "what if?" crap that can build up. I spent a good amount of money asking her questions about my love life. I knew how to get sex, but I was clueless on the soulmate part.

She would say things that sounded very simple, and it felt reassuring. The fact that she had me talk to my father, and he said he was going to help me with things, especially the restaurant, was freaky, but it was helpful.

Cheryl stopped seeing a future, and she started working on all sorts of preparations for the end of this life. She wanted to move in with me, but I couldn't do it. She would go to live with her sister, because I just couldn't handle thinking she would pass in my house. I would want to move if that happened. As things turned out, though, it became obvious she wasn't going to get out of that little rental on time. She was getting weaker in spurts. One day she looked OK, and the next she wouldn't feel strong enough to pick up the phone. On those days when she didn't want to see anyone, the best she could do was give her Santissima, the one that rattled around in my car for months, her offerings. Cheryl was lucky in a way because she had time to make peace with death.

We got the Santisima statue right after Cheryl got diagnosed. If she beat the odds or didn't, Santiima was still good to have on our side. We got in the car and drove to Long Branch, a town a little north of here. It's one of those places with a beach, but it also has a college and parts that feel like a city. Long Branch has rich parts by the water, over by where families like the Vanderbilts used to go to church a hundred years ago, and it has poor and regular parts over by the train station. This shop is way closer to the train station, and if I can, I like to park close to the front, so I can keep an eye on the car. You have to go to different types of shops for different types of things, so to get Santisima Muerte, you have to go to a botanica.

A botanica is a specific kind of store that's not for any one religion but for all sorts of religions, most of them related to Christianity, almost all of them from the South, from places where slaves and natives had to hide their old religions from conquerors. Botanicas are these places where you can buy a candle with a traditional angel like St. Michael or one for the Yemaya, an African goddess of the sea. When you walk inside your typical botanica, you see everything from feathers to crystals and glitter. You find all the stuff you need for all the ancient prayers that go back thousands of years. They can be a little spooky, but if your intentions are good, you don't have to worry. Even the stuff that looks scary as hell can be used in the right way to protect people you love or to call in some healing from God.

Cheryl, as you might have guessed, loved these types of places because she was into old-time magic done by real people who had been carrying that stuff from generation to generation. She could stay there for hours if you let her, looking at all the candles, oils and powders. She would stay just to shoot the shit, to talk about spells or hear about someone getting hit by an evil eye from a mother-in-law. It was in that kind of shop, not far from a thrift store and a bunch of churches, where we found the little skeleton lady, standing about 6 inches tall, dressed in a white veil with tiny little silver sequins running down the trim. There was a mirror in the shape of a triangle glued to her heart, and she had what looked like a fake bill rolled up and attached to her side. She had a silk rose across her chest, and at her feet was a coin, and next to that was some colorful beads. I was totally freaked out by the thing at first. "Tom, if you look at her long enough, you'll see she's beautiful." I laughed at Cheryl that day, but the truth is now I find myself looking over at Santisima sometimes thinking the exact same thing.

The bakery is still on the same corner where it has been for maybe twenty years. My landlords are still making their pastries with the ovens they ship in from Italy. Their kids are pushing the business forward, so the cannoli cream keeps flowing while the saints stand guard and the grandkids are born. They speak that blend of English and Italian that makes you feel like you understand even if you don't. It's the kind of place that uses sugar and eggs to make delicious things without calorie counts.

I care that Cheryl isn't here to eat cannoli and read my cards or make a fuss over Napoleon. I care that when I go to Long Branch, I don't have Cheryl to remind me about the haunted house pier that burned down under suspicious circumstances or the fact that Bruce Springsteen was born there. I hear he's a nice guy, but I never liked his music and as a piece of ass he was always too serious. Bruce was for straight guys and for rockers like Cheryl, not for gay boys like me, but I respected him, and I would play him for her. When I look around Long Branch these days, I hear way more hip-hop and salsa than I hear Springsteen, and that's cool, but I also hear Bruce with Cheryl singing along. Those were good times, and no matter how much I tried to enjoy them, I knew I couldn't; it's just part of being human. For Cheryl, time stood still in those moments in a way that I knew she felt, and she brought me into them. Her horizon was closing, her cards were dark, and she was getting ready for her moment of lightning.

Garden State Lifetime

When you miss someone, you think you would give a million dollars to hear from them again. I guess that's why a lot of people want to hear from their loved ones who have passed; it's like getting a piece of ourselves back. Going up to Dawn in Hackensack, I wanted to get more pieces of myself back, more backstory on whether my lives had a common thread to them. If we were playing out stories that spanned over lifetimes, then I figured I would go back to learn to see if I recognized anyone. Dawn said we could do a past-life regression as long as I did not mind being hypnotized. I had no idea if I would let her do it to me. I knew I might resist giving someone full access to my mind.

I was told I had to clear my head of all thoughts, and I almost told her to stop. I didn't think I could focus. I had to listen to her voice and nothing else. I had to respond to the questions and completely let go. Next thing I knew, I was a woman in Paris, wearing a grey wool suit. I couldn't see my face, but my hair was thick reddish-brown. I walked around my past life like it was a video game. Answering questions during the session was easy.

I was kind of amazed at how good I felt in that life, where I was an artist, a painter of some kind. I had a small apartment, and my front door was red, not gray or blue like most of the others in my building. It was great to see how creative I was. It seems I had a quiet but happy life, and my canvases were big and bright. Sunlight came through the glass doors of the balcony, making my little studio into this palace, and I worked in between coffee and cigarettes and long loaves of bread that I ate with olives or cheese. When I was looking out at this life, I felt this kind of contentment, something close to how I feel now when I look out at the pond or when I see the wisteria vines perfectly intertwined and blooming above the front porch.

I was surprised that I had lived in Paris. I don't know what I expected, but it wasn't that. In this life, as Tom Sharpe, I haven't taken that many long vacations or traveled all that much because of the kind of work I do, and maybe because I always heard my faer's voice in the back of my head saying I couldn't afford it.

"As you sow, so shall you reap." My father quoted that from the Bible all the time, and it meant everything from "Be a good person" to "Don't be lazy" to "You'd better save for a rainy day." It could even mean "Don't you have work today, smartass?" That line was everything to my father, and it tormented me as a kid and continued to do a number on me as an adult. I went on some trips for long weekends, but I didn't ever go try and learn another language. I could do that in Jersey, just speaking to the guys in the kitchen. Who was I to waste money traveling the world?

Later, after the past-life regression session was over and I was back down south where I know the roads, I thought about Paris. I thought about this life and how small it suddenly seemed, like maybe I should I renew my passport. Most of the time that felt kind of comfortable, like a good pair of shoes or my best-fitting jeans, but after that session it felt like I had been doing the same things, the same way, for way too long. If you want one cycle to die, you have to be willing to let a new one grow, and that past-life regression had given me a new angle on things. If I had been that woman in that gray wool suit, who was I now in my jeans and my -shirt?

I felt like I should travel more and get out of this rut. I thought about the times I did travel. I went to Germany once, before they took down the Berlin Wall, back when I was working at the home. I remembered how I didn't stay there long – two weeks – because I had to get back to work. I hated that job, and I really liked the guy I traveled with, a cutie named Scott. He worked at the home, too. I was out of the closet to my friends back then but not to the public. People would ask me just so they could gossip about me being gay. Scott was not gay, and that was fine; we traveled together like brothers. I wasn't going to hit on him even though his body was incredible. Scott was a good friend, and we went to Germany to see his father. Because of him, I got to pass through East Germany and West Germany, and I got to look up at Checkpoint Charlie in his tower with a gun pointing down.

I always felt like I had to get back, like my world was going to fall apart if I was gone for too long, and the older I got, the more intense that feeling was. Years after the Germany trip, I went to Italy for a friend's wedding, and all I booked myself for was a long weekend. I went clear across the Atlantic Ocean and was back in less time than most people take to go to Disney World. I had a business partner by then, and a mortgage. I had more responsibility, and I had people screaming at me through the phone because we were never making enough money or because one of the girls was stealing. The moment the plane doors closed, I felt this incredible calm, and I realized I should have at least taken a week.

I remember how I wanted to see some sights, and I thought I could fit in an afternoon trip to Pompeii while I was at it, because I was in the south in this tiny village, Monte San Giacamo. I really wanted to go to Pompeii, but I missed the bus, so I ended walking around town. Most of the time I was there, I was surrounded by my friend and his family. He had an aunt who found out how I liked my coffee, and every morning she had it ready by the time I got downstairs. Anyway, I broke out of there for a little me time, wondering why I didn't book the trip for longer. Now that I had missed the bus on my one day free from wedding activities, I felt kind of stupid for not staying longer. I tried not to worry about it, told myself three days was plenty, and I tried to look around at the buildings, to see what was hidden in the architecture. No one was around the little alley where I was walking, except for this old guy.

"Buon Giorno," said the man. I nodded and said, "Hello." No point in butchering their language.

"Good morning."

"Where are you from?"

"America."

"Where?"

"Jersey."

"Do you have a gun?"

"No, I don't have a gun."

"I thought everyone in Jersey had a gun."

"Well, that's because of the Mafia you sent over."

He nodded.

We understood each other.

He asked me about the book I was reading.

I said, "The pope says it's a book of the devil."

"Yeah. He would say that. Do you like it?"

"Yeah."

"Maybe I'll read it, then."

And he walked away.

I was holding "The Da Vinci Code" by Dan Brown. That was the first book I ever read cover to cover. I could not put it down. The book was so much about history, which I love, and it was about the secrets and lies that people tell to keep power. Since I was a kid, people used the Bible to hold things over my head. Reading the book was fun, it was fast, and the story was perfect. It mixed history with this twist I never imagined on my own. I didn't care whether the facts were 100 percent true; the story had a truth to it. I liked the book enough for it to open my mind at a staggering rate. For a kid who didn't read so well in school, who probably had some kind of undiagnosed dyslexia, this was a big step. After "The Da Vinci Code," I started to read book after book.

As Cheryl got closer to the day we called the ambulance, a lot of things also happened, at a staggering rate. I let Cheryl dog-sit Napoleon, which can be a nightmare if he starts howling. The first time he was good, and I was glad that I risked it. The second time he howled when he realized I would be gone for a while. Napoleon got to love spending time with Cheryl, and thinking about it now, I have to laugh. She would kiss that dog's ass. She cooked for him, sweet-talked him, whatever it took to make him relax. Eventually he got into it, and Cheryl would put tarot cards out on the floor, and Napoleon would step on the deck, and she'd use it to learn more about what he was thinking. I miss her a lot on days when I want to feel that comfort that she gave me with her readings.

Cheryl had a mix of Catholic and what people call "pagan" that was both sassy and deeply respectful. Cheryl called herself a "Cathowitch." Her witch style was deep, and it was also very North Jersey. It was fun, and it was real, made up of a life sandwiched between New York City and Philly, a place with churches from the colonial days and immigrants always bringing in these spirits, their saints, their visions. Cheryl loved all that old stuff, all those symbols and stories of people doing right over wrong.

She had these visions her whole life, so it was common sense to her that dying was not an end and all of this was telling the same story. Death was merely a transition to another kind of realm or maybe multiple realms. Even so, it was a big transition, and watching her go meant watching her sink into that world, while she disappeared in ours.

When she got to the hospital, she was calm, and I left to run errands. Maybe I didn't want to be there; maybe I knew I needed a moment to collect myself and do my routine. The doctors had her in the emergency room, probably thinking she was going to pass away any moment, but after my errands she was still there in the emergency department hallway. When it became obvious she was going to need some time, they found her a room. She was there for two weeks. The first one she spent going in and out for treatments, the very ones she had tried to avoid. The second week, the treatments came to an end. At first, she was wide awake, going through that barrage of radiation; then she was out cold. The goal was to shrink the tumor enough to send her home or to her sister's so she could pass there, but that wasn't going to happen. The radiation gave Cheryl so much pain that they gave her the morphine after a while, and then she lost consciousness, and she never came back. Her sister and I managed to clean out the tiny apartment she was renting on J Street while she was there. If by a miracle she made it, it was clear the time had come for her to go to her sister's. Of course, we knew she wasn't going to make it, but it was only in the very last hours and days that we started to admit it to ourselves.

Cheryl didn't want to die in the hospital – nobody does – but from the moment she got into the ambulance, this calm came over her. In the hospital room we decorated two of the windows with these light-up 8-inch skulls. It was almost Halloween, so we took the opportunity to decorate the room with all sorts of stuff that would have seemed weird any other time of year. The doctors had said we could make her comfortable, and the skulls did that. She had left Santissima home, but she made sure she told me, "Make sure the lights stay on, Tom." She had purple lights around her. I don't know the meaning of it, but I'm sure Cheryl had ten reasons, at least. I looked up what I could on the Internet. Purple is a power color. It can get rid of bad luck. It connects us to our higher self and the crown chakra.

Maybe Cheryl put those lights on there to call in her power, to give herself the strength. I don't know, because she never told me. There were lots of little things she never told even when she was repeating herself to me, trying to get me out of my mental ruts. I would run back to Cheryl and tell her she was wrong when she read for me. I would complain that the guy of my dreams was unavailable or someone was playing games with me.

"Do you remember what I said to you?"

"You said this could be the one."

"That's not what I said. You wanted to hear that, Tom."

She would hit the spells on and on, hitting something to no end with candles and cleansing baths, jars, eggs, so many things. She would listen to me and see where I was blocking myself. Sometimes she'd say something to my face; other times she kept it inside, shooting me looks.

"You gotta keep hittin' it, Tom."

"What if it doesn't work?""You keep hittin' it."

Cheryl was a romantic, she said, and she believed that if I wanted love so badly, I should have it. She knew that I had challenges, things to do with anger management and trust, but she wasn't going to stop helping me get out of my own way. One time she had me go to the dollar store and get a cardinal to make a prayer to St. Anthony. She said he liked me, him and Saint Michael, the archangel who slays the serpent. St. Anthony is from all these different ages, and the further you go back, the more he comes across like a magician; a gift giver. I understand now that he helps find lost things, too, so maybe it's not that I don't have love in my life, maybe it's that I can't see it.

Cheryl believed she could change my luck, and I believed her most of the time, but she never got her man, and it made me a little skeptical. She defended her own blind spots, saying you could never do magic for yourself as good as you could for someone else. To do magic right you have to see past the blind spots that you were born with, and that doesn't usually work out so well if you try and do it alone. Cheryl put a lot into me getting what I wanted, and I appreciated it. I didn't need her to be perfect or her magic to be like something out of the movies. I appreciated the effort, and she was going to have those skulls on her deathbed even if I had to put up a fuss. In fact, no one said a word about them, – well, not the people in charge.

"'Bruja'"

The housekeeping staff whispered it when they came by in the morning with linens or to clean up the wastebaskets. You don't hear too much from the people who do the cleanup at hospitals, but they talked to each other quietly, and all of them let out a little whisper when they noticed the skulls in the window. The thing Cheryl feared the most in life, being seen as a witch, as a spiritualist, was the thing that came out in the end. It came out of the mouths of the Mexican ladies, who were a little bit scared at first, but when they looked at her suffering, trying to smile at them, all the little whispers gathered around her like prayers.

Just weeks before all this happened, we were joking about naming the book "Belmar Bruja," and then out of nowhere the jokes gave way to a new reality. If the veil had gotten thin around Cheryl, allowing her to see the dead like never before, then the veil that she used to hide herself was also getting thin. At the salons, at the restaurant and around the corner at the bakery, people were asking about the Cheryl they knew. They were asking about how she was feeling, some of them swallowing their guilt about the mean things they gossiped about her. Others stayed nasty towards her to the end, never giving an inch of mercy as they bitched about me not covering their shifts.

In the hospital, though, the atmosphere was different, and Cheryl laid there, going in and out of radiation in this quiet way. She was claustrophobic all her life, and in her last days she was ushered in and out of one elevator and put right into another time and again. She kept thanking the staffers who wheeled her in and out of the elevators while she practically held her breath the whole time. I felt so bad for her, and for some reason it flashed back on me how Cheryl had said one of my employees was hexing me. She said that they were hoping Napoleon would bite me so I would get rid of him. Cheryl said people don't even need to do magic, that all words hold power. There was a storm of hate coming my way, Cheryl said, so she did a spell to keep the hexer at bay. I didn't ask her to, but she did it.

I thought about that lady being claustrophobic and how Cheryl was maybe paying the price for that spell she cast by feeling that same fear now, at the end. I saw Cheryl going up and down those hospital cars, and I felt like some of that was my fault, but she would have told me that was ridiculous. She thanked all the people as a way finding peace with the rides that she hated. She was already thinking like someone more on the other side.

Her eyes got shinier while the rest of her got more like paper. Her smile got tighter as the pain got worse, and then the painkillers they gave her got stronger, and that sent her to deeper extremes. Her smile would loosen up, and then it would fade, then it would tighten and get loose again. Cheryl was bobbing on waves, coming in and out her body, in and out of time. Sometimes her eyes would open; other times she went through all that with them closed like she was living half in a dream.

"Bruja," "witch," "priestess," "shaman": all of those words fit Cheryl up until the end, but we weren't allowed to say them out loud around people she didn't know. I did not give a fuck if the skulls made anyone uncomfortable, not even her mother. If Cheryl said her father sent me, then I was going to be that protector, that one who gives his little girl what she needs to feel safe. In that way, some part of me remembered my own father and how he treated my sister. It made me think of how being in her good graces would shield me from the worst of my father's temper.

I never hated my sister for all the power she had over my father. I never saw that as a competition or felt as though if he were less nice to her, he would be nicer to me. The older I got, the more I appreciated the way that he protected his sisters and the way he doted on his daughter. I realized that what he couldn't give me did exist in the man. I thought about it as I sat there, protective at Cheryl's deathbed, holding vigil with plastic skulls and strings of decorations in the shapes of ghosts. I thought about it more after the fact, when the months after her passing dragged on and all I felt was like I had lost my best friend. I thought about it a lot when we buried my Aunt Ree Ree, too.

The day when we buried Aunt Ree Ree, it was cold out. The simple church was full of people from the congregation, plus us family. The members of the congregation took the microphone offered up by the pastor and one by one, they testified to my aunt's stamina in service of God. They appreciated her discipline, the way she knelt down to scrub the floor of the church! The way she tested the pastor's knowledge of scripture when he first came to visit! The next-door neighbor and his wife, both of them young, with tatts and not looking like regular churchgoers, talked about how influential she was in their life, how she gave advice, when asked, over the fence. None of them knew what she had been through when she was younger, not like we did.

By the time most of them knew my aunt, she wasn't scared of much. Her father and mother had long since passed, and so had most of the life she had built up in her younger years. The farms had mostly turned into strip malls and McMansions. The old farm workers had disappeared, and in their places were neighbors who spoke Spanish at church. Aunt Ree Ree noticed the changes, but it didn't seem to faze her. She measured people by their actions, so Aunt Ree Ree accepted those superficial things as long as it didn't change the God-fearing aspect of the people around her. Aunt Ree Ree had settled into a peaceful life by the end, in some ways totally alone, but always surrounded by good neighbors.

Family is family, and Aunt Ree Ree was one of us, a Sharpe, but I looked out and saw that she had her own clan through the church. I was looking at the program designed by my cousin, and I smiled to see that it had cardinals on it. They didn't have the same meaning to Aunt Ree Ree as they did to Cheryl, but seeing them there made time stop still a little. It wasn't the big kind of time stop, like I've felt when someone was actively taking their first or last breath, but it was something close. Seeing the cardinals on the program made me feel like a regular bird could be magical, maybe even a sign of good things to come. If I stare out the window just after sunrise, sometimes they'll surprise me while I'm having my cup of coffee and that first cigarette, and then I'll think of people.

Aunt Ree Ree touched my heart in a special way because she lived a hard life without it making her hard on the inside. She would have hated Cheryl's Catholic-witch stuff, but she might have gotten past that and really enjoyed Cheryl. In a weird way they shared this way of living that was full of inner strength, the kind that is harder to see from a distance. With people like them, you have to take your time and get up close to catch all the small stuff.

By the time Aunt Ree Ree passed, she had buried her only son and her husband, and despite all that she still said things like, "Golly." She was always up to a little bit of "this and that" every day of her life. She grew up hard, like Dad and her sisters, but she wouldn't swear or talk about things like sex. She kept that kind of innocence about her even if she knew the facts of life. Aunt Ree knew how mean the world could get while scratching out a childhood under Grandpa's watchful glare. She once got it hard, for leaving one potato behind in the dirt. He screamed that they would all starve if they were lazy like her, and by the time he was done teaching her a lesson, Aunt Ree Ree never left another potato unturned in the ground.

She stayed in the fields most of her life, picking blueberries for the local farms. Long after she was comfortable enough, Aunt Ree Ree kept picking berries for the farms in the summer, going until her back ached and her fingers turned blue. She grabbed at the berries and got each one better than most others or any machine. She wouldn't talk about it much, except to answer questions, and sure enough my father would ask her how the picking was going whenever he saw her. He was loyal to her and she to him in a way that I never got. He would sound different with her, using the exact same words but in a different tone. He was like that with his sisters, and with my sister, too. That tone didn't exist for me or my mother or even my brother.

Aunt Ree Ree was a bridge between that softer part of him and the part of him I knew. Women and men in families bring out different things in each other. They bring out patterns that don't always make sense on the surface. My father was hard toward my mother, but he never laid a hand on her. That was about the best he could do, considering the example he saw and his natural temper and all. In my sister, he saw a lot of himself, a lot of his sisters, so again, the softness made sense when it came out. Anyway, I don't know how it all fits, and I can't figure out his psychology any better now than I could then, but I know that Aunt Ree Ree brought out that feeling in both of us. When they laid her to rest, I felt like my father might have been with us, looking out across the clearing to the road, bringing us a comfort we couldn't see. Another Sharpe was gone; another woman who made life softer and better had left my life.

THE STAR

Star Light, Star Bright

"How is it that you don't have patience for any breathing person, but for that child you have unlimited patience?" It was one of my salon wives talking, giving me a hard, pissed-off stare.

"Simple. She knows what we teach her."

"Yeah, so?"

"You've already been taught."

(Torrents of deafening silence.)

I held her look until she walked away. If looks could kill, I wouldn't be here telling any stories. Behind the chair with some of these personalities, it's amazing salons don't have daily visits from the cops. Think about it: six, sometimes seven days a week you're standing there with sharp tools in your hand Anything could happen. She was right; I don't have a lot of patience, wasn't born with it, didn't always see it in action. I don't lie about that being a challenge.

It depends on the schedule, the weather, on all sorts of things that make old habits die hard. One thing that helps is I work in front of a mirror all day, and I hate catching glimpses of myself looking tired and angry. The dogs helped me learn some patience, and somehow so did cutting that cord in the delivery room. I didn't magically transform all at once, mind you, but something started changing in me from that moment in the hospital.

When my goddaughter showed up in my life, it turned out I did have patience for at least one breathing person, and that was a big deal. It was like this amazing experience where nothing she did seemed to wear me down to the point of sheer frustration. None of her questions were annoying. Nothing she did ticked me off. Sure, I would have to correct her if she was rough with the dog or if she was spilling juice on the upholstery, but these were not huge problems. She was learning about the world, and the moment I mentioned something, pretty much anything, she listened. She actually listened, and that made me patient beyond my wildest dreams. It was like some kind of magic made its way into my world from the day she was born, and it kept on growing. The more that I acknowledged her as a gift from God, the more she acted like one.

Now, it wasn't easy to become a godfather, in case you were wondering. Me being Protestant and the baby's parents baptizing her Catholic – well, it wasn't a perfect fit. I was on Cloud Nine after they asked me to do the thing, but I had a nagging feeling I wasn't going to be able to do it on account of all the rules. Then the lady at the church confirmed my worries. She said I was going to be stuck as a "Christian Witness," and that I could call myself "godfather" but technically, I wouldn't be. I started to seethe. She was just so sure of her rules. My God, she was smug. Long story short, I thanked her and left. Then I started thinking and got on the phone.

I dialed the number and started to spill every detail about this baby girl and how I helped bring her into the world. I don't really know what I said, but I know I said it all. On the other side of the line a Catholic Father listened and didn't say a word. Eventually he asked a few questions, then we hung up, and I went back to work. The other stylists looked at me, kind of skeptical.

I thought it was over, and that the church lady was right: I wasn't going to qualify. I could hear her in my mind, smirking at me as she said, "I told you so." It stung at first, but then I got used to the idea. It took me a few days, but then I was ready to call her and admit defeat. I was finally prepared to call up the office, to let them all know they were right and I was wrong.

Then I got a call from the Father, and everything changed. I ran out of the salon as soon as I could and shot over to his parish where there was a letter waiting for me. It said I was a member of a certain kind of order, and that I was in good standing. It said that I, Tom Sharpe, was eligible and fully qualified to be a godfather. I thought I would cry. I almost fainted. Father, someone I knew from the clubs, had saved the day with a Medieval loophole. Nobody needed to know that the young Father was as queer as a three-dollar bill. All they needed to know was that I had a bona fide green light.

I drove as quickly as I could to the other church office and handed them the letter. I put it down politely but firmly. I didn't say a word while the church lady read the letter, signed and sealed. I did not break out into a smile. I watched her shift in her shoes. Then she seemed to read it again, until finally she looked up and said, "OK." That was it. Father had given me a loophole, and sure enough, it worked. I laughed and I cried in the car, and then I got to telling the parents, who told their naysaying relatives. Seems everyone was in shock. Seems no one thought I could do it. Whenever anyone asked me how I pulled it off, I looked them in the eye and said it slowly: "I cut hair for a living."

Truth is, the whole thing felt fated. I was still driving up north a lot to get spiritual advice when the baby was born, and she and her parents were in and out of my house all the time. I would see her mother and father having drama, and me having drama and I saw the baby taking it all in. I noticed she tried to cheer us all up. I mean, I couldn't figure out why she wasn't acting out like most kids her age would, like half the adults, including me, might. When my goddaughter came into my life, every time she smiled, I knew the meaning of hope, even if I wasn't in the mood for it. I needed to know more, so I asked some questions.

"She's a Crystal child."

"A what?"

"A Crystal child."

"OK. What about these Crystal children?"

"They're the seeds of a new world."

Then Dawn, the healer up north, went on to tell me about the different types of spirits coming into the world. She explained how most of us are regular souls, living out the same lessons from life after life. There are other souls, though, a lot of them being born lately, that are here mostly to help the rest of us. They're on the advanced course; they're the people you think of when I say, "Old souls." My goddaughter is one of those people, and it doesn't matter if she grows up to be a doctor or a makeup artist, she'll always be helping those around her. It's like it's in her spiritual DNA or something.

The Crystals have to be cared for, and sometimes they get special people in their lives who do just that. We were still in Dawn's living room, with those tall windows and classic hardwood floors, tons of sunlight all around us, when she gave me the breakdown. She said these Crystals were a second wave, and they needed protection. especially after what happened to the ones who came before them, the Indigos.

If I remember it right, the Indigos prepared the way by breaking down barriers and norms. They were fierce with blue auras and rebel attitudes. The Indigos came down and started trouble, shaking people from their patterns by challenging authority in every form. "You wouldn't recognize most of the Indigos now," Dawn said "They were put on Ritalin."

"The Indigos cleared the path for the Crystals, and they are a much softer energy," Dawn added. I asked if I was maybe an Indigo, because I knew I wasn't a Crystal. The answer from Dawn was a quick, "No." I had a regular soul and a regular aura. That was good enough for me. I had enough stress with my own life and didn't think I could handle being responsible for setting the healing of the planet in motion. Still, I had the ADD, which they say can be part of the Indigo expression, but I took Dawn's word for it. Not everyone with ADD is spiritually enlightened.

We talked about the planet shifting from old ways of doing things to new ones, and I was excited to be part of things, no matter my status. I knew my little goddaughter was special, and we had a bond, so maybe taking care of her would be enough for this soul for this lifetime. Still, I didn't understand what I would have to do for her, and it was making me anxious. Nothing came to me-no big answers, no bolts of lightning or voices.-that I really expected any, but they would have helped. I was thinking about fantasy movies or sci-fi flicks where the hero has his mission revealed to him by some oracle. Dawn just kind of looked at me and said she wasn't getting any particular message on my mission, but she could figure more out if I brought my goddaughter to the house.

I made my way down from North Jersey, cutting south along the Parkway, avoiding the traffic that gathered around the parts of the state that lead to the big-city bridges and tunnels. I was driving in and out of potential bottlenecks, remembering how I had cut the umbilical cord when she was born. I was second guessing this star child story and my role in it, asking myself all sorts of questions until there was nothing left to think about or ask. My goddaughter was probably more spiritually advanced than I, and that was easy enough to accept. I didn't see myself being of use until I remembered that I was older than her, and so maybe I could help her. I felt like a protector, a friend, a guide, even though I wasn't sure I was ready to be. I was taking this whole thing very seriously because that was probably the only time I would see someone born. That was the one time, as a gay single man who was not a nurse or a doctor, that I would witness the true miracle of life. Maybe I was complicating things, but maybe I was right to take it seriously. Days, months and a few years went on, and nothing about that child seemed typical, and nothing I did for her seemed particularly special.

Eventually, I couldn't take the curiosity, the rampant anxiety that I was screwing this up, so I brought my goddaughter up the Parkway, onto the Turnpike, and around a few jug handles on a field trip to Dawn's house. We got into the driveway, and I took her out of the car seat. I held her hand, and we made our way into the house. We got in there, and I had no idea what to say, so I said we were going to visit a friend of mine, and so my little brown-eyed angel went with that.

It was a sunny day and there was a nice amount of light coming through those tall windows again, showing off the lines of the room, making all the crystals and flowers sparkle. This wasn't some dingy back room or boardwalk spot with one of those "Psychic" signs. This house was calm, comfortable and perfect for having a chat. We were all there to have a nice, simple chat.

"You have a dream."

"Yes."

"The same dream."

"Yes."

"About a black cat and a white dog?"

"Yes."

"And the dog chases the cat away?"

"Yes."

"And Uncle Tom is there with you?"

"Yes."

"And what happens when you're in the dream?"

"He holds my hand."

"Does he ever let it go?"

"No, never. He just holds my hand."

I saw her all the time, and we talked about everything, and I had no idea about this reoccurring dream. I obviously didn't know it had animals in it, and that they would fight and she would be scared. I had no idea I was in the dream consistently. I didn't have to fight the animals. I didn't even have to holler at them. The only thing I did in the dream was hold her hand, and that small act made me a hero. I was in shock. I couldn't believe it was that simple, but it was. For once in my adult life, my presence was enough. It wasn't my personality or my wallet or even my jokes that made me special. Me being there while the world swirled around her was a gift.

We always think revelations are going to show up in these massive dramatic moments, but this kind of realization can sneak up on you. You don't even end up shaking your head as much as you kind of bob for a second, feeling like, "Oh. All right." "Nothing to do about it, no reason to get anxious, just be there for the child," was what my inner voice was saying.

I'm like anyone; I know that when it comes to giving gifts, it's the thought that matters, but I still fall into traps about getting the best gift, the perfect one. Simple celebrations transform into pressure where I agonize over giving the ideal present, wrapped in the right bow with exactly the right card. When I see the person's face, I want it to light up so I know that "BOOM!" I nailed the perfect gift. What I realized that day was that imperfect gifts worked just as well as perfect ones. Realizing I mattered so much made me realize I didn't have to be perfect to be loved. Somehow the meeting with Dawn ended, and I drove us back down the miles of highway, feeling blessed but still driving defensively. I played the kiddie music and sang a few words. I answered questions and kept it cool, but I was absolutely wild with relief on the inside.

Sometimes blessings come upon you softly like the sound of crickets on a summer night, or the breathing of a sleeping child as you get them out of the car seat and into the house.

It's those little blessings that slowly but surely change the course of a life. Maybe I'm impatient with most people because I know they've got agendas. Once you get a to-do list, you get an agenda, and once you get an agenda, you lose the moment. That's why we stop having patience with each other, because we are constantly battling over our agendas. I don't just mean doing the laundry or taking out the recyclables. I'm talking about the big agendas, like getting married, having kids, buying the car you always dreamed of by the time you hit a certain age. I got my few goals out of the way as early as I could in life. The ones I couldn't manage to get, like marrying my first love, I spent my time letting go. My only agenda for years has been wanting a life where nobody aggravates me, and since I drive, and work and live in the most densely populated state in the country, my agenda is never being met. Like every list that exists in the world, never expect it to all get done. Give yourself little gold stars for surviving the ones you do manage to cross off your list.

Making sure we mark the small wins is everything. When my goddaughter was little, she loved the stars, and when I think of her, I immediately think of the new beginnings in the Star card. I remember how we would watch these videos on the stars and galaxies, and she loved them. I took that as a sign, in a way. Back when she was barely a toddler, I would watch as she would fight to keep her eyes open while these puppets on some video were talking about scenes from telescopes. She didn't even speak back then, but the pictures of the different stars and planets held her attention, and they held mine, too. Having kids around forces you to pay attention to the world. In fact, having kids around makes you remember when you were small and new, back when you had this thing: curiosity.

I was so fascinated sitting with her, hearing these facts and figures about which planet moves in what orbit. I was taking in facts, wondering, "What is she thinking?" "What is it like to see that for the first time?" I didn't know if she could truly relate to it, because I knew I couldn't. It felt so big, so far away in the sky. We adults think we see things, but we see them through the lens of all the things we think we know. Kids are innocent, so they don't see what they know, they see questions. Kids are curious, and they can make you curious, too. We would watch the videos and hear the facts, and after I wondered what she was thinking, I would wonder, what am I thinking? What is going on in this world that I don't notice the little things?

Stars are new beginnings, in science and in tarot. In the cards and in real life, the stars can give you hope if you let them. You might have to be patient, but eventually the stars can bring you light. Ancient philosophers looked to the stars for answers, and so did the scientists that came after them. For all of history it seems we've been filling in the story of the stars. For all of our history we have been a little obsessed, wanting to know how they burn and how they stay on their paths. It's like some part of us can't help but wonder about those lights shining from so far away that to look at them is to look back in time. Of course, there's one star we circle around, and we love that one so much, it has its own name.

The Star feels like sitting in the backyard on a summer evening with a child, looking up. The Star in the traditional cards has a lady, kind of a goddess, and she pours water into the river and onto the land out of two jugs. The Star is about destiny and following the divine map, the one that is bigger than anything we comprehend. The Star as a card is about getting back that curiosity even when you think you know the drill, the heartache. The Star says, "Hey, are you ready ...?"

I remember my father pointing out the stars to me when we went out on the boat, back when I was just a little boy. He was always on the boat for some reason or another, day or night. He even used to race that thing. It wasn't much, a 24-footer from some local boatbuilding brand named Luhrs, but it was sturdy and respectable. He would take his tiny boat and bring it out against all these big boats and yachts, in these races. They're called "predicted log races," but it's hard to call them races when they're more like competitions. In a predicted log race, you set a course and figure out when you will get from buoy to buoy. You set the time, not to be the fastest, but to be the most accurate. You have to take into account things like wind, tide, currents and even boat traffic. Back then my father was still learning and going for certifications, eventually earning a professional captain's license. His plan was to use it for his own business when he retired. In the meantime, we kids were along for the ride.

We went out at night with my father, using a sextant to navigate and plot courses according to the stars. He had to master that skill for some advanced class, so he would gather his maps and his instruments and try and interest one of us kids in going with him. He had to work to convince even one of us to go because it felt like going to school with him. We had to pay attention to the stars and the markings he made, even if we weren't into it yet. I couldn't work a sextant now, wouldn't have a clue, but I can still hear my father saying, "If you know where the stars are, you'll never get lost." I guess that's why I like astrology. I sure as hell don't want a boat.

My father's dream was to retire and captain boats down to Florida for rich snowbirds. He worked on that dream relentlessly. For a working-class man of his time, the best retirement he could imagine was one where he still made some money in addition to a pension. It was a dream in the distance, and he imagined getting there buoy by buoy.

I never thought about my father's dreams when he showed us the constellations. I was totally incapable of appreciating that he had any hopes, even while he was pointing out Orion's Belt or the big bear, Ursa Major. I never for a minute thought when he was going on with that sextant and looking at the sky, how much it could have meant for him, Ensign Sharpe, to finally get a Captain's license after being denied promotions in the military as a younger man. I never thought about the mysteries of life or how they applied to normal people – at least, not that much, and not until I got a little older. I didn't think those mysteries applied to my father, of all people, until he was gone for many years. When I remember him now on the boat, I can hear the water lapping the sides. I can feel myself staring up at the massive display of the night sky while we gently rocked.

My goddaughter got me looking at the stars again, pulling at me to quiet down and listen to them. She reminded me how magical the stars can be after all the emotional luggage gets put down and we settle. The years took their toll on me, and time had turned the stars into faraway decorations and not much else. The stars had become a way of gauging the weather or making small talk in the evenings at some party.

It wasn't until we sang those songs about the stars and watched those children's videos about the galaxy that something about the stars came back to me. It brought back these memories I wanted to forget, things that would flash across my mind so fast I didn't know if they were real memories or passing indigestion.

Little details came back, like my brother singing to me after I got my first earring. I had just gotten back from this jewelry store in the mall, and I was exhausted from all the anxiety. The technician was acting like it was no big deal, while I was barely able to keep myself in the chair. Being out was one thing; showing it with an earring was another. I didn't even get in the ear that said I was gay, but any earring was enough to signal I was different. I was being rebellious.

I thought, "Daddy would be turning over in his grave," and in that same flash, the earring was in. The gun had hidden the needle from my eyes, and I had gotten lost in my thoughts, and here I was, on the other side. I had taken some control of myself. I looked in the mirror, and then I left. Every step I took out of the shop, I wondered if people could notice. I caught a glimpse of myself in the car mirror, and it looked fine, not too big. I drove home slowly, not sure what would come next.

Sure enough, my brother saw it within seconds of me coming home. We were both in the kitchen and he started singing, "Twinkle, Twinkle, Little Star" as soon as he saw it. Suddenly this seemed like the worst idea ever, with his eyes trained on this tiny starter earring, voice rising higher and louder. I felt this heat in both my ears, and I knew it was shame that was about to be anger.

"Twinkle, twinkle, little star," he was singing slowly, and as he got to the line, "How I wonder what you are?" I felt like it could have been my father's voice singing. I got tense, was half a second away from swinging, but then I realized I wasn't scared of my brother like I was of my father. I was free, and besides being sarcastic, I didn't want to fight him. All the years of fighting had to stop because we were the men of the family now. Never mind that he was bigger than me and would have kicked my ass.

"How I wonder what you are?" Wondering about who you are is what they call self-examination, and everyone needs it. Being who you are is different than being what you are. What you are is skin and bones and a limited number of years; who you are – that is a never-ending question. Who you are is about having a purpose. It's all right to be into what you are almost as much as who you are, but you can't get lost in either; you have to find a balance.

Whether you're cruising some country road or zipping along the interstates, there are exits to take and -turns to follow; otherwise, you will rust in place. You have to drive, and you can't rely on GPS, and there is no perfect map. You have to keep your eyes on the road, and keep the music on, if that's what it takes to get you through the gray days, the sleet, the branches and debris in your path. You have to deal with the other assholes on the road with as much kindness as you can.

You need to drive to work, and you need to help your friends pick up their kids from school. You need to stay sober enough to not lose your license, and you have to hustle hard to get it back if you do lose your way. No matter what road you're on, you will find yourself driving to someone's house in the middle of the night because they need you, and you have to be OK with that. You will lose sleep. You will drive while cranky. You will drive to places you don't care about and will barely remember, but in the end, it is your responsibility to fill your life with the drives that give you life. It is your responsibility to remember that there are bigger roads, like those up in the sky. They're not paved roads, just paths, and when these roads give out, those out there will probably still be running.

You have to figure out that life is all about the stars in some way, so give yourself sunrise drives and secret drives, and drives along the water during a full moon. Give yourself drives to places that make you want to get through all the others.

I can still remember one of those drives, going to this place called Paradise, in Asbury Park. That was the old Asbury Park, the one with a broken-down convention center, with derelicts and homeless people crowding around the shoreline. The next town over was full of private access beaches and mansions the size of your dreams, but Asbury Park was a place where things burned down and people collected the insurance money and then disappeared. Except for us gays, and the punks, no white people went and hung out in Asbury Park back then. I remember parking my car, hoping no one would break in while I was adjusting my hair, making sure I had my ID. I remember how clear it was that night and how the sky glittered until I got under the neon signs.

I remember driving the half-hour, pulling open the door, and the place would be packed and bordering on a little too warm. I remember this song, "Desert Rose" by Sting, and somebody remixed it into a banger. This version of "Desert Rose" would come on the speakers like a force of nature had been unleashed. I remember hearing that woman's voice in the song, floating above us, and how the whole place went wild from the very first note.

Even now when I drive, if that song comes on, I turn it up loud. Just a few notes and I am back there in the club, on a Y2K dance floor full of queens, butches, trannies and every other flavor of the gay spectrum. We didn't have as many names for what we were back then, but inside we knew who we were. We were something together that I don't think we were in small groups or alone.

That song would come on and stop the chatter, and like moths to some flame, we all got on the dance floor. Nobody told us to do it; we just grabbed onto some feeling. The floor would get crowded, and everyone would find their place. Then the song would start to really kick in, and everyone would let loose, dancing up against whoever they were next to. People were singing the chorus at the top of their lungs and I would kind of hum along, but at the top of my lungs. That was our anthem at that club, at that time, and it didn't matter how we lived our lives day to day, at that moment we were together. Staying in the closet wouldn't have killed me, but staying in the lane my family wanted for me would have. Dancing in that club, in that kind of town wasn't part of their script, and it was everything I needed.

I knew that Cheryl gave me the permission I needed to share those stories. And I know that having a goddaughter in my life has given me a reason to look back on them harder. She is going to do things and say things and know things that I won't, ever. I want a big, beautiful life for her, full of happy memories that outweigh any painful ones. I want her to be free to design her own life. I want her to know joy and to feel it at every stage, to live with no regrets. I want her to have friends like I had with Cheryl, the ones who let you talk or rage, the ones who let you be all the different versions of you. I want her to have friends that talk about the stars. I don't care if they're talking science or astrology or both – because all that's on a spectrum, too.

When I started writing this book for me and Cheryl, everyone asked me "Why?" "Why you? What do you have to say that's so special?" I didn't really know. But I wouldn't say that. All I could do was promise them a shocker or give them a defensive, "Wait and find out." Wait and find out – sure, no pressure at all.

I had promised Cheryl I would try, and nothing else mattered. If you had to tell your story, you would have to ask yourself, what is it all about? You would have to wonder, why does it matter? You wake up, go to work, run errands, make lists and cross days off the calendar, year after year. You have to find something that shines so deep in your life that it makes all the pain worth it. That's why most people never write it all down, because to make sense of it all, you can't hide from the pain. This world is defined by your memories. I want to know, what memories are you leaving? I mean, that's what you have to ask yourself. To be clear, that's what I'm asking you to think about, right this second. You don't have to write it down like I did. You don't have to think about it the next time you see a shooting star and someone says to make a wish. You don't have to answer me at all, but if you don't, someday you probably will.

The Final Drive

There's a place around here named Crystal Lake. I pass it all the time but don't think too much about it. It's just another place where people get left when the family can't handle them. The place mostly catches my eye around Halloween because of all the ghosts they say live on the property. Before the place became the Bayville Convalescent Home, it had lots of lives, first as the Royal Pines Hotel in the roaring 1920s, and later as a women's hospital for babies being born in the 1940s. Now it has some updated name for a long-term care facility, the kind that takes wards of the state. It's the kind of place where people rock to themselves and scream at the shadows.

I had a friend who worked there around the same time as I worked in a home, and we would compare notes. Everything seemed to be about the same; patients were needy, and staff was overworked. Everyone had an attitude, and some people thought you were their long-lost child. Where I worked, the buildings were all new and kind of boring. At Crystal Lake, the nursing home started off as a mansion, and there wasn't a boring thing about it. I never thought about its history too much until my friend worked there. She said it was this place where the notorious gangster Al Capone kept his mother. They say in the beginning he built tunnels and ran booze from the creek to a smaller house on the property, and that the rich and powerful would show up to drink.

The building at Crystal Lake towers over the pine barrens almost ten stories, throwing a big shadow on the pygmy tree line. That's not tall for a city, but around here, that building is a skyscraper. The highest floors are where they have these skylights, and supposedly they keep the craziest wards of the state up there now. When it was a hospital, that's where the women gave birth, since electricity was scarce back then.

At the top, the doctors could see, and the women could scream, and nobody would hear them, so in a way, everyone won.

The building for Crystal Lake never fit the landscape, and even the lake wasn't natural. I heard of them draining the lake at least twice looking for money Capone might have planted there. They never found anything down there but the bottom and those tunnels. My friend said it was true about the ghosts running around there, that you could feel things without even trying. One of the ghosts shows up with flowers. Only the dying person sees the flowers, but everyone on the floor can smell them. From what my friend said, it was creepy even in daytime, and that made me happy never to work there.

The lake is now dark, and the cement work is in disrepair. It's crumbling, and everything Capone worked for is gone. I wonder if that's what happens when you make your money from his kind of career. "As you sow, so shall you reap." I wonder if buying something like that for your mother makes up for all the shit you did to get her there. I think about being a big-time gangster and how crazy it would make me to watch all my possessions crumble, even from the other side. It makes me wonder if that's why ghosts happen, because they can't get over life going on without them. It's a losing game to be a ghost.

I imagine standing there, just after death when all time ceases to matter, and seeing how many of my small decisions could have changed the world for the better and realizing how many times I got it wrong. I imagine what it's like to see my summer palace become a place where senile adults are medicated and put into beds, by overworked single parents and bored teenagers who can't wait to be done with their shifts. There's a lot to what we leave behind and what we're remembered for, and our legacy is something we set in motion, it's not something we control. That doesn't change if you're filthy rich or dirt poor. "You're born with a name, and you die with a reputation." I can still hear my father saying that line. I think I get it now, at a whole new level.

"All right, I don't know how this is going to go." she said as the ambulance rolled up to the house, and she hung up on a call to her friend Sondra. That "all right" meant, "I am not 100 percent happy with this, and maybe I'm scared, but I am going to dig deep and let it be." That "All right" was everything to Cheryl: a prayer, a note to God. I feel that "All right" repeating in me from time to time, sometimes for no reason. When I pass Crystal Lake, I feel it in my bones, that all of this passes, and that we don't get to decide how it ends or who remembers us. We don't decide where it ends or how, and we don't decide who picks us up or who cleans up our mess.

Cheryl knew there could be hell to pay at the end of life. She knew that every little suffering wasn't an accident. It wasn't really a lesson, either. Each little thing that came at the end was like a wave coming onto shore during a storm. It was a crash that came down with force and changed everything, but it was all part of some ocean. Cheryl didn't expect miracles at the end, and she wasn't about to try and change her suffering. She gritted her teeth and got ready for the final wave to get her across. She thanked the workers even if she felt like the walls were going to close in all around her as she took that last ambulance ride. That acceptance was powerful to watch.

"So be it."

That's what Cheryl said as her last ride pulled up to the house. She said it was all right, but to the scene in front of her, which was calling her into it, she held her ground and used her words. With all her courage and magic set to the max, she got in and started to live out the motions of active dying. By the end, she didn't need to say anything, and neither did I. We looked each other in the eye as the final ride, the final days all came to pass. It was tragic, and still it was completely normal. The final moments of Cheryl's life were like a movie where even after you know the ending, you can't help but watch the person live out the details.

I don't like to imagine myself dying because nobody does. I don't like the idea of leaving behind people who depend on me. I don't care about judgment so much, but I don't like change. They say that at the end, everything we lived runs like a story inside our head, and then it dissolves and then we pop out of this bubble. We pop out, and the only thing we notice is that we have no body. They say that no matter what comes later, we pop out of the flesh and into this unfathomable light. They say that light is who we really are, and all these faces are costumes.

"Don't touch her."

"Why not?"

"It's a memory you don't want."

My mother was in the casket, and my aunt was at my side. I remember her saying it and me still reaching out to touch her. I didn't enjoy the feeling at all. My mother was warm and soft, and this was something cold, like leather. My aunt stood there while I pulled my hand away, straight like a rod. She stayed there, knowing the memory I had just made for myself, knowing she was right. My aunt knew I didn't need to do it, that I never needed to feel that level of aloneness. She knew I never needed to feel like the best thing in the world could leave me and become something else.

I think about it sometimes, how it felt to touch that body that was no longer my mother, and I have to let it go every single time. I remind myself that there is another side and that wherever that is, my mother is calm and content there. I think about how she might be there when I pass, standing in her dress that she always wore, welcoming me home. Then I pet the dog or flick on a radio station. If I'm on the highway, I put the car on cruise, and then for a minute or two, I don't think about nothing, and the only thing I see is the lines of the road. The exits don't matter so much, and the other drivers, they become almost nothing.

Closing the Circle

By the time you learn this story, I might be gone. Cheryl sure is. Who knows, by the time you read this that Santa Muerte statue might be in her rightful resting place, or buried by accident, right next to me. It's a cheery thought in a way, to think that you might get to know us even after we're gone.

There's no way to tell how life goes except to know it goes on, and all the going forward doesn't happen in straight lines. Life moves in these circles, patterns repeat, and still, they change a little. Prayers go out and over land and into the air and find their own ways. It's like we all know it's simple, but we make it complicated. That's what I liked about the first time Cheryl showed me a circle. It wasn't like I was ignorant of circles as shapes, as clocks or wheels, but I never knew them as a way of making a prayer.

"Set it clockwise."

"What?"

"Clockwise, so it draws the power into your space."

"What happens if I do it the other way?"

"Everything will go backward."

(Terrified look.)

"Thy will be done," on earth as it is in heaven – that's one way of saying to God, "Hey, I'm good to live by your rules." People like Cheryl have no problem saying that, since you'd have to be crazy to think anyone but God is calling the shots.

But the Witch types add their own will to the picture; they set their own ground and call in their power so the things they want can actually come to pass. They can funnel it past Jesus or Buddha or anyone they want. Key thing is that they call their power in, and they connect that power out, into the stars. They connect themselves into mystery, and they do it all by starting a circle, big enough for a bunch or just big enough for one.

"As above, so below." "As in heaven, so on earth." – sounds kind of the same, sort of timeless, right? And so I have no judgment on religion or ways. I have no sense of what's going to happen to me or to you by the time we meet here. All I know is we went on a trip, and I never once cursed or got angry. I never shot you a look of pure disdain.

In fact, I brought you on this trip out of love. So, I'll let you go now, from the north, to the east, to the south and the west – leave here with a thank-you from me and mine, and from Cheryl and hers. Tonight, when you watch the moonrise, or maybe tomorrow if you catch the sun coming up with all those pink and orange colors, know that we had a flame for a minute, burning between all of us, behind all of it.

www.ingramcontent.com/pod-product-compliance
Lightning Source LLC
Chambersburg PA
CBHW060128130626
46556CB00006B/2268